Cunt (kŭnt) n.
A Declaration of Independence

Inga Muscio

Patricia Bradshaw

Seal Press

CUNT: *A Declaration of Independence*

© 2002 by Inga Muscio
Foreword © 2002 by Betty Dodson
Introduction © 2002 by Derrick Jensen

Published by Seal Press
A member of the Perseus Books Group
1700 Fourth Street
Berkeley, CA 94710

All rights reserved. No part of this book may be reproduced or transmitted in any form without written permission from the publisher, except by reviewers who may quote brief excerpts in connection with a review.

Credits are listed on page 365, which constitutes a continuation of the copyright page.

Library of Congress Cataloging-in-Publication Data
Muscio, Inga.
  Cunt: a declaration of independence / Inga Muscio.
      p. cm.
  Expanded and updated 2nd ed.
Includes bibliographical references (p. 357-364).
  ISBN-10: 1-58005-075-1
  1. Women. 2. Women—Social conditions. 3. Women--Psychology. 4. Women--Identity. 5. Body, Human—Social Aspects. 6. Sexism in language. 7. Feminism. I. Title.
  HQ1233 .M87 2002
305.4--dc21

                                        2003267081

ISBN-10: 1-58005-075-1
ISBN-13: 978-1-58005-075-3

15 14 13 12 11 10 9

Cover design by Rachel Ramstad and Ingrid Emerick
Interior design by Maren Costa
Printed in Canada by Transcontinental Printing
Distributed by Publishers Group West

In Loving Dedication:

To everyone with Cuntlove in their hearts,
especially my Sacred Mother.
I thank you for giving me life.

Contents

Author's Note

Unless otherwise stated, throughout this book the words "gentleman," "man" and the like are used to refer to the tightly knit, male social power structure as it is recognized in American patriarchal society.

Let it be known that the author is fully cognizant of the fact that many men in this world strive for women's rightful place in society. Without the work, study, love and support of certain members of the male sector of humanity, this book would not have been as thoroughly articulated as it was.

The author is grateful and indebted to many members of this sector of humanity, both living and dead, of which her loving father, brothers, nephews, Malcolm X and Robert Graves are merely six.

The author would also like to acknowledge that masculine and feminine nouns and pronouns impose unrealistic limitations on lived human experience. The author looks forward to the time when our vocabulary reflects the reality and complexity of our multi-gendered human nature.

All that said, the author continues to be free to talk some serious shit.

Cunt (kŭnt) n.

Foreword

A friend sent me a book with a note that said, "Dodson, you're gonna love this woman." The bright yellow cover had a pink daisy with "cunt" written in its center. I dropped the book into my handbag to read on my trip to San Francisco the following day.

The plane landed before I knew it. My nose was buried in this bold, brave declaration of independence written by a young woman named Inga Muscio, who was surely my spiritual granddaughter.

Over the next four days, during business meetings and social dinners, I kept asking friends about the author who had the guts to title her book *Cunt*. Did anyone know her? The book jacket said she was a recluse, but I figured a cuntlovin' woman like me could get through to her. I left my phone number with her publisher, knowing everyone comes to New York City at some point.

Although Inga and I span two generations of feminism, we share a lot in common. Both of us embrace the old Anglo-Saxon noun, "cunt," that claims the innate power of the sex organ it names.

In my first book, *Liberating Masturbation*, which was self-published in 1974, I had a chapter titled "Becoming Cunt Positive" followed by sixteen full-page pen-and-ink portraits of my friends' cunts. Inga begins *Cunt* by informing us about her reconciliation with the word and the anatomical jewel it names. She points out that when popes or politicians refer to female genitalia, "the term 'vagina' is discreetly engaged." She writes that the word originated from a term meaning "a scabbard or sheath for a sword," and rightly concludes, "Ain't got no vagina."

From the nineteen-sixties to the present day, I have objected to the term "vagina" because it refers to the birth canal and leaves out the clitoris, the primary source of women's sexual pleasure. As a budding feminist author in the seventies, I was furious to discover the vast number of women struggling, and mostly failing, to have an orgasm from penis/vagina intercourse and blaming themselves. I proclaimed that "frigid" is a man's word for a woman who can't have an orgasm in the missionary position in a few minutes, with only the kind of stimulation that's good for him.

Among the many things that excited me about *Cunt* was how it took me back to my feminist awakening. My perspective was grounded in the sexual revolution of the sixties and seventies. Abandoning marriage and monogamy and claiming my sexuality radically altered my life. This new feeling of empowerment gave me the courage to have the first one-woman exhibition of erotic art in New York City. I began writing articles and speaking out about the importance of women embracing masturbation so we could develop and define our own sexuality.

I designed a workshop I called "Physical and Sexual Consciousness Raising." My feminist commitment evolved into helping women learn to become orgasmic by experimenting with different forms of clitoral stimulation. I ended up leaving my art studio for what became a twenty-five-year career running masturbation workshops.

Inga is a product of the eighties and nineties, when many mainstream feminists wanted to censor pornography and the anti-violence movement merged with an anti-sex movement. My worst fear while reading *Cunt* was that I'd be engulfed in a PC feminist rant, an anti-sex diatribe focused on ending violence against women. But I discovered that Inga's adamant anti-rape stand was not anti-sex. Instead, she offered ways for women to deal with rape beyond impotently stomping our feet, hating sex and blaming men.

I silently cheered when she said we needed to learn self-protection, suggesting practical techniques for protection like the one she uses for dashes to the store late at night: she calls a friend to let her know she is going out, puts rocks in her pocket, jumps on her bike and goes. For me, the best part about studying martial arts and self-protection in the seventies was learning to avoid dangerous situations in the first place.

I have observed the women's movement for the past forty years, and we've routinely avoided the subject of sexual pleasure. From Women Against Pornography to the current V-Day campaign to end violence against women and girls, sex continues to be equated with violence. As if ending violence for biological women alone could ever change anything.

Every Valentine's Day, the one day that celebrates lovers, the *Vagina Monologues*, which spawned V-Day, is performed around the world. Yes, we can say it's a beginning. Or we can say that the good old boys have thrown us another bone. The adorable Dr. Ruth saying "penis" or "vagina" or "sexual arrrrrrousal" entertained us, but merely saying the words publicly provides no new information that improves our sex lives. I tend to question anything or anyone that gets corporate sponsorship, for it wouldn't get corporate sponsorship if it truly challenged the status quo. Corporate feminism is a far cry from the early feminist movement of the seventies. Back then we sat in a circle, which broke through the traditional model of a leader or expert standing in front of a group. We shared the truth about our lives, making "I" statements instead of giving advice. As we spoke, we began to realize that how we were living was indeed the result of the current political climate. This new awareness gave rise to the powerful feminist statement of the seventies, "The personal is political." Unfortunately, this brilliant concept has rarely been applied to our sexuality.

As long as we continue to insist that sex is a private matter, public discourse by most feminist authors, scholars and women's studies educators will continue to focus on rape, incest and abuse. Many feminist leaders avoid discussing the subject of pleasure for different reasons. If they celebrate sexual pleasure, they will be attacked by right-wing factions. On the other hand, going public with their sex lives is still considered threatening within the mainstream feminist movement. Having no sexual pleasure would be as embarrassing as having too much, or the "wrong" kind. Until more feminists have the courage to openly claim and enjoy their own sexuality and sexual pleasure, the women's movement will remain stuck in a joyless discourse which does not improve society.

I've been told by corporate feminists that talking about sexual pleasure when there is so much sexual violence against women is inappropriate, insensitive and politically incorrect. And who is to blame for all the sexual violence in the world? Dare I ask why so many feminists think biological women have cornered the market on being victimized by violence? Will I sound too insensitive in mentioning the violence caused by poverty, hunger and wars that affect women, men and children of every gender?

In *Cunt,* I found a young feminist brave enough to claim her body, her cunt and her sexuality. She openly supports masturbation, which is the bottom line of pleasure. Although the acceptance of masturbation has made headway over the last few decades, it has not been nearly enough for me. My idea of sexual liberation is linked back to the suffragette movement and my hero Victoria Woodhull's declaration of free love. *Cunt'*s subtitle is *A Declaration of Independence*; I want sexual independence. I want to free sex from the old religious morality of heterosexual marriage as the only viable lifestyle. I want to see the end to the double standard that allows men an abundance of sexual choices while they pose as monogamous married men and insist on faithful wives.

Inga and I have both endured abortions. The comparison between them shows some progress. One of mine was an illegal kitchen-table abortion in the fifties with a metal tool scraping out my uterus without any anesthesia. One of hers was gently induced with massage and herbs, which was far more civilized. Both of our unwanted pregnancies were with men we liked. Unfortunately, we had been thinking with our clits and forgot about birth control. Sex is a powerful force.

Inga did eventually make to it New York, and she called me. Over dinner, one of the first things I asked her was how she handled telling strangers the title of her book. She replied that she simply said, "It's a women's studies book." How clever of her. In the seventies, I felt obliged, or maybe challenged, to say the name of my book every time someone asked.

We had a good laugh when I told the story about the cab driver who inquired about my line of work. When I said I had just written and published (and was now distributing) a book, naturally he wanted to know the title. Full of feminist fervor, I proudly said, *"Liberating Masturbation,"* and he drove smack into the car in front of us that had stopped at a red light. From that day on I made it a point to use the second title, *A Meditation on Selflove,* whenever I was in a moving vehicle.

When I sold the book to Crown, the title was changed to *Sex for One,* but that didn't fool anyone. If people hesitate to buy my book for fear the salesperson will think they are going home to masturbate, how do folks handle asking for *Cunt?*

As we talked, Inga and I agreed that one of the big, glaring problems today is the pitiful state of sex education in our schools. Currently religious groups have imposed their own beliefs on public-school students with government-funded, abstinence-only programs that limit sexual expression to heterosexual, monogamous marriage. Our teens are being told that birth control usually fails, and abortion and homosexuality are morally wrong. And, as ever, masturbation is never mentioned as a safe alternative to penis/vagina intercourse. While religious leaders claim we have a choice as to whether or not we follow God's laws, our teens are not given a choice.

We also agreed that until America accepts sexual diversity as the law of the land and includes lesbians, gay men, bisexuals, transsexuals, genderqueers and intersex people, we will remain in the Dark Ages of human sexual expression. We all need to come out of our sexual closets. We need to be able to talk about sex without shame and take pride in how we choose to enjoy our bodies and genitals. Otherwise the public discourse on sex will continue to focus on abuse, rape, incest, disease and dysfunction. It's time we begin to discuss sexual skills that will help us experience pleasure.

I believe that thought creates form, and I hold the image of a future filled with women who are cunt-positive and orgasmic on their own terms. My declaration of independence includes sexual and financial self-sufficiency. We will have an equal voice in government and decision-making. Raising our children to be fair-minded and sex-positive is our best hope for the future.

The intergenerational friendship between Inga and me is time-binding, a concept of Alfred Korzybski, a mathematician who wrote a book called *Science and Sanity*. Time-binding is building upon the knowledge of each generation, accumulating it and passing it on in order to learn from our mistakes and avoid repeating history. Just as I was inspired by sex-positive Victoria Woodhull, I hope I have inspired Inga, and that she will be there to inspire the next generation of young women.

Inga and I continue to stay in touch, time-binding our ideas of sex-positive feminism. She says I remind her of her grandmother, and I tell her she is the granddaughter of my dreams. When we talk together, our age difference disappears. We are feminists who want equal rights for women all over the world, and that includes sexual pleasure.

Betty Dodson, Ph.D.
New York City, June 2002

Introduction

Cunt is a necessary book, one of the most important books in
print today, not only for bio and trans-women, as it
obviously is, but for men-folk and dyke boys as
well. And it is important not only for those
whose cunts or other body parts or lives have
been scarred by the deathly culture in which we
find ourselves immersed. When you count rape
survivors, domestic violence survivors, those who
love those survivors, wage slaves, survivors of public or private
education, all of us now living on a planet which is being killed
before our eyes, it certainly encompasses more or less all of us.
Cunt is also for those who, against all odds, may actually retain
shreds of their original sanity.

    Cunt is a celebration, not only of cunts but of all life. Cunts
are life, as are pricks, kneecaps, elbows, fingernails, the tails of
tadpoles, redwood needles, and the sandy red soil we taste
between foreteeth and tongue. *Cunt* explores this life, rolls this
life gently between fingertips, more gently across the soft skin
of lower belly and more gently still between still-softer thighs.
The book tells us—whole or scarred—how to live, as life tells us

how to live, as our bodies tell us how to live, as fingertips, elbows, pricks and cunts tell us how to live. As the soil tells us how to live. They're all the same. Only different.

I first read *Cunt* last year, long after it had changed the lives of many people. It took me a day. I picked it up as the sun cleared the trees to the southeast, and didn't put it down till the book was done and the sun was well on its way back down the blue hill above. It was a day that changed my life. I have read the book several times since, and each time have learned more about the women in my life, more about my own life, more about life in general. And I've learned about the culture, about the way men are trained to terrorize women and children. And I've learned what women, and children, are doing about that.

We may as well acknowledge that we're all fucked.

I don't mean this in the delightful sense of lovers coming together, meeting in the middle of their hearts and minds and bodies, but in the sense that we're in far more trouble than words—even words as powerful as Inga Muscio's—can say. Wild salmon are disappearing, as are great apes, coral reefs, native earthworms, wild forests, wild places of all stripes. Last week two more huge chunks of Antarctica fell into the sea. Dioxin contaminates polar bear fat, and it contaminates mother's milk. Three corporations control more than eighty percent of the beef market, and seven corporations control more than ninety percent of the grain market. Military scientists have placed computer chips in the brains of rats, and can force the creatures to go left, right, backward, forward by pushing buttons on keyboards. Imagine the fun the scientists would have if they figure out how to do this with women's hips.

We're fucked. We all know the numbers. We know that twenty-five percent of all women in this culture are raped within their lifetimes, and another nineteen percent have to fend off rape attempts. Which means of course that unless one guy is excruciatingly busy, an awful lot of men are rapists. We know that as many as twenty-two million American women have been molested by relatives, with six million of those molested by their fathers. We know also that 565,000 American children are killed or injured every year by their parents or guardians.

We know, too, that there are more slaves in the world today than came across on the Middle Passage. And we know that in the 1830s a slave in the American South cost between $500 and $1000, the equivalent of $50,000 to $100,000 today. And now a slave costs about $50, making them not even a capital but a simple expense, to be used up and thrown away.

We're fucked.

This is where *Cunt* comes in. If we're so fucked, one might reasonably ask, why not just go ahead and off ourselves? *Cunt* gives the answer (as do our cunts, pricks, elbows, kneecaps, and as do all the wild and free creatures on the planet): life is good. Life is really, really good. Not mediated life. Not televisions, cars, stereos, jobs, professional sports, colognes, perfumes, skyscrapers, steel, asphalt, brick, mortar. But life. Waking up with the sun on your face. Tasting your lover's sweat. Smelling their scent. Stubbing your toe, petting a dog, french-kissing a tree (but only if the tree agrees), helping your mother plant her garden, feeling your body grow heavy at the end of a hard day, and waiting to catch up to your dreams.

But to merely reside in the sensual as the world burns isn't good enough. Nor is it good enough merely to mourn the losses both inside and out. Both of these are necessary, but not sufficient. And here *Cunt* helps again. If things are so bad, one can also ask (this time unreasonably, I think), why not just withdraw into the sensual, why not just party (or cry)? Because, I think *Cunt* makes clear, this question reveals nothing neither more nor less than an inability to love. If you're in love, with your life, with your body, with your lover, with the tree outside your door, with the world that gives rise to all of these, the fact that we're all deeply, deeply fucked doesn't matter a damn to your actions: if you're in love, you act to protect your beloved.

In the end, *Cunt* is about love, as are cunts, pricks, elbows, as is the soft flesh of puppies' ears, as are the spines of thistles and the sharp edges of blades of grass.

If we are to survive, we must reclaim our planet from those corporations which—and people who—are destroying it. But even before this, we must reclaim our own bodies and our hearts from that same grasp. *Cunt* helps us do that, helps us find our way back to our cunts, pricks, elbows, kneecaps, and perhaps most important of all, our hearts.

Derrick Jensen
May 2002

Preface

"Cunt" is very arguably the most powerful negative word in the American English language. "Cunt" is the ultimate one-syllable covert verbal weapon any streetwise six-year-old or passing motorist can use against a woman. "Cunt" refers almost exclusively to women, and expresses the utmost rancor.

There's a general feeling of accord on this.

Except for some friends who know all about this book, no one calls me a "cunt" to communicate what a cool and sublime human being they think I am. Up until a certain time in my life, I never employed "cunt" to express respect or admiration.

I qualify these statements because my relationship with "cunt" is no longer what it once was.

One day I came home from third grade and asked my pops, "What's a wetback?"

With resignation and a sigh, Dad elucidated a brief history of "wetback." He concluded, "Don't you *ever* say it."

A list of words I was similarly not to utter was forthcoming:

nigger, beaner, kike, wop, jap, injun, spic. The only formal cuss word included on his roster was "cunt."

Coming as I did from a family where us kids were allowed to strew profanities like rice at a wedding, I was mighty affected by all this. Why, in my father's way of thinking, could I call someone an asshole but not a wetback nigger cunt?

The foreshadowings of a mystery.

In my childhood home, the 1965 Random House Dictionary was as much a part of dinnertime as laughter, arguments 'n wanton table manners. Throughout dinner, my siblings and I were required to spell and define new vocabulary words. It was a custom I enjoyed very much.

I was raised to appreciate the power of words.

Little did I know that when I grew up, out of the billion and one words in the 1965 Random House Dictionary and beyond, there would exist no word that I could use to adequately describe myself.

This wouldn't be much of a problem except that there are millions of me's: articulate, strong, talented, raging, brilliant, grooving, sexy, expressive, dancing, singing, laughing women in America, of all shapes, hues, ethnicities, sizes, sexual orientations and dispositions.

We are everywhere.

But what are we.

The only dimly representational, identifying term that advocates truly authentic recognition for the actual realities of women in this world is "feminism." This is a relatively youthful word. Our actual realities, on the other hand, are rooted deep.

We are born with them in our hearts.

Inherited them from our mothers.

Grandmothers.

Under the influence of this dilemma, I've asked myself if there might be a word as old, as universal and as deeply rooted as women's actual realities in patriarchal society. Hidden somewhere in the English language, could there be a word with power steeped in our history, a word which truly conveyed the rage and hope of *all women?*

And lo and behold, I return to the one formal cuss word on Pop's roster:

cunt.

This book is about my reconciliation with
the word
and
the anatomical jewel.

In Part I of *Cunt,* "The Word," I assert that the context in which "cunt" is presently perceived does not serve women, and should therefore be thoroughly re-examined.

English is considered the "universal language" because it represents the victors of history's present telling. Seizing this language and manipulating it to serve your community is a very powerful thing to do, and—based on a variety of specific elements, such as ethnicity, musical tastes, credit limits and/or sexuality—it is done a lot in America. Creating a general, woman-centered version of the English language, however, is just insanely difficult.

Womankind is varied and vast.

But we all have cunts, and it does not matter if they are biological, surgical or metaphorical. A cunt's a cunt.

While one word maketh not a woman-centered language, "cunt" is certainly a mighty potent and versatile contribution. Not to mention how *deliciously satisfying* it is to *totally snag* a reviled word and elevate it to a status which all women should rightfully experience in this society.

When viewed as a positive force in the language of women—as well as a reference to the power of the anatomical jewel which unites us all—the negative power of "cunt" falls in upon itself, and we are suddenly equipped with a word that describes all women, regardless of race, age, class, religion or the degree of lesbianism we enjoy.

Part II, "The Anatomical Jewel," examines why having a cunt in this society might just be worse than being called one. Our cunts bleed and have weird, unpredictable orgasms. The birthing process is painful and messy. Lordisa knows what our cunts are up to. Generally speaking, we don't understand them, we don't like them and we often think they're ugly.

A different, more sublime way of looking at this is that our cunts are the symbolic and physical zenith of our existence.

When our cunts bleed, *we* are *bleeding people*. Clairvoyant dreams visit our sleepytime heads. Sometimes, the swaggering braggadocio of human males causes our wombs to clench up in spasms of pain. When cunts have stupendous orgasms, we may reel for days, and have a fetching smile for every person we meet when we're walkin' down the street. When cunts get filled

up with sperm, women sometimes get pregnant and experience
either the trauma of aborting, or the courageous and under-
appreciated tribulation of devoting *the rest of our lives* to another
human being. When men fuck our cunts against our will, we
often feel like a diarrhea shit has been offed upon the very
essence of our soul, and may live *the rest of our days* cleaning it
off in whatever way we see fit.

An aisle in all American grocery stores is devoted to various
commercial products, dreamed up by corporations owned and
operated by men, which are designed to "care for" and deodorize
cunts. An entire branch of Western medicine, male style, exists
because of the infernal, confounding magic of cunts. Doctors
who treat cunts have special names.

Famous cunts in history have caused empires to rise and fall.

Sex industries throughout the world enjoy exorbitant profit
margins because of the wonderful things cunts do and represent.

When women endure cultural customs such as clitoridectomies, chasity belts, Mississippi Appendectomies (i.e., forced
sterilization), infibulation, forced prostitution, slavery and rape,
cunts are where? Why, in the spotlight, of course.

Yes, though they often play supporting roles to cocks, cunts
deserve star billing in the marquee of every woman's life.

Cunts are very important.

Unfortunately, cunts are important to all the wrong people
for all the wrong reasons.

Cunts are not important to women because they are the
very fount of our power, genius and beauty. Rather, cunts are
important to men because they generate profits and episodes of
ejaculation, and represent the precise point of vulnerability for

keeping women divided and thus, conquered.

History, the media, economic structures and justice systems have led women to the understanding that delighting in a love affair with our cunts will get us no further than Sitting Bull, had he opted to have a passionate love affair with the Seventh Cavalry.

Which, of course, he did not.

Why should Sitting Bull love the Seventh Cavalry? The Seventh Cavalry consistently represented the undoing of his people.

Why should women love our cunts? They, too, consistently represent the undoing of our people.

The main contention here, of course, is that the Seventh Cavalry did not reside between Sitting Bull's legs.

"The Anatomical Jewel" makes up the bulk of *Cunt*. The fact that women learn to dislike an actual, undeniable, unavoidable physical region of ourselves results in a crappy Sisyphean situation, warranting an intense focus of attention.

Part III is called "Reconciliation." One definition of reconciliation is the re-establishment of a close relationship that has experienced estrangement somewhere along the line.

My cunt is *mine*.

In order to re-establish a close relationship with my cunt, I must take responsibility not only for what it is to me today, but for everything it has become due to the seemingly endless throng of spin doctors, past and present. My cunt serves me in ways *cavernously* unrelated to generating profits, procuring episodes of ejaculation in males and representing the precise point of vulnerability for keeping women divided and thus, conquered. It is therefore my responsibility to insure this reality resides at the forefront of humanity's consciousness when history is rewritten once again.

We women have a lot of responsibilities.

Here are a few:

Seizing a vocabulary for ourselves.

Actively teaching ourselves to perceive cunts—ours and others'—in a manner generating understanding and empathy.

Taking this knowledge out into the community.

Learning self-protection.

Seeking out and supporting cuntlovin' artists, businesses, media and role models.

Using our power as consumers.

Keeping our money in a community of cuntlovin' women.

We arrive at reconciliation by confronting learned, internalized misogyny and re-educating ourselves on our terms. Three of the most important aspects of reconciliation involve fighting with our minds, art and money to create a cultural consciousness that supports and respects all women. The power and potential of these weapons—minds, art and money—are exalted in Part III.

Closing Regards

One of *Cunt*'s aspirations is to contribute to a language and philosophy specifically designed to empower and unite *all women*.

I do not, however, expect my personal experiences necessarily to pluck on the heartstrings of said *all women*.

I am white, so many complexities of individual and
institutional racism are not present in this book like they would
be if I were, say, a Filipina-American writer whose ancestors
founded a ranch outside Houston before the treaty of Guadalupe
Hidalgo was signed in 1848.

I am a lesbian who wouldn't oppose a tumble in the hay
with my housemate's boyfriend's twenty-year-old brother who
lives in Peru and is *achingly* beautiful, so likewise with rigid
strictures of hetero- and homosexuality.

I am an American citizen from a mid-middle-class family
that was supported solely by the sweat of my mother's brow. As
such, I have never been without shoes, food, education, shelter
and other fine trappings of subsistence.

When I was three, an accident with a street-cleaner bristle
blinded me in my right eye. I've lived through the deaths of my
father and youngest brother. I started writing as a child to
survive a spiritually blighted landscape. I obsessively devoted
my life to writing so I wouldn't go insane after my brother died.
I'm a vegetarian, but I like watching people eat spareribs.

All this greatly influences my perspective.

As does a prayer my mother has hanging in her kitchen,
now, then and in the hour of her death: "You are a child of the
universe, no less than the trees and the stars. You have a right to
be here, and whether or not it is clear to you, no doubt the
universe is unfolding as it should."

From the poetry of Sappho to the zines of riot grrrls,
personal experience has proven to be a very effective way for

women to communicate. Sharing individual knowledge contributes to the whole, and has been a foundation of women's power, in cultures spanning the globe, since time out of mind.

Here in America, at the dawning of the post-patriarchal age, a growing understanding of our differences and commonalities continues to emerge full force. Because we now have more means to communicate than ever before, histories based on personal experience are increasingly poised to unite *all women*.

Women are blue-black as the ocean's deepest knowledge, creamy-white 'n lacy blue-veined, freshly ground–cinnamon brown. Women are Christian motorcycle dykes, militantly hetero Muslim theological scholars, Jewish-Chinese bisexual macrobiotic ballerinas and Chippewa shawomen who fuck not just lovers, but Time and Silence too.

Women are drug addicts, anti-abortion activists and volunteers for Meals on Wheels. Women have AIDS, big fancy houses, post-traumatic stress disorder and cockroach-infested hovels. Women are rockstars, Whores, mothers, lawyers, taxidermists, welders, supermodels, scientists, belly dancers, cops, filmmakers, athletes and nurses.

There are not many things which unite *all women*.
I have found "cunt," the word and the anatomical jewel, to be a venerable ally in my war against my own oppression. Besides global subjugation, our cunts are the only common denominator I can think of that *all women* irrefutably share.

We are divided from the word.

We are divided from the anatomical jewel.

I seek reconciliation.

Part I
The Word (w û r d) n.

a tidy little prelude

On the choice occasions popes and politicians directly refer to
female genitalia, the term "vagina" is discreetly engaged.

If you will be so kind, say "vagina" out loud a few times.
Strip away the meaning and listen solely to the phonetic sound.
It resonates from the roof of your mouth.

A "vagina" could be an economy car:

"That's right, Wanda! Come within five hundred dollars of
the actual sticker price, and you'll win this! A brand new
Chrysler Vagina!"

Or a rodent:

"Next on *Prairie Safari,* you'll see a wily little silver-tailed
vagina outwit a voracious pair of ospreys."

Say "cunt" out loud, again stripping away the meaning. The
word resonates from the depths of your gut. It *sounds* like
something you definitely don't want to tangle with in a drunken
brawl in a dark alley.

A "cunt" could be a serious weather condition:

"Next on *Nightline,* an exclusive report on the devastation in
Kansas when last night's thunder cunt, with winds exceeding
122 miles an hour, ripped through the state."

Or a monster truck:

"The City Arena is proud to present the Coors Crush 'Em

Demolition Round-Up competition, where Randy Sam's *Beast of Burden* will challenge Mike Price's undefeated *Raging Cunt* in the 666 barrel jump."

Moving from phonetics to etymology, "vagina" originates from a word meaning sheath for a sword.

Ain't got no vagina.

Cuntist Mystique

I came across the power of "cunt" quite accidentally. After writing an article for a newspaper, I typed in "word count," but left out the "o." My editor laughingly pointed out the mistake. I looked at the two words together and decided "Word Cunt" seemed like a nice title for a woman writer. As a kind of intraoffice byline, I started typing "Word Cunt" instead of "word count" on all my articles.

The handful of people who saw hard copies of my work reacted strongly and asked why I chose to put these two words on my articles. After explaining my reasoning to editorial assistants, production magis, proofreaders and receptionists, I started wondering about the actual, decontextualized power of "cunt."

I looked up "cunt" in Barbara G. Walker's twenty-five-year research opus, *The Women's Encyclopedia of Myths and Secrets,* and found it was indeed a title, back in the day. "Cunt" is related to words from India, China, Ireland, Rome and Egypt. Such words were either titles of respect for women, priestesses and witches, or derivatives of the names of various goddesses:

In ancient writings, the word for "cunt" was synonymous
with "woman," though not in the insulting modern sense. An
Egyptologist was shocked to find the maxims of Ptah-Hotep
"used for 'woman' a term that was more than blunt," though
its indelicacy was not in the eye of the ancient beholder, only
in that of the modern scholar. (Walker, 1983, 197)

The words "bitch" and "whore" have also shared a similar
fate in our language. This seemed rather fishy to me. Three
words which convey negative meanings about women, specifically, all happen to have once had totally positive associations
about women, specifically.

Of the three, "cunt" garners the most powerful negative
reaction.

How come?

This was obviously a loaded question to be asking myself,
'cause the answer evolved into quite the life-consuming
project.

According to every woman-centered historical reference I have
read—from M. Esther Harding to bell hooks—the containment
of woman's sexuality was a huge priority to emerging patrifocal
religious and economic systems.

Cunts were anathema to forefather types. Literally and
metaphorically, the word and anatomical jewel presided at the
very nexus of many earlier religions which impeded phallic
power worship. In Western civilization, forefather types practiced savior-centered religions, such as Catholicism. Springing
forth from a very real, very fiscal fear of women and our power,

eventually evolving into sexual retardation and womb envy, a philosophy and social system based on destruction was culled to thriving life. One of the more well-documented instances of this destruction-oriented consciousness is something called the Inquisition. It lasted for over *five hundred years*. That is how long it took the Inquisition to rend serious damage to the collective spirit of non-savior-centered religious worshippers.

The Inquisition justified the—usually sadistic—murder, enslavement or rape of every woman, child and man who practiced any form of spiritual belief which did not honor savior-centered phallic power worship.

Since the beginning of time, most cultures honored forces which were tangible, such as the moon, earth, sun, water, birth, death and life. A spirituality which was undetectable to any of the human senses was considered incomprehensible.

One imagines victims of the Inquisition were not hard to come by. Women who owned anything more than the clothes on their backs and a few pots to piss in were religiously targeted by the Inquisition because all of women's resources and possessions became property of the famously cuntfearing Catholic Church. Out of this, the practice of sending "missionaries" into societies bereft of savior-centered spiritualities evolved.

Negative reactions to "cunt" resonate from a learned fear of ancient yet contemporary, inherent yet lost, reviled yet re-demptive cuntpower.

Eradicating a tried and true, stentorian-assed word from a language is like rendering null the Goddess Herself.

It's impossible.

Ancient, woman-centered words and beliefs never, like, *fall off the planet*. Having long done taken on a life of their own, they—like womankind—evolve, and survive.

Chameleon style.

For women this has involved making many, many concessions, such as allowing our selves, goddesses, priestesses and words to be defined and presented by men.

Many words found in woman-centered religions, such as cunt, bitch, whore, dog, ass, puta, skag and hag, along with the names of just about all goddesses—over time—assimilated bad connotations. As matrifocal lifestyles became less and less acceptable, "cunt" survived, *necessarily* carrying a negative meaning on into the next millennium.

Words outlive people, institutions, civilizations. Words spur images, associations, memories, inspirations and synapse pulsations. Words send off physical resonations of thought into the nethersphere. Words hurt, soothe, inspire, demean, demand, incite, pacify, teach, romance, pervert, unite, divide.

Words be powerful.

Grown-ups and children are not readily encouraged to unearth the power of words. Adults are repeatedly assured a picture is worth a thousand of them, while the playground response to almost any verbal taunt is "Sticks and stones may break my bones, but words will never hurt me."

I don't beg so much as command to differ.

For young girls in this society, coming into the power we are born with is no easy task. As children, our power is not culled out of us as it is for boys. Still, culling power is—above and beyond all social conditioning—a very surmountable *task* to which womankind collectively rises higher each day.

But we need a language.

A means of communication demands and precedes change.

I posit that we're free to seize a word that was kidnapped and co-opted in a pain-filled, distant past, with a ransom that cost our grandmothers' freedom, children, traditions, pride and land. I figure we've paid the ransom, but now, everybody long done forgot "cunt" was ours in the first place.

I have lived the past couple years of my life writing a book called *Cunt*. When people ask me what I do, sometimes I bypass the whole conversation and say I'm a taxidermist. Reactions to a book called *Cunt* always lead to an intense grilling. Ain't never encountered ambivalence. At this juncture, I am still absolutely unable to gauge reactions to this word.

Living with the title of this book as such a huge fixture in my day-to-day life has been a very weird anthropological study unto itself. "Cunt" is a bad, bad word, but *damn* if it don't *intrigue* people when it's the title of a book instead of a meanspirited expletive.

Since everybody already knows that the diabolization of "cunt" is an absolute reality of our language, nobody has to waste time and energy defending its honor.

A cunt by any other name is still a cunt.

"Cunt" is a highly satisfying word to utter on a regular basis.

Every girl and lady who is strong and fighting and powerful,

who thrives in this world in a way that serves her, is a rockin',
cuntlovin' babe doing her part to goad the post-patriarchal age
into fruition.

"Cunt" is the crusty, disgusting bottle in the city dump pile
that is bejewelled underneath and has a beautiful genie inside.

Here is a nice story about the transformation of destructive
negative, crap-ola into constructive, positive brilliantiana.

Once upon a time, civil rights activist Dick Gregory went
into a restaurant and ordered some chicken. Three or four men
who wore pointy white hoods for their nighttime fashion
statement presently came into the restaurant and said, (I'm
paraphrasing here) "Yo, boy. Anything y'do tah dat chicken,
we're gone do tah yoo."

Mr. Gregory looked at the chicken on the plate before him
and was silent.

The men repeated, "Anything y'do tah dat chicken, boy,
we're gone do tah yoo."

Everybody in the restaurant stopped what they were doing
and stared.

Mr. Gregory sighed, picked up the chicken and gave it a big
ol', sweet ol' kiss.

Perhaps, as some "historians" may have it, I fabricated the
historic considerations in reassessing the way we presently
perceive "cunt."

Even if "cunt" were simply four spontaneous letters
someone strung together one day 'cause his wife didn't have
dinner on the table when he got home from a hard day's labor

offing witches or indigenous peoples, it is still *our word*. Demographically, the women who have *no chance* of negatively being called "cunts" throughout life can be found in totally cloistered nunneries and maybe Amish communities.

Based on the criteria that "cunt" can be neither co-opted nor spin-doctored into having a negative meaning, venerable history or not, it's ours to do with what we want. And thanks to the versatility and user-friendliness of the English language, "cunt" can be used as an all new woman-centered, cuntlovin' noun, adjective or verb.

I, personally, am in love with the idea.

Part II
The Anatomical Jewel

(jōō′ əl) n.

an eentsy bit of math

If it were my job to mathematically figure out which women despise more: being called a cunt or having one, I'd be hating life.

I'm glad that is not my job.

Instead, my job at present is to discuss some of the different ways 'n means women learn to hate our cunts, which still isn't the most savory task on earth, but it is attainable.

Women comprise over 50 percent of this country. Women comprise just over 50 percent of this planet. There's plenty of power in numbers. If we don't have power, it can't have anything to do with mass.

I conclude it must have to do with some stuff inside ourselves.

To know oneself *truly* is to love oneself. Whereas women do not learn the veritable nature of ourselves in this culture, the likelihood that we love ourselves and/or one another is highly suspect.

All cunts belong to *all women*.

The responsibility sits between our legs.

Blood and Cunts

One fine spring day, after the lunchtime recess in sixth grade, Miss Cothran announced that all the boys were to join Mr. Rogers out on the playground for a game of softball, while all us girls were mandatorially invited to accompany her to the cafeteria.

My friends 'n me knew what was up. We had heard about the infamous Period Movie around fourth grade. Most of the boys were no less familiar with this legendary film and teased us relentlessly as they filed out to the softball diamond.

In the cafeteria, the girls from Mrs. Wolff's class, Mr. Rogers's class and mine assembled into tittering rows. The school nurse stood in the front of the room, between the pull-out movie screen and a table displaying all of the various disposable bleeding paraphernalia we would one day come to know so well. She explained the ways to affix pads to our panties and dabbled a little into tampondom; then the Film Projector Monitor was called to do her duty, and the Period Movie started.

To date, it is the most intellectually impaired film I've ever seen, taking into account the *combined* fatuity of *Basic Instinct* and *Ace Ventura: Pet Detective*.

A cartoon of the female form demonstrated how this dot in your head travels down to your cunt and makes you bleed. The doctorly sounding male narrator insisted that we not take baths or exercise during this "special time," but be sure to keep *spotlessly clean* with lots and lots of soap and showers because menstruating girls tend to stink up the room if they're not completely at one with personal hygiene. He also informed us that any pain or discomfort we might feel resided "in our heads," and had been collectively imagined by womankind for thousands of years.

Were we told anything about how our uteruses are almost exactly like the moon, shedding their linings, growing new ones and shedding all over again? Did the Period Movie teach us *thing one* about how miraculously cool and sublime the human body's reproductive system is when you're a girl?

Fuck no.

All I truly gleaned from this experience was that my cunt was the yucksville reason I had to sit in that stupid cafeteria watching some hack nurse show me how to safety pin a three-mile-wide wad of cotton to a pair of brief underpanties even my grandma wouldn't be caught dead in, while the other half of the sixth grade population was out in the sunshine playing softball. This was the first formal instruction in estrangement from my cunt—within a lifetime's barrage—that I consciously recall.

With all the prepubescent hoopla surrounding periods, I was inclined towards totally vivid nightmarish visions of complete humiliation that would usher in my initiation to womanhood. A recurring one was related to the shower scene Carrie endured—where she was pelted with tampons—in the Hollywood/Stephen King rendition of menstruation commencement. I was *wholly unprepared* for the simplicity and intuition I encountered at the inauguration of my blood.

In seventh grade, I was walking home from school with Teresa and Joyce. We were halfway down Tunnel Street and suddenly I *knew* I was bleeding. It was the first time I remember *knowing* something in this manner. I told Teresa and Joyce, "Hey, I just started my period," and that was that. I went home, grabbed a pad out of my mom's store and bled on it.

Tampons didn't come along until my fourth period, when Amy Ajello instructed me in great detail over my teen talk phone line. It was tricky holding the phone to my ear and inserting a tampon for the first time but, thank god, I managed, 'cause pads creeped me out the door. Whenever I wore one, I imagined Jimmy Vallejo and Andrew Vasquez pointing at the gigantic bulge moshing up my ass as I walked down the hall. In my vision, they howled, à la Beavis and Butthead, and everyone else, of course, would hear about it and I'd be the laughingstock of the whole middle school.

Shame kept a close watch on me and all my girlfriends.

It was shameful to bleed, to be seen bleeding, for blood-soaking paraphernalia to be visible on or about one's person at any time whatsoever, to speak of bleeding, to look like we were bleeding, to be excused from P.E. because of the crippling cramps which sometimes accompany bleeding, to display frailty, vulnerability or mood swings because we were going to be bleeding soon and to express any emotion other than contempt and disdain in reference to our blood.

No one, least of all my peers—who, verily, whispered about this proscriptive subject in hushy undertones, behind closed doors, in only the most trusted of boyless locales—thought bleeding a pleasant reality.

Girls are told bleeding is a *bad thing,* an *embarrassing thing,* a *secret thing* that we should hide and remain discreet about come hell or high water.

Boys are told to go outside and play sports while the girls learn about some creepy, cootie-laden mystery that makes blood ooze out from our you-know-whats.

Given my swimmingly fetching cultural milieu, getting used to this bleeding business took quite a while. In the meantime, I fervently asked people why the hell this happened to us girls. Various sources consistently informed me that it was (big sigh) "just part of being a woman" (big sigh), or the good ol' standby curse we inherited from Eve.

My period was not only a "curse," but for the first years of bleeding, I was completely incapacitated with mind-numbing spasms of pain. For at least one day out of every month, I didn't go to school or work. I lay in bed and cried, unable to do anything about the agony of my uterus. Frequently, because of this "imagined" pain, I fainted and puked.

I find it fascinating that men's description of the pain enkindled by a knee to the groin sounds awfully similar to what I have experienced for up to thirty-six unflagging hours. And yet, imagine the hue and cry if men were informed that the horrifying symptom of pain accompanying a swift kick in the nuts was purely psychosomatic.

A coupla years after my period started, the newspapers across our fair nation announced that women *weren't* imagining those intense pains. *Scientific studies* proved that the pain *is real!* As you might surmise, this was but a *load* off my mind.

After all those days I vomited because the mid-section of my body was clenched in a fist of throbbing excruciation; when I sat in the bathtub crying for five hours straight; when I couldn't get out of bed or leave the house for fear of fainting in public; suddenly, because a group of men took the time to study a group of women and found there was indeed a rational reason for these symptoms to wrack our bodies once a month, I was allotted the pale comfort of knowing this pain *actually* existed!

Oh, joy.

Cynic that I am in such arenas of contemplation, I wonder if perhaps this generous allotment wasn't bestowed upon womankind because pharmaceutical companies came to the magnanimous conclusion that sales for pain relievers would skyrocket if only they invested in a little "research" to counter the "in her mind" myth and re-condition the general public into believing there was a veritable malady at hand.

In the spring of 1995, I had the momentous honor of inter-viewing Barbara G. Walker at her home in New Jersey. Among many other things, she told me about menarche parties women in her community have for the newly menstruating. Ms. Walker described a menarche she attended a few months prior to our interview. The honoree wore a red dress. Her mother made a beautiful, red cake for her. A bunch of women,

young and old, brought her red gifts wrapped in red paper. The
older women talked about the symbolism of the moon and the
miraculous joys of both bleeding and not bleeding anymore,
while the younger women who hadn't yet started to bleed duly
expressed reverence for the honoree, and enthusiasm about
starting their periods.

I mean, wouldn't that be wonderful?

Wouldn't you feel like a total princess if your mom or
whoever did that for you? Wouldn't that put a whole new slant
on bleeding from the get go?

I was deeply moved by Ms. Walker's account, but in all
honesty I must acknowledge my bittersweet envy. My mom's a
dang smart lady, and I admire her above and beyond all women
on the planet, but it was a bummer to realize that if she hadn't
been so busy dealing with the social constraints of single
motherhood during the early '80s, sans the aid of a supportive
community of women, she might have had the inspiration to
hostess a menarche for my sister and me. Whereupon, I
sincerely doubt I would've spent almost a decade of my life
teaching myself to love the blood that coursed out my stunning
cunt every month.

Throwing menarche parties for our younger sisters, nieces
and daughters is a very simple and profound way of effecting
positive change for the next generation.

Get off your ass and do it.

If Pippi Longstocking were the nation's covergirl, rest assured
that women would have a superlative role model in the fine
science of accepting ourselves. Ms. Longstocking is extremely

the anatomical jewel

outspoken in response to negative social beliefs:

> [T]he children came to a perfume shop. In the show window was a large jar of freckle salve, and beside the jar was a sign which read: DO YOU SUFFER FROM FRECKLES?
>
> "What does the sign say?" asked Pippi. She couldn't read very well because she didn't want to go to school as other children did.
>
> "It says, 'Do you suffer from freckles?'" said Annika.
>
> "Does it indeed?" said Pippi thoughtfully. "Well, a civil question deserves a civil answer. Let's go in."
>
> She opened the door and entered the shop, closely followed by Tommy and Annika. An elderly lady stood back of the counter. Pippi went right up to her.
>
> "No!" she said decidedly.
>
> "What is it you want?" asked the lady.
>
> "No," said Pippi once more.
>
> "I don't understand what you mean," said the lady.
>
> "No, I don't suffer from freckles," said Pippi.
>
> Then the lady understood but she took one look at Pippi and burst out, "But, my dear child, your whole face is covered with freckles!"
>
> "I know it," said Pippi, "but I don't suffer from them. I love them. Good morning." (Lindgren, 1970, 18-19)

Unfortunately, Pippi Longstocking is *not* the nation's covergirl.

※

All the way through my teens and into my twenties, I loathed my period. "Menstruation" was synonymous with unmitigated physical pain on a monthly basis.

But then I got to thinkin'.

Maybe because I was in college, and what are you supposed to do in college if not think? Maybe because I noticed a marked difference in the way women reacted toward menstruation at this point in human development. Maybe because for the first time in my life, I found myself surrounded by women who were greatly intrigued by the workings of our bodies. Maybe because by the time I went to college I'd taken enough psychotropic plant forms to feel more or less At One with the Universe, instead of lost at sea in the swimmingly fetching cultural milieu I'd previously more or less accepted as reality.

During this period of thinking, I read books and watched the moon.

All women throughout time have had the *opportunity* to see the moon. From Africa and Asia to the Americas and Europe, plenty of these ladies started noticing that the moon grows, recedes and grows again, over and over every twenty-eight days. Those not detached from their menstrual cycle couldn't help but trip out on how their own blood rhythm also occurred over the span of approximately twenty-eight days.

This is how the moon links one up with a form of history none of the textbooks can possibly touch upon: a *psychic* history with all the women who've ever bled on this planet.

By reading some books, investing in a lunar calendar and poking my head out the window every night or so, I figured out how to tell time by the moon. I learned her phases and moods. The springtime full moon has a much different luminescence than the autumntime full moon. When I went to a party on a dark moon, I generally had a shitty time. When I went to a party during the moon's waxing phase, or better, when it was full, I had a whopping good time.

And on and on.

Soon after me and the moon got to be buddies, the strangest thing happened. The simple act of *hanging* with the moon invoked beliefs my brain had never computed before. Suddenly, all the period propaganda shoved down my throat since that fateful day in sixth grade was far away and beyond ridiculous.

Lo and behold, my period stopped hurting!

I designated the first day of my blood a Special Time where I consciously guarded my quiet. I soaked in mineral salted baths, read Pippi Longstocking, mended clothes (before this, shortening a skirt involved the use of duct tape and an iron) and cooked Creole Tomato Soup.

I quit taking ibuprofen. My period mellowed out even more. For the first time in my life, I actually *enjoyed* bleeding. I gauged myself with the movements and rhythms of the moon. I still got cramps, but I didn't faint or puke at all.

Hip, hip!

One month I had pretty bad pains and took some ibuprofen. The following month, the pain was even worse. Then I did an experiment. Some months I took pain relievers and some months, I didn't. Every time, the month *after* I took pain relievers, I'd have, as Holiday Golightly would say, the Mean Reds.

Though the medication brought *immediate* relief, the following period was excruciating. Taking menstrual-pain drugs became a vicious cycle. I never realized it before, and it was so obvious once I saw it, but I needed more and more ibuprofen to keep the pain at bay each month.

This little experiment resulted in an *absolute mistrust* for everything I had ever learned about being a woman in this culture. I began the arduous task of questioning, re-evaluating, researching and rewriting the entire information-cataloging system in my brain.

For two years, I did not watch television, read newspapers or any magazines which did not reflect a standard of woman-hood with which I identified. Dr. Leo Daugherty, one of my esteemed instructors at the Evergreen State College, told me that for one whole year he read books only by women writers, and I did that too.

All this activity started with my period, but it soon encompassed my entire life and history as well as my way of perceiving the lives and histories of every woman with whom I came into contact.

The way I had learned to deal with my bleeding ways was a reflection of what our society teaches us about everything cuntlovin' and female and rhythmic and sexual. These are things which must be somehow "controlled" with shame, embarrassment, taboo, violence or drugs. In order to serve the destructive tendencies of our society, everything that is cuntlovin' must be sequestered away far into deep recesses of the collective unconscious *somehow*.

c
u
n
t

Therefore, like our cunts, our blood is weird, messy and ugly. The negativity surrounding menstruation is an illusion that falls, falls, falls away the instant perspective shifts.

And all this mental activity started with me and the moon.

The moon has consistently proven herself to be every woman's ally since the beginning of time. The moon renders fearful illusions of social conditioning petty riffraff that gets in the way of a cuntlovin' lady's life. The moon fucken rules.

Once you decide your body is your fine-tuned hot rod to tool you around this earth as you desire, buy a lunar calendar (I highly recommend the one published by Luna Press). Put it where you'll see it every morning. Slap it up by the coffee maker, the bathroom mirror or above your bed. Wherever. Look at it every day. Notice where the moon is on the calendar. As often as possible, notice the moon in the sky. That's all you have to do, nothing fancy, just notice the moon. The clincher here is *consistency*. Watch the moon grow and recede every month. Be able to eventually wake up in the morning and know where the moon will be that evening without looking.

This is aligning yourself with the moon. Since, like I say, the moon has been teaching us ladies about our insides since we developed the eyeballs able to see that high, there's no wrong way to do this. The moon will teach you just as it taught your distant ancestors.

When you get your period, make a (red) mark on your moon calendar. What did the moon look like when you got your period? What did it look like last month? Sooner or later, you'll get a rhythm going with the moon. You'll have your period every new moon or every waxing moon, or maybe one month you will get your period on the full moon, the next month on the waning moon, next on the new moon and next on the waxing moon. It varies just fantastically. There is no way of knowing what your cycle is until you lunarly track it. Even then, it is likely to traverse the moon's phases throughout the year, but if you keep a good record and watch what goes on between your cunt and the moon, you'll be able to predict, *to the day*, when you start your period, *even if you are "irregular."* Again, I can't stress enough: This takes time. You may not have a full grasp on your cycle for six months or even longer.

Patience is this: a virtue.

As you begin to groove with your fine cunt workings and the moon, you'll be able to perform all kinds of neat-o miracles. You can figure out if you're in for a hellish period. Nasties like yeast infections can be easily nipped in the bud because you're so *utterly hip* with yourself. What were once faintly clairvoyant premenstrual dreams take on more lucid clarity and depth. Sex becomes more intense and ecstatic. Menstrual cramps diminish. You can determine when you will and won't get in the family way—if you investigate the matter fully.

Our society creates a hospitable climate for cuntpower to be generated into profits amassed by large corporations. Pharmaceutical and feminine hygiene companies, plastic surgeons and weight-loss centers are designated to care for our bodies in our stead. We learn to rely on various "experts" and authority figures who patronizingly inform us how we should respond to our bodies. We are not offered the opportunity to consider how we'd like to respond to bleeding, nor are we presented with how women menstruated in the past or in other cultures.

Becoming responsible is about quitting the "expert" addiction, feeling and listening to what is going on inside of us and responding in ways that feel good and right to us. Learning to be responsible for your body *takes time*. It's taken you *all your life* to learn how to alienate yourself to the point of total irresponsibility.

If it took society, say, twenty-five years to teach you that you have no control, it'll take you less than a tenth of that time to learn yourself otherwise. In the long run, that's not much time at all, but still, it does indeed amount to roughly two point five years.

It is of utmost importance to be patient with yourself, your ignorance and your curiosity. Any stockbroker in her right mind will tell you: The return on an investment is wholly dependent upon the investment itself. By the time we're twelve or so, society has convinced the vast majority of women that it is in our best interest to remain incontestably oblivious to our bodies, outside the realm of tormenting ourselves into reflecting a certain standard of physical beauty. Therefore, it is entirely reasonable that we never pause to invest in ourselves on terms that we ourselves define. Our subjugation continues because women are estranged from our actual realities.

Taking responsibility for one's bleeding ways is part of the reality-based revolution founded between the soft, luscious thighs of every woman on the planet.

A more material aspect of this revolution is downsizing the percentage of our funding to corporations that exist for no other purpose than to constrain women in the throes of body-alienation and perpetuate our deleterious relationships with our cunts.

Here is my story about that.

I went to Anystore U.S.A. to buy a box of tampons. I had but eleven dollars to my name. I went down the aisle where I would find "feminine hygiene" products, bitterly playing that term through my mind.

Why are words like "hygiene" and "sanitary'—which imply that a woman's cunt is unclean—acceptable in our society? Why are these people trying to sell me feminine deodorant spray? That's like hawking floral air freshener to a lady who lives in a rose garden.

Also, excuse me, but what's so clean about dicks?

One never hears of sanitary jock straps, deodorant condoms, perfumed Hershey-Squirt protection pads or hygienic ball wipes, whereas I've heard tell of need for such products.

So anyway, with thoughts such as these playing through my mind, you can imagine my dismay on tampon-buying excursions. If I happen to be in a good mood, it's simply annoying. If I happen to be in a bad mood, I am a green monster who lives in a trash can with a grand piano. On this occasion, I was in a bad mood.

I grumbled down the aisle, openly sneering at all the products on the shelves. New Freedom this and Light Days that.

Comfort, security.

Plastic applicators.

Discreet disposal pouches printed with flowers that do not exist.

I positively *fumed* as I scanned the prices. Five, six, seven bucks for *a box of cotton*. Sixty, seventy bucks a year.

Why the *flying fuck* should a woman have to *pay* some huge corporation over and over because the lining of her uterus naturally, *biologically* sheds every month?

Amongst my small circle of friends, I tally seven hundred dollars spent on tampons and pads a year. I estimate the women in my apartment building spend thirteen thousand dollars a year to swell the already enormous profit margins of "feminine hygiene" companies.

Reluctantly, I made my selection: a box of Tampax Slender Regulars for $7.19. I stormed my way to the check-out line. In front of me was a young man who said hello.

I replied, "Do you realize that I will have barely three dollars in the whole wide world after I purchase this box of tampons because my period is coming and I find it unsavory to bleed in all my clothes and on every seat I occupy for the next few days?"

He told me that he'd considered this very conundrum. His girlfriend had bitched about the same thing at length.

We fell into a check-out line conversation on the matter, comparing men's hygienic expenses to those of women and also, how the moon is totally disregarded in our culture in relation to womb-type activities.

The couple behind us—a well-to-do looking pair in their lawn-bowling sixties—kept clearing their throats, saying ehh-hemmm and harrummphh. The woman, especially, gave me extremely disdainful looks for speaking so tactlessly and loudly in the Anystore U.S.A. check-out line.

A few days later, I related this experience to my friend Panacea Theriac, who, at the time, had just organized a small women's health collective in Olympia, Washington.

She said, "Oh, Inga! I've been using sea sponges! Have you heard about them?"

I said no.

Panacea told me all about them. She bought three sea sponges for $1.59 apiece. Besides their obvious economic virtues, she said, you use them over and over, so they're more ecologically desirable; when your sponge gets soaked with blood, no matter where you are, you just haul it on out, wash it real good with hot water and mild soap, then pop it on back in; you never have to trouble yourself with remembering to bring a tampon reserve; they're totally comfortable and fun to play with in the bathtub. Also, you can squeeze the blood out into a jar, fill it with water and feed it to your houseplants, who, Panacea assured me, "absolutely adore the stuff."

I asked her about Toxic Shock Syndrome and whether sea sponges harbor yucky things that can make a girl sick.

Panacea said that it is very, very important to keep your sponge *super duper clean*, washing it thoroughly every time you use and re-use it.

Trusting my friend as I do, I bought a couple of sea sponges at the local health food co-op and gave them a whirl. The only problem I've had is that when a sea sponge is full, it is *full*. If you laugh or yell when the sponge has absorbed its maximum capacity, your nice white panties will get a big red how-do-you-do on them.

Other than that, sea sponges are the coolest. I've developed an endearing friendship with my sponges. They are miraculous little plant bodies that once lived in the ocean, which is also ruled by the moon. And they don't carry that impersonal, flushable, bleached personality tampons possess.

Sea sponges can be found at almost all Anystore U.S.A.-type stores, usually in the make-up or bathtime section. If you're lucky enough to have a health food co-op in your town, they're sure to have them. At under two dollars apiece, they pay for themselves after one month.

Keep them clean. Boil a new sponge before you use it for the first time. Store them in a little cotton bag. Wash them and let them dry completely before putting them away for the month, but *always* wash them again before using. I've heard that you can use more than one at a time if you bleed a lot, but I've never tried this. I wouldn't recommend using the same sea sponge for more than a few months because the natural fibers wear down after a while and it gets kinda disintegratey.

A friend of mine who uses sea sponges once told me about an experience in a public restroom. She was at a busy nightclub, waiting in line with eight or so other women to use the toilet. There were four stalls and at least that many women at the sinks, primping and washing their hands. Suddenly, all normal bathroom conversation came to a crashing halt as a voice from behind one of the stall doors pealed out, "I'm coming out with my sea sponge, so if you're gonna gross out, shut your eyes." A woman then emerged from her stall, sea sponge in hand. With all eyes upon her, she washed it carefully at the sink, went back into the stall and finished up her business. One woman actually did close her eyes, but everyone else stood transfixed, witnessing the woman's ritual with her sea sponge. When the woman came out again, she fielded quite a number of questions about where to get sea sponges and how to use them. The whole room of women came together for a few moments, laughing and talking about our blood.

I enjoy imagining how the culture of restrooms would be different if our periods weren't all hush, flush 'n rush.

The Keeper is another fabulous gizmo for catching blood flow. It is a natural rubber cup with a stem that has a small hole in the end. The cup fits over your cervix, and when it's full, little drips of blood flow through the stem, letting you know it's time to tend to your Keeper.

I have never tried The Keeper because I don't like things covering my cervix, but I still average around two emails a month from ladies extolling the The Keeper's virtue. It is, I've been informed by sources all over the globe, reusable, incredibly comfortable and convenient.

Using sea sponges and the Keeper are very good ways for women to cut down on contributions to large corporations that don't readily promote the idea that cunts are sacredholy, and responsible for the entrance of every human being walking this earth.

But some ladies just don't like internal blood-soaking devices at all. Some ladies like to bleed *onto* something.

Even though me and my period have come to terms quite nicely over the years, I still can't put anything up my cunt on the first day of my period. My uterus rebels if a stray pubic hair finds its way up my canal on that ultrasensitive first day.

So I asked my grandmother, "What did ladies bleed on

before Kotex dreamed up those thick-as-white-wall-tire pads and elastic security belts?" She blinked her desert tortoise eyeballs before replying, "Child, where do you think the phrase 'on the rag' comes from?"

So smitten was I with not spending my money on tampons, I started safety-pinning rags to a pair of boys' underwear. (Why are BVDs so comfy, while Maidenform makes all these panties that cost too much and skooch up one's ass?)

I cut up a towel for my rags: A few are around four inches long and six inches wide, and the rest are five inches long and two inches wide. I wrap the wider width rags around my underwear, placing as many of the thinner ones between the wide rag and the underwear panel as I'll be needing.

It takes some practice to figure out how to get the rags situated just so. I can't really offer any suggestions, as it depends on how much you bleed, how you walk, sit and stand, what kind of fabric you choose, how you decide to affix the rags to the undies, etcetra and etcetra.

Many health food stores sell ready-made flannel rags with velcro fasteners.

If you sew, design your own rags.

If you don't sew, contact Bloodsisters, Lunapads and Glad Rags. Their information is in the Cuntlovin' Guide at the back of this book. Heck, these organizations are *so dang cool*, get in contact with them, regardless. They feature cuntlovin' bleeding products, reading materials, panties and many other revolutionary products.

And then, of course, there's the trusty Blood Towel.

I've had the same Blood Towel for seven years. It is blue. Terra cotta shadows stain it everywhere.

Linus from *Peanuts?*

Me and my Blood Towel.

When I'm on my period I sleep with my Blood Towel between my legs. We all know you're not supposed to wear tampons or sea sponges to bed, and rags and pads always seem to mosh up the ol' ass. Maybe a Blood Towel isn't the most alluring thing to wear to bed, but it sure is comfortable and keeps the sheets clean.

In the morning I walk around the house with my Blood Towel wrapped around my waist. It catches the flow when I sit down. I use it to wipe the insides of my legs. Otherwise, the blood splatters on my feet, the floor. I step in it and get it everywhere.

Sometimes I don't clean it up right away.

Messy, messy. Fingerpaints in kindergarten messy.

I like to do this for a very good reason:

Because I can!

Isn't it amazing.

By the simple act of not wearing panties, I can stand in the middle of my kitchen and *change the way it looks*. Without moving a muscle, a pool of blood appears between my feet.

Like magic.

Bleeding on sea sponges, the Keeper, rags and Blood Towels may *seem* undesirable when affiliated with commonly accepted standards for absorbing blood flow. But these "inconveniences" are founded solely upon our indoctrination in this society. Spending time with your blood is a constructive action. Bleeding every month is a part of life that we are taught to ignore. When we choose, literally, to *see* it, we open up to our actual reality as cuntlovin' women.

Rinsing a sea sponge or the Keeper out in the bathroom of a fancy restaurant or washing bloody rags by hand may not be as "convenient" as flushing all one's cunt ambrosia away into the city sewer system, but it reconnects a cuntlovin' woman with her body and, indirectly, with the bodies of every cuntlovin' woman, living and dead, who has ever known the sensation of blood flowing out of her cunt.

You have a ritual for bleeding on throwaway cotton. *You and only you* know your bleeding technique. Sure, it takes time to learn another one but the nice thing is:

Human beings are the most highly adaptable mammals on the planet. You'll figure out a system.

If, for example, you were to decide that using rags and sponges was impossible except when you are home at night, that'd still cut your dependency on large corporations' products anywhere from 20 to 50 percent.

In some situations, I use tampons (preferably, the un-bleached kind found in food co-ops and healthy rainbow sister stores). But instead of being *solely reliant* on tampons, instead of coughing up the money every single period, it takes me three to five months to empty a box.

When I *unconsciously* relegated the right to be in charge of how I bleed to various commercial and corporate entities who have no interest in me as a living being, much less as a woman, the distribution of my power did not serve me. Feminine hygiene corporations fund the lives of a small percentage of men who *remain* in power because they are so good at convincing us ladies that the most *natural and convenient* thing for us to do is to give them ours.

Speaking of men.

As individual husbands, fathers, brothers, sons and lovers, rather than as the most affluent team of business associates on the planet—are involved with this bleeding situation in a deeply subconscious way.

Men do *themselves* a *great service* learning about women and the moon. Unless they're incarcerated, it is just about impossible to avoid interacting with us.

Bleeding ladies are taught to be, at best, intolerant of a month-to-month physiological occurrence which clocks the time of our bodies. We therefore act mighty peculiar. Disliking something unavoidable takes its toll after a while. Some people call this PMS.

If, at every stage of life, society commanded men to despise their hard-ons, how pleasant would they be when this bodily function that they are incapable of desisting occurred?

Society fails to acknowledge that our bleeding cycle affects men's lives tremendously. This is further compounded by the fact that women who live or work in close proximity to one another tend to merge bleeding cycles. Chances are, every woman in a given household or workplace is bleeding at the same time. Sometimes men are surrounded on all sides by cranky, bleeding cunts.

To the incognizant, we seem entirely unpredictable. We may

bite a man's head right off for the smallest vagrancy.

They know this.

There is no way for them not to know this.

But chances are, they don't understand, and act like jerks 'cause their courage is tested. When most men who don't understand women see how really scary we are, courage usually segues to fear. This results in anger, frustration, violence and the perpetuation of general disrespect towards women. Bottom line: Men are afraid of our blood.

How's this for some serious chicken shittedness:

Keep away from women in their courses,
and do not
approach them until
they are clean.
But when they have
purified themselves,
You may approach them
in any manner, time, or place,
Ordained for you, by God.
(*The Koran*, Sura II, 222)

The ancient world's most dreaded poison was "moon-dew" collected by Thessalian witches, said to be a girl's first menstrual blood shed during an eclipse of the moon. Pliny said a menstruous woman's touch could blast the fruits of the field, sour wine, cloud mirrors, rust iron, and blunt the edges of knives. If a menstruous woman so much as laid a finger on a beehive, the bees would fly away and never return. If a man lay with a menstruous woman during an eclipse, he would soon fall sick and die. (Walker, 1983, 643)

Can't say that I blame men for fearing our bloody cunts. We be powerful people when we bleed.

When women bleed, all of the frustration and anger we've stored in our bodies for the month is physically manifested in a sudden and swift change in hormone levels, resulting in an openness and vulnerability that cannot be described. Menstruation is a monthly purging and cleansing. We hear, taste and smell things that are usually indiscernible. Whether we consciously recognize it or not, we feel threatened when our heightened senses are assaulted.

I assert that menstruating women intuitively want to be *left alone* or with other bleeding women, as many of our great-great grandmothers firmly believed.

A number of societies certainly have the right idea prohibiting highly sensitive menstruating women from entering churches where a son-sacrificing, war-mongering, sadistic god is worshipped. Unfortunately, this prohibition is enforced because of the belief that menstruating women are "unclean" and not because we'd rather spend the sabbath quietly paying homage to ourselves and the moon.

A few friends and I spoil each other silly if we're hanging out on the first day of someone's period. We fry up sweet 'n sour tofu, give massages, play Toni Childs and Sade or bring each other chocolate-covered strawberries. Mostly, we sit quietly and stare out the window and demand absolutely nothing of each other.

The social requirement that we fulfill the responsibilities of our non-menstruating selves at all times throughout our cycle is the source of our alleged PMS.

We're taught to distrust everything about our very compelling blood mystery. Yet the clickety-clack, passive-aggressive business world of men and machines is the absolute antithesis of everything our senses crave on the first few days of our blood. In our souls, we still know this. In our DNA, we want to be quiet with ourselves. In this society, where a day to ourselves might very well mean no one to care for the children and no food on the table, bleeding women are naturally irritable.

The evils of our blood recede when—however fleetingly— we're free from the demands of this unfeeling world. When we sit reverent and peaceful. When those around us respect our silence. This is when the negative becomes positive.

Every woman has a different way of honoring her blood.

Every so often, Bambi, my housemate, has a ritual of painting fantastic gold leaf menstrual homages, framed in total baroque. Bambi's not a painter, she's a musician. Her period tells her when it's time for another painting. "I seem to make one every eighteen months or so," says Bambi. She has no idea why she started painting with her menstrual blood in gold.

Some women cook fabulous dinners for themselves, some save up money to take in a weekend by the sea.

When you open yourself up to learn how to honor yourself, the *how* part just falls into place via your imagination, passion and lifestyle.

It takes a lot of time, focus and energy to realize the

enormity of being the ocean with your very own tide every month. However, by honoring the demands of bleeding, our blood gives something in return. The crazed bitch from irritation hell recedes. In her place arises a side of ourselves with whom we may not—at first—be comfortable. She is a vulnerable, highly perceptive genius who can ponder a given issue and take her world by storm. When we're quiet and bleeding, we stumble upon the solutions to dilemmas that've been bugging us all month. Inspiration hits and moments of epiphany rumba 'cross de tundra of our senses. In this mode of existence one does not feel antipathy towards a bodily ritual that so profoundly and routinely reinforces our cuntpower.

Reproductive Control for Cunts

Just because I don't envision myself in a romantic, sexual
relationship with a man anymore, doesn't
mean I never have.

 The first time I got pregnant, I was
nineteen and living in the agricultural
community on the California coast where
I'd lived all my life. A mere two weeks
separated me from my move away from
home to Seattle. Making such a major move
with a tiny human growing inside my body seemed a pretty
contradictory way of setting off on my own.

The thoroughly unsavory "option" of hanging around town
for nine months and then giving my child to an adoption agency
didn't hold my attention for more than two puffs off the continuous cigarette I'd had in my mouth since I got back my test results.

So I went to Planned Parenthood for a clinical abortion.
In the waiting room, there always seemed to be fifteen or
twenty other women, no matter how many left with the nurse.

Evidently, it was "abortion day."

We were shuffled through the clinic like beef cows. All of the women had the same horror-stricken, empty look on their faces. It was one of those situations where one can assume one holds the same expression as everyone else without looking in the mirror. I sat there for an hour and a half, nervously leafing through *People* magazine, in a desperate attempt to give a rat's ass about the lives of Darryl Hannah and Whitney Houston.

When they called my name, I probably would have shit my pants if there had been any digestion going on in my intestines, which there wasn't. It's hard to eat when you're pregnant with a child you do not want.

My boyfriend accompanied me into the exam room. I was told to strip and lay on the table, feet in the stirrups. I still remember the ugly swirl designs and water marks on the ceiling. After a while, the nurse came in and explained what would be happening.

She referred to the machine used for clinical abortions as a "suction device," which is a more professional way of saying "vacuum cleaner." In theory, if not design, this machine is quite like the Hoover Upright, the Dust Buster or the Shop-Vac in your closet at home.

The nurse didn't mention how useful vacuum cleaners are for cleaning up messes. In our society, a pile of kitty litter on the floor is treated much the same as an undesired embryo. The main difference, though hardly recognizable to Western science, is that kitty litter is sucked from cold linoleum and an embryo is sucked from a warm-blooded living being's womb.

Instead, because I was crying like *La Llorana,* she said, "Are you sure this is what you want?"

What other goddamn choice did I have?

I muttered, "Just do it, please."

With the ugliest needle I'd ever seen, she shot something into my cervix. I don't think my cervix was residing under the belief that it would someday have a large needle plunged into it, and so protested accordingly. The pain was overwhelming; my head swam into the netherworld between intense clarity and murky subconscious.

Then I heard a quiet motor whirring.

The lady told me to recite my ABCs.

"A, B, C, D, E . . ." Something entered my cunt, deeper, deeper, deeper than I imagined anything could possibly go.

"F, G, H, I, O, W . . ." The walls of my uterus were being sucked, felt like they were gonna cave in. I screamed, "O, P, X, X, D, VOWELS, WHAT ARE THE VOWELS? R? K? A! A's A VOWEL!" And then my organs were surely being mowed down by a tiny battalion of Lawn-Boys.

"S, did I say S?" My boyfriend was crying too, didn't tell me whether I said S or not.

There was a white-wall-tire pad between my legs then, and blood gushed out of me. The motor had stopped whirring. I was delirious. I asked, "What do you do with all the fetuses? Where do they go? Do you bury them?" The lady ignored me, which was fine, I had to puke. She led me into a bathroom and I vomited biley green foam. Then I went to a recovery room, lay down and cried.

There was another nurse woman in there, she patted my hand, reassured me, "I know just how you feel."

"You've had an abortion before too?"

"No, but I know how you feel."

I told her to get the fuck away from me.

For two weeks, there was a gaping wound in the center of my body. I could hardly walk for five days.

Then, stupid me, a couple of years later, I got pregnant again. I still lived in Seattle, but was just about to move to Olympia, to begin school at Evergreen.

I couldn't really envision myself having an academic edge with a bun in the oven, so I faced the reality of going to that machine once again. This time I was more terrified than before. I knew all too well what that rectangular box and its quiet motor had planned for my reproductive system.

Have you any idea how it feels to willingly and voluntarily submit to excruciating torture because you dumbly forgot to insert your diaphragm which gives you ugly yeast infections and hurts you to fuck unless you lie flat on your back anyway? I was to withstand this torture because I was a *bad girl*. I didn't do good. I fucked up.

I had the same choice as before, that glowing, outstanding choice for which we ladies fight tooth and nail: the choice to get my insides ruthlessly sucked by some inhuman shitpile, not invented by my foremothers, but by someone who would never, ever in a million years have that tube jammed up his dickhole and turned on full blast, slurping everything in its path.

Abortion #2 took place in a clinic that was under so much political pressure, I wasn't even allowed to recuperate. Twenty minutes after the vacuum cleaner was out of my body, I was dressed and walking home.

Felt like a piece of shit.

On one of Olympia's main thoroughfares is an abortion clinic. I passed it every day on my way to and from school. Almost always, there were old women, young girls and duck hunters standing on the corner outside the clinic, holding signs in their hands showing you pictures of a dead fetuses with some words underneath to the effect that this may have been the next president of the United States of America.

Whenever I saw those people out there, especially the young girls, I'd see myself yanking the bus cord—in all probability, snapping it in two—vaulting off the bus, crossing the street and morphing into a walking killing machine, kicking in faces, stomping on hands. There were times when I gripped my wrist so I wouldn't yank that cord.

At this point in my life, I'd begun to study different kinds of medicines and healing methods. One thing I learned in college was that knowledge helps me transcend anger. Upon examining my desire to physically assault individuals whose convictions were in direct opposition to mine, I delved into histories and applications of medicines far and wide. At the same time, I was hanging around with a group of women who were asking a lot of compelling questions about our reproductive systems. We found many of the readily available answers to be thoroughly unsatisfactory, and started discovering our own.

In this research, we found one constant: healing starts from within. It appeared to be some kind of law. No, more than a law. Is breathing a law? Is waking up every morning a law? If so, maybe the notion of healing coming from within is a law as well.

I had never been comfortable with the idea that healing comes from the physician or his bag of tricks, because I learned years before, when I had my own health challenge with polio that healing has only one source. The doctor can aid the body by removing foreign particles, injecting chemicals, setting and realigning bones, but that does not mean the body will heal. In fact, I am certain, there has never been a doctor anywhere, at any time, in any country, at any period in history who ever healed anything. Each person's healer is within. The doctor is at best one who has recognized an individual talent, developed it and is privileged enough to be able to serve the community by doing what he does best and loves doing. (Morgan, 1991, 91)

This concept is completely alien, even deviant, in our culture. In this society, we look to the outside for just about everything: love, entertainment, well-being, self-worth and health. We stare into the TV set instead of speaking of our own dreams, wait for a vacation instead of appreciating each day, watch the clock rather than listen to our hearts. Every livelong day we are bombarded with realities from the outside world, seemingly nonstop. Phones, car alarms, pills, coffee, beepers, ads, radios, elevator music, fax machines, gunshots, bright lights, fast cars, airplanes overhead, computer screens, sirens, alcohol, newspapers. One hardly has the opportunity to look inside for love and peace and other nice things like that.

Western medicine, that smelly, deaf dog who farts across the house and that we just don't have the heart to put out of its misery, is based on a law opposed to the one the rest of the universe seems to go by, namely: Healing Has Nothing to Do with You, Just Follow the Directions on the Label.

In America, we don't (nor are we encouraged to) look inside ourselves for healing, finding truths or answers. If you want to know something, you find out what the Person in Charge of This Area says. The weather is not to be discerned by looking at the sky, the mountains in the distance, or by listening to the song of the wind. You will find it in the Report of the Meteorologist. And likewise, if you are pregnant and don't want to be, you don't look to yourself and the immediate, personal resources in your immediate, personal world, you pay a visit to the Abortionist, who will subsequently predict the climate in your body for two weeks, guaranteed.

And so, la dee dah, once, twice, three times a cuntlovin' lady, I got pregnant again. It was the same boyfriend as the other two times only now we were breaking up. It was the fuckedest one of all because I didn't want to be with this man and I shouldn't have fucked him, but it was his birthday and he was obviously fun to romp with and blah dee blah blah blah. No force on earth could make me feel like I wanted this child. Furthermore, I promptly decided there was to be no grotesque waltz with that abhorrent machine.

So, I started talking to my friends about abortion alternatives. I lived in a small town with a high population of like-minded cuntlovin' women, so that was one thing in my favor right there. Against me was the fact that I was eight weeks along, which is too advanced for an organically induced miscarriage. According to naturopathic physician Loraine Harkin, six weeks of pregnancy is the outside limit for herbal abortions. Since they are effective about 60 percent of the time, she says it's important to schedule a surgical abortion since a fetus is most sensitive to the harmful effects of herbs and drugs in the first eight weeks of pregnancy. I made an appointment at the women's clinic (the one with the protesters, who'd since moved on to haunt other neighborhoods) as a back-up in case my way didn't work out.

My dear friend Judy, the masseuse and scientist, was my biggest resource. She and Panacea found some herbal tea recipes a Boston anarchist-feminist group printed. (I tried to contact this group, but they had evidently disbanded.)

Judy came to my house almost every night and massaged my uterus where you are not supposed to massage pregnant women who want to keep their babies. She also did reflexology by rubbing either side of my Achilles tendon on both feet.

I knew a naturopath in Olympia, who was one of my sources of inspiration in learning about healing from within. She taught me this thing called "imaging." It may sound terribly New Age, but through imaging, I got rid of this weird bump I'd had on my labia *all my life*. Since imaging goes on in your own head, I can't tell you how to do it specifically. The basic idea is: *Every* night, when you are falling asleep, graphically imagine the part of your body that's giving you problems *changing*. For the bump on my labia, I imagined all this beautiful soft flesh growing over and absorbing the bump. When I was pregnant, I *vividly, consistently* (I do believe these are the operative words when imaging) imagined the walls of my uterus gently shedding.

Eight days passed from when I started inducing miscarriage to the morning my embryo plopped onto the bathroom floor.

Judy's daily massages and my continuous imaging of the

lining of my uterus shedding away at every moment of my days, I feel, were *the most crucial* elements of my success story. I was absolutely focused on miscarrying and I *felt* Judy's gentle, yet firm massages prodding things along quite nicely.

It was an incantation.

Me and my women friends did magic.

Esther's love made magic. She supported me and stayed with me every day. Bridget's thoughtfulness made magic. She brought me flowers. Possibly most magical was the fact that, after the first coupla days, I possessed not one filament of self-doubt. With that core of supportive women surrounding me and with my mind made up, I was pretty much invincible.

I stress this because in America, we tend to hold that popping medicine in our mouths and swallowing is the extent of our involvement in the healing process. We believe that if we get better, it's because the *medicine* worked magic, not the *person*. Many women I know have tried to induce miscarriage and failed because they took certain herbal potions and went about their lives as if everything were normal, waiting for the herbs to work their wonders. To successfully induce miscarriage, one must devote One's Entire Life to the attainment of this goal. *I place an enormous amount of emphasis on this point.* When I induced miscarriage, I breathed, ate, shat and slept thinking of nothing else but the lining of my uterus shedding.

The herbal teas and other oral and topical applications I prescribed to myself were *little helpers*. They served to further direct *my own focus* and *aid* me in achieving my goal. Herbs are *particularly* good little helpers because plants easily and synergistically jive with one's own magic and are quite willing to work with you if you respect them.

The herbs I chose were blue cohosh root and pennyroyal leaves. The information I am providing is to illustrate how I, *one specific individual*, induced a miscarriage. There are hundreds of emmenagogues and abortifacients that grow on the planet. The two I decided to use were chosen after a lot of dicussion and reading.

After a week of non-stop imaging, massages, tea drinking, talking and concentrating, I was brushing my teeth at the sink and felt a very peculiar mmmmbloommmp-like feeling. I looked at the bathroom floor and there, between my feet, was some blood and a little round thing. It was clear but felt like one of them unshiny superballs. It was the neatest thing I ever did see.

An orb of life and energy, in my hand.

And Jesus H., wasn't I the happiest clam? It hardly hurt at all, just some mild contractions. I bled very little, felt fine in two days. I wore black for a week and had a little funeral in my head.

Organically inducing a miscarriage was definitely one of the top ten learning experiences in my life thus far.

You know, it's like when Germany invaded Poland. I once read how in the ghettos of Warsaw, the people fighting the Nazis were real amazed at first that a Nazi soldier would die if you shot him. They *suspected* that Nazis could die, but *felt* like they were somehow superhuman.

That's how I felt after I miscarried a child without paying a visit to the beef cow clinic and that sickening vacuum cleaner. I felt the way I imagine any oppressed individual feels when they see that they have power and nobody—not men and not their machines—can take that away.

c
u
n
t

Terminating a pregnancy in any manner is a harrowing, traumatic experience. At the time, my emotions were an odd juxtaposition of untold grief and profound exhilaration. When the sadness settled quietly into my heart, I felt *so happy* to be a woman. I looked at all my women friends with such an intense, burning rush of joy. My cuntlovin' friends and I did something *amazing* to *affect my destiny* in the most conducive possible way.

I learned that the fight for human rights does not take place on some bureaucratic battleground with a bevy of lawyers running from congressional suite to congressional suite, sapping resources into laws. The war for peace and love and other nice things like that is not waged in protests on the street. These forms of fighting are a reaction to oppression, giving destructive power that much more energy. The real fight for human rights is inside each and every individual on this earth.

While traversing along this particular train of thought, I realize I just might sound like a woman who has never experienced the unspeakable horror of back-alley abortions, and I am. I also realize that it might seem as if I'm ungrateful to all the cuntlovin' women who fought their hearts raw for legal abortions, which I am not. The fact that there now exists a generation of women who can actually consider clinical abortion to be an oppressive diversion from our own power is *based wholly upon* the foundation that our mothers and sisters built for us. I sincerely thank the individuals who fought so hard that I may have the luxury of the belief I now hold. Evolutionarily speaking, it is quite natural for this fight to progress into a new arena, for the fight is not over, it has not ended. The squabble between pro-lifers and pro-choicers serves only to keep our eyes off the target, and nothing more.

Without the women in my life, both living and dead, I would have been roadkill simply ages ago. All women benefit from concentrating our energy on the power within our own circle of friends, creating informal health collectives where we discuss things like our bodies and our selves.

Abortion clinics, in their present incarnation, will be completely unnecessary when we believe in our own power, and the power of our immediate communities. The abortion issue can become a personal, intimate thing amongst cuntlovin' women friends.

Can you say Amen.

Nobody here is saying abortion is a form of birth control.

It isn't.

Having an abortion totally sucks. Practicing a birth control lifestyle is a fabulous all expenses paid, carte blanche vacation in Tahiti compared to terminating a pregnancy.

Birth control is preventative medicine (referring, of course, to the nurturing, woman-centered definitions of "medicine"). It is actively sustaining a lifestyle that grosses and nets the fewest possibilities of conceiving a child. Having an abortion, on the other hand, is terminating the progress of something that is already quite under way.

However, since the morning-after pill has been cleared by the American Food and Drug Association, abortion and birth control have kinda merged a bit.

The morning-after pill was not available to me the three times I was pregnant. If it had been, I do not know if I would have taken it, because I am deathly fearful of pills, and am unclear on the long-term side effects we're talkin' here. There is definitely an allure in a pill one can take "just to be safe." Absolute knowledge of conception is a non-issue. Take the pill, have your period, and if it's a little heavy and clotty, figure ya mighta been, but then again maybe not.

Kinda preventative, kinda terminator style.

Yeah, the morning-after pill runs 'long a misty boundary.

One thing I'm pretty certain about, though. Featuring this pill as a fabulous star in one's birth control lifestyle would rend untold—quite possibly irreparable—damage to the lining of one's uterus. Since it's now accessible, I am concerned that women could start relying on it too heavily.

My opinion of the morning-after pill also runs along a misty boundary. It's damn important for a lot of reasons. But to the day I keel over, I'll be a diehard, furrow-browed skeptic whenever male-run industries are involved with us womenfolk's business.

That said, I know of three birth control lifestyles that are 100 percent safe and infallible.

The first—abstinence—is no fun and extremely unhealthy, so forget that one.

Masturbation *is* fun. Lordisa, is masturbation fun. It's also liberating, empowering and a superlative form of safe sex. You cannot get pregnant or become HIV positive even if you are in a circle jerk with everyone and her sister. Besides all of these outstanding qualities, masturbation is an *absolutely peerless* cure for the hiccups.

Masturbation is a high art. I have a cuntlovin' friend who

masturbates without touching herself. She ornately concentrates on an erotic adventure until she comes her brains out. She's rolled her eyes and moaned on public transportation and in long lines at the grocery store. Comin' her brains out. Another friend of mine goes the manual route, but has specialized her timing and precision in elevators.

For those of us less mentally talented and/or dexterous, there are vibrators, dildos, Ben Wa balls, butt plugs and massage wands shaped like everything from dill pickles to elephants with trunks raised clit high. Also, of course, the five holy and munificent fingers on each hand.

Sex exclusively with girls is also fun. Unless pregnancy is on the agenda, or something immaculate occurs, lesbians do not usually conceive. Women do not have sperm. Thus, women cannot accidentally get each other pregnant. HIV, though, is another scenario. Women are able to pass HIV to each other. The research done thus far on the possibility of acquiring HIV woman to woman is inconclusive, but the risk should be taken seriously. Trust no one but yourself, and always practice the safest possible sex.

In conclusion, the only 100 percent safe and infallible birth control lifestyles worth considering are: masturbation and/or sex exclusively with women. When neither of these lifestyles coincides with a cuntlovin' woman's reality, the prevention of unplanned pregnancy is often an issue.

There are ways for cuntlovin' women to deal with this issue without the pill, barriers against the cervix, hormone implants or whatever other "choices" male-centered medicine's birth control industry has palmed off on us.

What, exactly, is the lifecycle of a *woman's* body *doing* under the jurisdiction of a medical science established, defined and implemented by people who *do not have cunts?*

It's like suddenly, one day in the Middle Ages, people figured men should be in charge of women's bodies since they were in charge of pretty much everything else.

In context, at the time, perhaps it made sense.

It does not make sense anymore.

Maybe we lost contact with our archives somewhere along the way. Maybe we kinda went ahead and played along like we were dumb. Maybe we got beaten and raped and tortured and enslaved into submission.

That is the past.

It's something to reckon with, but also: it's gone.

Face it, forget it.

Focus on the present: the age of communication.

We gots us the Internet.

You can e-mail government officials in Pakistan and plead mercy for the fifteen-year-old girl sentenced to death for killing the man who raped her. You can find the chemical compound for Depo-Provera and see how that chemical compound affects the human body. You can hop on Diamanda Galás's website and find out what in good Lordisa's name she's up to now. You can download all the recipes for chocolate chip cookies on the planet earth and follow a different one each month when you and your friends are PMSing.

And that's just the Internet.

Living as we do in an age of communication, it is pretty much acceptable to go, "Hey Gramma, what'd you use for birth control, how did you bleed, what was sex like back then, how many lovers did you have, how many abortions, when, where, how, why?"

Bam, connection with history.

Our communication environment fosters vast, far-reaching and intricate networks of women who utilize fanzines, small presses, schools, record companies, magazines, television shows and movies. Women from all socioeconomic stratas communicate in mediums that in the past were either not accessible or not invented.

It is *perfectly socially acceptable* for you to write down every thought you've ever had about *anything*—from your gorgeous prize wisteria, to the insane relationship you have with your hair, to your all-consuming love for the clitoris—then slap the words together with some cool pictures, make five hundred copies, staple each and sell them to every woman you do and don't know for a buck a pop.

Bam, everybody profits.

All these situations are now in context and they now make sense.

We are able to share knowledge, history, experiences, recipes and remedies like our motherkin could not. As more and more women communicate, a new language and sense of community evolves. Equipped with language, a means of communication and the desire to talk to one another, our voices, histories and dreams whirling dervish into regenerative cuntpower.

The story of you gives the life of me personal power in my body, my eating and health habits, and in my political, spiritual, emotional and ethnic beliefs.

Without you, I am ignorant, oppressed, alone.

Without you, I am powerless.

As we all know, up to this point American women have tended

to rely upon methods of birth control founded upon a body of knowledge created by men.

This holds true, even after it's religiously proven to us like water torture on our foreheads from the cradle to the grave: Men have a vested *financial* interest in controlling our lives, histories and bodies. Men dearly love, cherish and respect women until death do us part as long as we're:

consumer

wife

teacher

helper

bitch

concubine

accountant

housekeeper

orphan

punching bag

counselor

nag

nurse

threeholestopenetrate

cook

mother

daughter

prey

Whore.

Tangle, tangle, tangle, mother, grandmother, sister.

We been told for centuries, he's father, lover, husband, brother, son, and really, truly does have our best interests in mind.

Pa-shaw.

"Our best interests" are naturally, unquestionably pre-defined by a social power structure that, at the turn of the twentieth century, witnessed an ad for *Lysol* with a recipe for douching to keep wives from experiencing "embarrassing odors" during intimate moments with their husbands.

Nowadays, most women who think about this kind of stuff—and have the opportunity—matronize the offices of women healthcare providers. Women go to male gynecologists—I can only imagine—because it's a family tradition or there's no better option. For me, personally, anyone who didn't have a cunt and tried to look at my cunt in an exam room, would get a silly slap upside the head with a cold speculum.

I know women *do* choose to go to male doctors because I see their names in the yellow pages: Richard, Ted, Micahel, James, Peter. I can only assume this means there is a demand for male gynecologists.

I don't know any women who go to male doctors, though.

A lot of women have decided that the whole way we interpret healing in our culture is based entirely on a male construct. These women go to women naturopaths who rely on healing straight from Big Mom's Bosom.

Her thuja oil, for instance, which—with the expertise of a healthcare provider—can cure chlamydia. Her red raspberry leaf tea that tones and strengthens the uterus. Her acidophilus bacteria in yogurt that cures yeast infections by restoring the natural acidity of your cunt.

And then there is you.

You who are a child of the universe. Whether or not it is clear to you, you came from Big Mom's Bosom too. Birth control and health care are very much integral aspects of your spirituality, self-esteem and power. Not only do you have vast wonders of communication at your beck and call, but Big Mom provided you with a mind and a will—the most omnipotent panaceas on the planet—to wield.

The naturopath I mentioned earlier asks new patients to document everything they eat for a week and fully detail personal and family medical histories. On the first visit, she conducts an interview to get the psychological and emotional context before doing *any* physical examination. She procures a whole picture of what's going on before ever touching someone's body. You know: holistic medicine.

This lady taught me a lot.

We learn to respect everything our doctor tells us. Doctor knows best. Perhaps. But the doctor learned about healing in a destructive school of thought. The doctor learned to isolate and napalm physical ailments. Vicariously, through the doctor, we too learn to deal with our bodies and health destructively.

We kill headaches with aspirin, which also weakens immunity to headaches.

Meditation and yoga soothe the stress that causes head-aches, while a plethora of herbal teas calm the spirit.

We kill infection with antibiotics, which also weaken immunity to infection.

Keeping cuts clean and drinking lots of fresh water to flush out the system make topical infection a non-issue. Internal infection and viruses are nipped with garlic, witch hazel, cayenne pepper, echinacea, goldenseal, chaparral. These and many other plant substances feed the immune system, which fights its own battles.

Accessing Big Mom's resources, while passionately communicating and accepting your power to heal yourself is constructive-assed, cuntlovin' medicine.

There are two basic, commonly accepted models of birth control. Both are, to greater or lesser degrees, based on the destructive model of "healthcare":

1. Chemical manipulation of the hormones.
2. Barriers placed between the os (opening of the cervix) and sperm.

I will suggest a third method of birth control, based on a philosophy intrinsic to a cuntlovin' woman's life.

Chemicals, i.e., Napalming

Three unplanned pregnancies be damned, I'm gonna go for broke here and assert I'd be hard pressed to come up with more systematic and refined forms of chemically induced oppression than synthetic hormonal birth control products. Birth control pills, Depo-Provera and Norplant all function in pretty much the same way—they control a woman's reproductive cycle by manipulating hormones.

Depo-Provera and Norplant were introduced on the market in the 1990s. It has come to light in recent years that the side effects of hormonal implants are far-reaching and extremely detrimental. Unfortunately, at least a decade will pass before the pernicious effects of these "new developments" are firmly established.

Because the pill is the oldest of the three, more is known about its insidious effects on a woman's body. The pill diminishes sexual desire, causes undue weight gain through laboratory generated manipulation of the hormones, obstructs the natural cycle and menstrual flow, represses ovulation, causes heart problems, irritability and migraines, has been linked, unlinked, re-linked to cancer, and synthetically dictates one's entire physical agenda. The pill creates a constant state of false pregnancy. Women on the pill do not have a natural menstrual cycle. Bleeding occurs when placebo pills instigate a false period.

The reproductive cycles of women on the pill are choreo-graphed and maintained by Ortho-Novum factories.

Depo-Provera and Norplant are simply newer products of an industry that profits from control over women's lives. Any "developments" in the birth control industry will always reflect a cavalier attitude towards our bodies.

A lovely woman named Marcy Bloom, the director of Aradia Women's Health Center in Seattle, Washington, once smoothly countered my rant against the pill. Ms. Bloom's is a very thoughtful and judicious perspective on the issue:

What you say about the pill is true. However, it is the most successful method of birth control as well—that's the Catch-22. For some women, the pill is the only method that works, or the only one they're willing to use because either they don't want to touch their bodies, or their lover is very resistant to using condoms. Sometimes the pill is the only psychosocial method a woman is willing to use, because all other methods require a woman to touch herself.

First off, let's get the Condom Matter behind us.

A gentleman who doesn't have the physical and/or emotional sensitivity to use condoms *couldn't possibly* possess the self-confidence required to fully procure the infinite soundings of pleasure from the depth of a woman's being, via the endlessness of her cunt.

At least not with his dick.

Insecurity about a physical lack of sensitivity in their bodies overrides their lover's mental and physical health. Cro-Magnon sociopsychological beliefs (i.e., "Women are the ones who get pregnant—they should deal with birth control.") also contribute to this ignorance.

This says nothing about what kind of dumbass would completely disregard the threat and reality of HIV.

Men who refuse to use condoms do not deserve to be fucked by anyone but other men who refuse to use condoms.

Taking *any* hormonal birth control product because we don't want to touch our bodies beats all our much-needed revolutionary, resurrectionary cuntlovin' synapses into hibernation 'n

the anatomical jewel

submission. This makes it difficult for a woman to just plain and simple love being a woman. By encouraging a physical aversion to our own bodies, the pill only adds to the unspeakably large number of ladies inclined towards cunthatred presently existing within the body of womankind.

Loving, knowing and respecting our bodies is a powerful and invincible act of rebellion in this society. This fundamental, entirely crucial act is not possible while we buy into destructive philosophies at the root of hormonal birth control products.

I've had countless discussions with birth control advocates who regard synthetic hormones as a right which allows us freedom.

What is the frame of reference we draw upon to reach this conclusion? Are we not basing this on the experiences of our ancestors who were dicked around, relatively speaking, no more and no less than we are to this day, but had access to quite a bit less information?

The only reason hormonal birth control products are considered a "right" is because women haven't yet decided to construct an entirely woman-based frame of reference with all of the information our ancestors could not communicate to each other through the Internet, zines, books, periodicals, shows, conventions, sporting events, festivals and fax machines.

The main freedom involved in using hormonal birth control is freedom from thinking about—and ultimately facing—our reproductive power. This "freedom" essentially results in an ignorance of our bodies which costs us, individually and collectively, dear, dear, dearly. We cannot love ourselves if we do not know ourselves.

There is bliss, but no freedom, in ignorance.

We have the means to educate ourselves and rely wholly upon rights and freedoms that totally jive with the rhythm of womankind in every way. If you are on hormonal birth control products, you *cannot* educate yourself about your body because *your body is not under your own Goddess-given jurisdiction.*

I return to the same argument I offered about using sea sponges, rags, the Keeper and Blood Towels. We've learned to place patriarchal rhetoric at the nexus of our thoughts. We're all reared in a society where the real, honest to goddess power of women intimidates just about everybody. Especially people who, historically and futuristically, have not a hope in hell of seeing blood course out from 'tween their legs, or of giving birth to members of the human race.

What it boils down to is this: If it didn't *originate* with women or the Goddess, if it does not *spiritually, emotionally, physically, psychologically and financially benefit* women, it does not serve women.

So fucken chuck it.

Barriers (Isolation)

Women-initiated barrier methods—such as the diaphragm, cervical cap and various spermicide-soaked sponges—do not eclipse a woman's cycle. A woman using barrier methods ovulates and bleeds. Barrier methods require physical contact with one's cunt, and that's *always* a good thing.

I, personally, have not had good experiences with barrier methods when I've been sexually active with men, which is neither here nor there.

Barrier methods have been used for thousands of years. Lemon halves and sponges or mosses soaked in spermicidal herbs were used by some of our greatest grandmas. Mass-produced cervical caps were around in the 1930s, and home-jobbies were used in many ancient cultures.

The sole reason I am negatively disposed towards the use of barrier methods is that the industry that creates them is not run by women.

If it were run by women, the following story just could not, ever, happen.

Once upon a time, there was something called the IUD. This stands for intrauterine device. The IUD was implanted in women's uteruses and inhibited the natural growth and shedding of the uterine lining. It made the uterus an inhospitable place for an egg. IUDs caused uterine cancer, infertility and—when they didn't cause death—tore the insides of many women's bodies asunder.

After wreaking havoc on hundreds of thousands of American women's uteruses and lives, an IUD called the Dalkon Shield was finally taken off the market in 1976. This was not an act of graciousness on the part of A. H. Robins (the corporation responsible for the Dalkon Shield). They were removed from the American market because six hundred lawsuits were pending against the company. These six hundred were but a spit in the ocean compared to the 306,931 lawsuits filed by 1986. And these three hundred thousand–plus lawsuits represented a mere 8 percent of women potentially harmed by the device. (Bloss, Cornell, Moon, Tomsich, "The Dalkon Shield," 1997)

Meanwhile, what do you do with 697,000 surplus IUDs? The instruments of terror were sold to USAID (United States Agency for

International Development). These 697,000 IUDs were then "distributed"—willingly or not, I couldn't venture to say—to women in impoverished nations, who, unlike American women, did not have the relative luxury of a legal system. (Raymond, 1993, 15)

Condoms are a barrier method of birth control I advocate for three reasons: They were designed by and for men, they work, and they are proven to reduce the risk of acquiring HIV.

I've never heard of condoms that make men's dicks shrivel off their bodies. I assert that this is a calibrated reflection of who produces what for whom.

If a collective of women designed a method of barrier birth control, produced it in a women-run company and ran advertisements depicting positive images of cuntlovin' women from all ethnicities and walks of life in women-owned mediums, I would jauntily support it.

At present, however, there is no such method of birth control, and I do not trust the birth control industry. I do not believe the needs of women are taken into consideration at all. I do not like knowing a multibillion-dollar corporation that inherently cannot regard our bodies as holy-rhythmic, gets all its money from us.

The birth control industry is a Big Business. We are mere consumers in this context. Our bank accounts are much, much, much more important than our bodies. If birth control is indeed "the womenfolk's responsibility," let's seize our responsibility with vigor, shall we.

Cuntlovin' Ovulation Alert

In no way do I claim to be a health practitioner.

Nor—as my Macintosh PowerBook with internal modem would gladly testify in a court of law—am I of the Luddite persuasion.

I am a woman and a writer who has thought about and experimented with the workings of her cunt with passion and vigor.

When you start teaching yourself about your cunt, you get a rhythm going. It is your rhythm and only you understand it 100 percent. When you breathe deeply and stay with this rhythm in your body, you will notice it encompasses every aspect of your life.

What I am about to discuss is not "the rhythm method." The objective here is not to understand the rhythm of your ovulatory cycle. The objective is to tap into the rhythm of your ovulatory cycle as a means of perceiving a broader rhythm inside yourself that shows you how powerful you are every day of your life.

Long before physicians started "curing" people with charming procedures like putting leeches all over their bodies, birth control was a normal part of life. There are as many forms of birth control as there are cultures in the world. It wasn't until popes and missionaries preached the sinfulness of sex outside of reproductive purposes for a couple hundred years that people started distrusting their medicinal regimes. Lots of people still practice their own kind of reproductive medicine, only now it's invalidated and called "voodoo," "black magic" or "folk medicine."

The big problem with forms of birth control founded in the people, the plants and the moon is that no one trusts them. They all completely depend on the individual woman and her community in order to be effective.

Few in our society have trusted the individual woman and her community to take absolute control. En masse, women haven't trusted ourselves or subsequently been trusted for over two thousand years.

The nice thing, though, is everything's changing. It's not *impossible* for small groups of women all over the nation to learn about our cunts and trust each other together. In the mite of a moment, we can get online. We can post what we know and find what we're looking for. We can sit in a cafe with our three best friends and discuss our erotic fantasies. We can purchase books that tell us all about our cervix.

Assuredly, the best place to start learning and trusting is the place from which you entered into this world.

Your Cervix: Axis and Ally

Everything your uterus produces—blood, eggs, babies and a variety of miraculous secretions—eventually passes through your cervix before leaving your body.

Your cervix is the doorway of humanity. Have you ever seen it? If you haven't, you dang well should. Viewing your cervix will not be a disappointing experience, I promise on a stack of holy *Beloved*s by Toni Morrison.

Go to your local women's health clinic with probably a five or ten dollar bill. Ask for a small, medium or large plastic speculum, and hand the nice health clinic lady the five or ten dollars. Along with the speculum, ask her to give you an instruction sheet. If you live in one of the more woman-negative states like Utah, Florida, Texas or Mississippi, you may need to purchase a plastic speculum through the mail.

Read the instructions that come with your speculum. If you're lucky enough to have a supportive women's clinic in your community, ask any questions you may have before leaving. If you buy a speculum through the mail, either call the company you ordered it from, or call the woman-positive health clinic nearest you by referring to the appendix in *A New View of a Woman's Body*, a book I vehemently urge you to purchase in a later chapter.

With your speculum, you can further investigate and learn of your wondrous cunt. Besides the speculum, you will need a flashlight, possibly some lube, a hand-held mirror and maybe some gentle patience. Practice opening and closing the spec a few times before inserting. Keep in mind that speculums were not designed for self-exams. It can be frustrating trying to get that thing to work right the first one or nine times, but try to relax. Tight cunt muscles don't facilitate this maneuver.

To insert a speculum: Lie down with some pillows under the small of your back. Spread them legs. Hold your cunt lips apart with two fingers of one hand. Insert the speculum sideways, longest handle facing your body. If things are parched down there, employ the lube, but use it sparingly. One of the main objectives here is to be able to see your juices in their natural element. Ya' won't be able to distinguish the lube from the juice if you lay it on too thick. Once you get the speculum in about halfway, turn it so it lies flat. Don't open it up when it's sideways. Gently insert it on in to the hilt and open it up. Wheee! There's a little lock mechanism on these things; click it into place when you get it opened as wide as you can.

Mind, this is not *the most comfortable* sensation in the world, but it shouldn't hurt at all (unless you have an infection or open sores or something), so long as you don't pinch any o' that tender skin as you open the speculum. However, if you're not used to having things in your cunt, especially hard, plastic things, you may experience more discomfort at first. Keep trying. Remember to relax.

Once the speculum is in, opened and locked, grab that flashlight and mirror. If you can't see your cervix, either you have a long cunt canal or a shy cervix. For the former scenario, try the exam again just before, right after or on the lightest day of your period. This is when your cervix is most visible. For the latter, bear down like you do when taking a shit. That cervix will overcome its stage fright in a matter of seconds. If lots of flesh is bulging around the speculum, you probably need a larger size.

Take a good long gander. Note the shape, color and texture of your cervix. It changes appearance according to where you are in your cycle. If your cervix looks kinda bluish or is indeed bright blue, it's time for a pregnancy test. If you're ovulating, you may see mucous, your cervix will be pulled higher up, it may be softer and larger than usual and the os may be open slightly. The os looks like a Q-tip wouldn't pass through it, but it is altogether capable of dilating to accommodate the head and shoulders of a new human being.

Cuntjuices: Know Your Ambrosia

Look, touch, smell and taste your cuntjuices. *Never* gross out on tasting yourself. You are an acquired taste. Acquire it. You swallow your spit without a qualm millions of times each week. It's filthy in comparison to your delectable cuntjuices.

This is another very good way of getting a rhythm going. You taste differently when you're about to bleed than when you're ovulating, and it's completely up to you to make distinctions.

A woman's body releases an egg once a month. This egg sits around in your uterus, waiting for some sperm to show up. It is not stupid. After twelve to twenty-four hours, it figures no sperm's gonna take it on a hot date and it makes an exit without further ado.

Sperm can live in your body anywhere from seventy-two hours to five days. What this means is, if some sperm finds its way into your uterus up to *one working week* before your body releases its egg, you *can, feasibly*, get pregnant.

When an egg is present, you are ovulating. Generally, not always, but *generally*, a woman ovulates halfway through her menstrual cycle. Therefore, if you had your period when the moon was new, then there's a good chance you'll ovulate when the moon is full.

Another indication that you're ovulating is a slight twinge of pain in your lower abdomen. It doesn't feel like a menstrual cramp, it's more of a tight, pinched-nerve-type pain. If you masturbate, you can sometimes feel it after you come.

Also, I should probably add that when you are ovulating, you will often become insanely horny. You may feel the urge to couple with the kitchen-table leg, though I wouldn't necessarily take this as an ovulatory symptom.

The *most* reliable way to tell when you are ovulating is by intimately familiarizing yourself with the posh setting of your cunt by interpreting messages from your cervix.

Stick your finger—middle finger's best—up your cunt, swipe it around and around your cervix, being careful not to neglect the underside, where secretions like to settle. If you are ovulating you will find a nice blob of snot on your finger. There's no seemly way to describe this. It's snot, quite un-mistakably, plain and simple, snot. It has no odor or color, it's just clear snot, and as such, tastes a little salty. This snot's function is to create a warm, cushiony thoroughfare for sperm to travel to your egg.

The unique characteristics of ovulation snots are created by a rise in the hormone estrogen. Before you ovulate, the discharge on your finger is milky and creamy. Right after you ovulate, when you stick your finger up your cunt, you'll find sticky, tacky, maybe curdy, white stuff. If the sticky white stuff is there, with either a little snot mixed in or no snot at all, figure you just ovulated. Estrogen decreases at the approach of your period and progesterone rises, making your cunt dry up a tad. As you get used to checking your cuntstuff, you'll be able to recognize what's what.

Now, if you're gonna be making expeditions in your cunt with your fingers, *keep those fingernails clipped and wash your hands!* If anybody else is of the mind to explore your cuntal regions with their digits, make goddamn sure they keep their nails clipped and hands clean too. Many minor infections are attributed to the hairline lesions caused by fingernail scratches. If you're prone to these minor infections, examine your lover's fingernails and hand-washing habits.

I've made it my business to peruse my cuntjuices once or twice every week when I'm not bleeding. The best time to do this is while taking a shower, when my hands are already quite clean and I'm already quite naked. I've incorporated this investigation into my shower ritual, so on any given week, I know exactly where I am in my cycle. When you make knowing your cunt's cycle an important part of your *normal* bathroom regime, it becomes rote.

After a few months of familiarizing yourself with your snots and milky or curdy or tacky white stuffs, ask yourself this question: "How can I get with child if I know exactly when I am fertile and, therefore, take precautionary measures?" Precautionary methods may involve the use of condoms, engaging in sexual activities that do not involve dick 'n cunt intercourse or investigating erotic fantasies based on titillation and masturbation.

Cuntlovin' Ovulation Alert is of obvious benefit to women who *want* to get pregnant. It's also a divine service for women who aren't at all preoccupied with the possibility of conception. Your cunt's rhythm affects perspective, mood and creative and erotic expression. What is day-to-day life, but perspective, mood and creative and erotic expression? Knowing and grooving with your cunt is *such* a huge assistance in these matters.

Cuntlovin' Ovulation Alert furthermore helps you:

1. Plan and navigate your way through any given week.

2. Anticipate and deflect negative interactions with
    people you care about.
3. Love yourself, which in turn effects positive changes
    for future generations of women. Counting you, that's
    one more cuntlovin' woman in the world who is
    contributing to an environment of cuntlove.

Cuntlovin' Ovulation Alert dictates compassion and respect
for all women.

Once you get to the point where you anticipate what juices
your cervix is letting loose, emotional and psychological
rhythms inside you become more lucid.

After that, there's no stopping you.

You rule.

We are at the juncture of examining the repercussions of truly,
candidly understanding our cunts.

Let's say now you've made some serious decisions about
your body. Let's say you've developed a keen interest in
reigning at the helm of your body's rhythm. Optimally, let's say
you're open to falling in love with yourself in a way you only
remotely considered in the past.

According to my little theory, a highly developed sense of
compassion for your physical self has a rippling effect in the
subconscious. It leads to the development of a psychic sense of
compassion for everyone with a cunt. Once you understand
your personal rhythm, you intuitively connect yourself with all
the people who share a similar rhythm.

These people are womankind.

Which leads us to honoring the single most excoriated group of women in the world.

Not virgins.

Not mothers.

One more guess.

Whores

I am thankful to have been blessed with a fairly well-developed sense of entitlement during the composition of every chapter in *Cunt*.

Except this one.

This one's been difficult.

I've never *been* a Whore.

I've read and thought about and talked to Whores. As a woman living in this society, I'm *consistently reminded* I am a *potential* Whore whenever a man is not escorting me, which is rather most of the time. None of this, however, is the same as consciously *experiencing* Whoredom firsthand. If I were a *truly* resourceful and courageous individual, I would've learned how to be a Whore for subsistence while I wrote this book. Alas, I am an impractical chickenshit in this regard.

Whores are a very important part of *Cunt*. Every time I've tried to explain why, though, I've met this insecurity inside myself. It is a very cranky insecurity that says stuff like, "You don't know what it's like to *be* a Whore, you dang fool. Can't base no chapter on sneaky suspicions."

But Whoredom is a massive part of our history and power as women. When fully instructed in the art of sacred sexual power, Whores are the people who can teach us all the stuff we grow up not learning about sexuality, our bodies and our innate sexual power. Our cultural ignorance and intolerance of Whores keeps Whores from realizing the full potential of Whoredom. It likewise robs women and men of Teachers who can help us understand women's sexual power.

Whores were a central part of religion, spirituality and everyday life in times when the Goddess—a *truly* sexual being—was overtly worshipped. It took a lot of work, study, devotion and commitment to become one of the Goddess's sexual priestesses. People were free to visit the temples of Whores, and did so to learn, to love, to open up physically, to heal.

I ruminated over this chapter for a long time, and prayed the Goddess would help me. Like always, She came through. This time She manifested Herself in a woman named Carol Queen, a writer, sex activist and Whore.

You won't find Carol Queen in the acknowledgment section because I know people don't always read the praises in books, and I want everyone to know:

Carol Queen fucking *rules.*

Woman, you saved my ass and

I thank you

from the bottom of my heart.

Ms. Queen's book, *Real Live Nude Girl*, published in 1997 by Cleis Press, casts resplendent light on the history of sacred Whoredom. Carol Queen reveals that the depravity surrounding

Whoredom is not based on the fact that Whoredom exists, but rather, it is based on the *perception* of Whoredom's existence.

> My "ardent worshippers" and I have no temple today in which to perform a dance that sometimes seems more profane than sacred. In a culture that does not worship the Goddess any longer, these are degenerate times indeed, but not because a once-holy act is still being negotiated in hotel suites, in massage parlors, on city streets. In fact, if prostitution is ever eradicated, it will be a signal that Christianity's murder of Eros is complete, the Goddess's rule completely overturned. Perhaps most prostitutes today are unaware that their profession has a sacred history, and doubtless most clients would define what they do with us as something other than worship. But I believe that an echo of the old relationship, when he was the seeker and she was the Source, are still present when money changes hands today. (Queen, 1997, 190)

It would be *so wonderful* to visit a Sacred Whore temple. Kick down some cash to mix with and undulate in the ol' Goddess's love juices for a while.

Damn, I'm so seethingly jealous of those olden time people.

I daresay the loss of our sacred sexual temples grieves the heart of Carol Queen threefold.

Whoredom has existed, in various guises, for thousands and thousands of years. A main artery of the Goddess's lifeforce, it is too powerful to annihilate.

Whoredom has been successfully vilified.

Whoredom is presently accepted as a very, very bad thing, while its history debases this idea beyond all reckoning.

Sound like any old word that is the title to a book you've been reading lately?

In our present mode of collective consciousness, a Whore is simply a person who exchanges sex for financial resources.

I accept this to be true, but only if it's recognized as one *part* of a much broader cultural-financial order that women participate in for survival. There is no difference between a woman who marries a very powerful man because it is the only way she is guaranteed a "place" in society, and a streetwalker who's never known the illusion of a "guarantee."

Some women opt to be Whores because procuring semen from men's bodies is a bona fide way to make a living in a society where we are viewed as highly expendable citizens.

Ms. Streetwalker exchanges womanly wiles for subsistence.

Some women—such as the late Princess Diana, who once referred to herself as the highest paid prostitute in the world— don't actually *opt* to be Whores, but realize nonetheless that that is exactly what we are.

Ms. Powerwife exchanges womanly wiles for a fancy house in the hills.

In this way of thinking, the issue is *class* rather than Whoredom.

Hugh Grant and Eddie Murphy could lecture on this subject.

Sacred Whore temples flourished in ancient India, the Middle East, Africa, Europe, the Americas and Asia. The word "whore" was a title, used in much the way our word "reverend" is employed today. "Whore" is associated with many words including hus-band, hussy, *puta* (Spanish for "whore"—in Vedic, *puta* means "pure" or "holy"), *ghazye* (Egyptian), *devadasi* (Sanskrit), *horae* (Greek) and *hor* (Hebrew). Whore-priestesses were revered because they taught "a combination of mother-love, tenderness, comfort, mystical enlightenment and sex." (Walker, 1983, 820)

Mary Magdalene was a Whore and Jesus dug her because she taught him the most sacred thing a man can ever hope to learn in his lifetime: how to fuck. Stud that he was, Jesus knew to humble himself to this woman.

I imagine the sex was spectacular.

Let's interpret the notion of Jesus visiting a Whore in a cuntlovin' way. Let's pretend Jesus and his Apostle frat brothers didn't visit Mary Magdalene after a hard night tossing off forty-ouncers and tipping cows in the holy land.

From all the things I've heard about Jesus, he sounds like a pretty decent sort. He looks nice in most of his pictures. You can *tell* Adolph Hitler and George Washington were dickheads just by looking at them. Looking at Jesus, he seems cool. By and large, Jesus evidently had a lot of love and compassion swimming around his heart. He had a pretty huge impact in certain parts of the world, yet left it when he was only thirty-two. You gotta figure Jesus didn't waste a lot of time dinking around. Even if he *did* dink around, he doesn't seem like the kind of guy who'd take an impersonal toss in the hay for a budgeted degree of arousal.

I seriously doubt Jesus perceived Mary Magdalene as anything less than an esteemed Teacher. In Jesus' time, Whores were still prophets of sexual power. They taught people how the

physical body is a conduit of energy. If Jesus was able to manifest the love in his heart in all the physical actions the bible
alleges, Mary Magdalene was certainly one of the people in his
life responsible for helping him figure out how to do it.

Though Whores were integral and respected in many times and
places, the fear and/or awe of female sexuality certainly rivals
Whoredom in age.

I don't know if that big dyke Lilith was a Whore or not, but
she was certainly too sexually aggro for Adam and God's liking:

Hebraic tradition said Adam married Lilith because he
grew tired of coupling with beasts, a common custom of
Middle-Eastern herdsmen, though the Old Testament
declared it a sin (Deuteronomy 27:21). Adam tried to force
Lilith to lie beneath him in the "missionary position"
favored by male-dominant societies. Moslems were so
insistent on the male-superior sexual position that they
said, "Accursed be the man who maketh women heaven
and himself earth." Catholic authorities said any sexual
position other than the male-superior one is sinful. But
Lilith was neither a Moslem nor a Catholic. She sneered at
Adam's sexual crudity, cursed him, and flew away to make
her home by the Red Sea.

God sent angels to fetch Lilith back, but she cursed
them too, ignored God's command, and spent her time
coupling with "demons" (whose lovemaking evidently
pleased her better) and giving birth to a hundred children
every day. So God had to produce Eve as Lilith's more

docile replacement. . . . The story of Lilith disappeared from the canonical Bible, but her daughters the *lilim* haunted men for over a thousand years. Well into the Middle Ages, the Jews were still manufacturing amulets to keep away the *lilim*, who were lustful she-demons given to copulating with men in their dreams, causing nocturnal emissions. Naturally, the *lilim* squatted on top of their victims in the position favored by ancient matriarchs. (Walker, 1983, 541-42)

The *lilim* that haunted men in their dreams were manifestations of a growing terror of female sexuality. In our society, this fear has gone past fruition and is presently rotting.

I feel pretty cheated about Whores for a number of reasons:

1. Whores generally subsist within men's domain, under conditions men have formulated for the past odd thousand years, and are largely inaccessible to women.

2. Most Whores are completely unaware of how important they are to society, and subsequently do not have the opportunity to learn how to be all-compassionate, all-loving, all-giving and all-receiving incarnations of the Goddess.

3. I've never been with a Whore because any Whore who knows she's one of the Goddess's priestesses would cost my entire disposable income for six months.

I do, however, have a frame of reference because I know what it is like to be in the arms of the Goddess.

One time I got blessed by this Goddess incarnation named Ammachi. She's not a Whore, but she's by far the closest personification of an olden time sacred temple priestess I've ever personally encountered.

Ammachi is a woman from India who comes to America and has these ashram things. The first time I went to her ashram thing, I had no idea what it was about. I saw a bunch of mostly white people dressed in white clothes who bugged me with their "Oh, I am so very holy and drink herbal tea constantly" vibration.

But the music was amazing.

Ammachi sat in the front of the room on a bunch of pillows. Musicians, attendants, children and flowers surrounded her. Thousands of flowers, like when Princess Diana died. She sat there with her eyes closed, and chanted. Probably, she was meditating. Wearing a flowing white sari, she was covered with chiffon, silk, everything soft and whispery. I figured she understood the concept of an ashram far better than I, so I did the same as her. Closed my eyes, sat and listened.

This lasted a long time, but like in a dream, I don't know how many minutes and hours passed.

Then there were the rustling sounds of people standing up. I opened my eyes. Everyone was forming a double-file line that led to Ammachi.

My friends told me she was gonna bless people, so we queued up. The line was very, very long, snaking throughout the entire large building we were in. If it had been a line at the post office that I *absolutely had to stand in* for some reason or another, I woulda sold my soul to the person in front to give me cuts. But this line was different. The music and nice quiet felt good. Being blessed by an incarnation of the Goddess is also much more alluring than overnighting IRS forms.

Before I knew it, I was next.

An attendant led me to her and kinda helped me kneel down right. Ammachi seized me gently—if you can imagine that—and pulled me into her lap. She cradled me, murmuring sweet chanting sounds into my ear. Her body engulfed mine and I relaxed—almost melted—into her. My face buried in her shoulder and neck, I breathed in her smell.

This is when I really, truly started to freak on the wonder of Ammachi. After holding hundreds of people in this manner, you would think she'd start to kinda stink. I was nowhere near the beginning of the line. The sun set and went down, down, down to Australia while I stood in that line. A lot of people were in her arms before me, but the woman smelled like flowers. Not perfumey at all. Like if you covered every inch of your bedroom floor with freshly cut bouquets of jasmine, gardenia, roses, hyacinth, carnations, sweet peas and freesia is what she smelled like. And this smell wasn't coming from the flowers around her, it exuded from her skin, the fabrics of her sari and veils. It filled my whole body, permeated my pores. Her smell made me so giddy the attendant had to help me stand back up again. She stared deeply into my eyes and pressed flower petals and chocolate kisses into my hand.

I stumbled away like a drunk.

Like I just had one 'dem orgasms to raise the dead.

Lordisa.

For a whole week afterwards, my entire apartment smelled

like Ammachi. Everywhere I went, I smelled her smell. Walking down the street with one of my friends, the smell of Ammachi would assail me. I'd go, "*Damn*, do you smell that?" And my friend'd go, "Car exhaust? What?"

As Ammachi's smell faded from my life, I started thinking about what happened when she blessed me.

It was the first time in my life I felt *loved*. Physically, emotionally, psychically, spiritually, *deeply loved* from the epidermis of my skin that featured a couple of ugly zits, to the core of my heart that is still traumatized by the death of my brother, abortions, meanspirited lovergirls and other nasty hurts. It is a consciousness-broadening freak-out to feel love in this way.

"What," I wondered, "is the difference between Ammachi and a Whore?" Ammachi gave me unconditional love, no questions asked. She healed me and helped me understand more about love. I was one of many people cradled in her embrace that day. Ammachi needs money to keep spreading her love, and I bought plenty of Ammachi paraphernalia to support her.

She doesn't offer erotic love to people, but any cuntlovin' Whore will tell ya, eroticism is a *part* of sexual love.

After Ammachi blessed me, after her flower smell took over my life for a week, after I sat down and thought about it long and hard, I realized her gift. She clues people in on what love really, really is. That way, it's easier to know what love really, really isn't. She helps people identify love, so we can call it into our lives. In the grand panorama of my life, I was in Ammachi's world, in Ammachi's arms, for mere moments.

Those moments changed me forever.

This is some serious-assed power founded in cuntlove.

The nemesis of this power is sexual cuntfear. One of the many, many, many casualties of our culture's negative sexual fear sits in a jail cell awaiting execution as you read this.

Aileen Wuornos is an ex-Whore on death row in Florida. She murdered seven men. She is the only "serial killer" ever to plead self-defense.

Not long after Ms. Wuornos walked through the prison doors, I attended Diamanda Galás's performance of a vocal composition entitled *Shrei X*. Ms. Galás's three-and-a-half octave range left me reeling in pain. Her haunting, stunning presence shattered all my fear.

I interviewed her the next day and asked, "What inspired *Shrei X?*"

Well, one thing was Aileen Wuornos. It's a long story. There's a documentary out called *The Selling of A Serial Killer* about Aileen Wuornos. It's a very, very interesting movie. She's a real hero of mine because without taking a predatory stance, you're fucked. In her case, literally.

If you're a prostitute and somebody rapes you, it's just fucken a shitty feeling. Aileen would go through the sex part and then the John would want to do something else, like fuck her up the ass and put alcohol up her ass. She got to where she went over the edge and said, "No more." She reached Critical Mass, said *No,* and started killing people who were abusing her. And because she was seen as being predatory, she got the death penalty. She's not seen as somebody who has the law on her side for the job that she was doing. A job that is, very effectively, if not legalized, condoned, as long as she pays out the cops. She didn't *have* any protection and it got to where she had to protect herself. So she protected herself and went to prison. As a woman, she's obviously powerless, but she's *really* powerless. A lesbian prostitute is seen as totally powerless trash.

The silence at the end of *Shrei X* is the silence that her dumbfuck lawyers sang to her because she was found guilty. Guilty, guilty, guilty.

Because Ms. Wuornos is perceived as being "totally power-less trash," because Ms. Wuornos resides in an exceptionally cuntfearing society and because Ms. Wuornos's case yielded quite a bit of media interest, her "lawyer" seems to have come to the conclusion that he could make a pretty penny selling her "story." *Especially* if his client is put to death. After watching *Aileen Wuornos: The Selling of a Serial Killer*, one is rather confronted with the idea that the people who one would traditionally expect to support Ms. Wuornos—namely her attorneys—are plainly itching for her to be executed as a ferocious serial killer.

Which she is not.

Aileen Wuornos is an economically challenged woman who defended herself and needs a decent, intelligent lawyer to get her the fuck out of jail.

If I may be so bold, I would like to dedicate a portion of Kinnie Starr's song "Buttons" to every Whore who suffers under the influence of our sexually retarded, destructive culture:

> and we could call it out when it doesn't suit us both 'cause
> there's a magnitude of choices and a really big boat
> and that big boat floats on a restless ocean
> singing about the chances of protective devotion
>
> for the girlfriend who stands on a street waiting on a trick
> some man demands that she lift her skirt quick
> she's got a mother, a daughter and a lover
> you tell me why she shouldn't have safe cover
>
> 'cause if the laws made sense
> she would have a legal fence
> to keep her clientele clean
> and she could still pay the rent
> she's got a mother, a daughter and a lover
> you tell me why she shouldn't have safe cover

A few years ago a friend of mine was twenty-five cents short for bus fare. None of us had change either. She turned to a gentleman at the bus stop and asked if he could spare a quarter. He responded, *"What?* What *you* askin' me for a quarter for? Girl, you got a *goldmine* between your legs."

This sentence rang in my ears for years.

Cuntlovingly decontextualized, "a goldmine between your legs" is a wonderful sentiment. Like what you find at the end of the rainbow. The idea of women having a goldmine between our legs was so appealing to me, I wrote a little blues song about it:

you gotts a goldmine between your legs,
a goldmine between your legs,
no need to be poor in the u.s.a.
you gotts a goldmine between your legs.
honey why you givin' it away?
we all know them boys'll pay
equal pay for equal labor,
not only love but charge your neighbor.
no need to be poor in the u.s.a.
you gotts a goldmine between your legs.
my momma's broke and all alone
even though she made me a home.
if only she'd charged dear old dad
momma'd be drivin' a shiny jag.
no need to be poor in the u.s.a.
you gotts a goldmine between your legs
does hubby make more money, honey?
wouldn't it be really funny
if he didn't get no fine puss-say
unless he lined your coffers, hey hey.
you gotts a goldmine between your legs,
goldmine between your legs,
no need to be poor in the u.s.a.
you gotts a goldmine between your legs.

All ladies have the power to cash in on the goldmine between our legs. Not necessarily with the objective of financial security or spiritual fulfillment, but for the most important reasons of all: future generations and our cuntlovin' selves.

On a less metaphorical level, nothing but good and fabulousness would come from erecting temples in honor of women's sexuality, filled with women and women-trained male Whores who offered us lessons in how to love and be loved.

Whores were in business back before the Red Sea ever thought about parting. Whores have no labor unions, no health insurance, no retirement fund, no unemployment insurance and no legal rights. Since a chain is only as strong as its weakest link, the nonexistent rights and freedoms of women who understand the power of cunts conceivably more than any other group of women in our society bespeaks the constitution of the chain we ladies are dealing with here.

Is it a mere coincidence that women so specifically, physically associated with cunts have no rights in this culture?

Get out.

Without honoring Whores, we cannot truly understand and transcend the dynamics of violence, destruction and ignorance fostered in our cuntfearing society. The fact that some women are considered "bad" is a puritanically based value judgement that reinforces a fatal division between women. Many women allow our lives and sexual expression to be dictated by the threat of being perceived as "Whores." Because of thinking like this, our society is brimming with women who have a hard time understanding, for instance, that

Whores *can be and are* sexually assaulted.

"How," one might ask, "can a woman who accepts money for sex *be* raped?" Or perhaps, "What does a woman who puts herself in that position *expect?*"

The fact that either question is considered *at all plausible* reflects the self-defeating ignorance we ourselves perpetuate.

The measure of respect Whores receive is in direct proportion to the measure of respect all women receive. Until there is an established, respected place for Whores is this society, no woman will have an established, respected foundation of power.

There is no circumventing this.

Until there is a shift in consciousness about the potential of Whores, we will continue to live in a society which offers no formally acknowledged Teachers to awaken us to our power as sexual beings.

Ain't no getting 'round this one either.

The fact that Whores are no longer exalted and respected is very much a reflection of our culture's collective sexual retardation and fear of women's innate sexual power.

The aptly named Carol Queen is my personal prophet on Whoredom's future in our society.

To guide another person to orgasm, to hold and caress, to provide companionship and initiation to new forms of sex, to embody the Divine and embrace the seeker—these are healing and holy acts. Every prostitute can do these things, whether or not s/he understands their spiritual potential. For us to see ourselves as sacred whores, for our clients to acknowledge the many facets of desire they bring to us, can be a powerful shift in consciousness. We show the face of the Goddess in a culture that has tried for millennia to break and denigrate Her, just as some today claim *we* are broken and denigrated. They are not correct, and the Goddess will not be broken. In our collective extraordinary experience we prostitutes have healed even those who do not honor us. Were the attack on us over, we could begin to heal the whole world.

After seven thousand years of oppression, I declare this the time to bring back our temple. (Queen, 1997, 204-5)

Whoredom is a constant.

Perception fluctuates evermore.

I don't know about you, but I like the idea of respecting things that have been around a lot longer than me. I drive old cars and live in old houses. I gravitate towards old souls and listen to what old folks say. My favorite games—chess and backgammon—are old, old, old.

So you see, if I were to find Whoredom and the Perception Surrounding Whoredom at a garage sale, I'd definitely buy the Whoredom.

Even if it was dented up, needed a new paint job and cost a coupla bucks more.

Orgasms from Cunts

Thanks to the perception surrounding Whoredom in our
culture, no one teaches us how to fuck. We grow up
and either figure it out for ourselves or settle into
some habitual bog of sexual expression.
Whatever.
Sexual expression must be made manifest in
the physical world, *somehow*. Since it cannot be
completely repressed, people sometimes hide stuff
and get into weird things like eating shit. Sexual expression is a
current of kinetic energy running through our bodies. It
whirligigs up our cunts, charges through our entire being and
slam dances on out into the world back through our cunts.

Comin' our brains out.

Sometimes we holler 'n shake the windows in their panes.

Our cunts are powerhouses.

Cuntlovin' women who make the conscious decision to
oversee the smooth operation of our powerhouses know all this.

One of my prized possessions is my 1965 Random House
Dictionary. It lived in my parent's house before I. Though

technically it belonged to everyone, I took it with me when I moved away. No one complained. Ever since I could read, that dictionary and I were inseparable.

When I was ten, I invited a boy I liked very much over to our house. We hung out in my room, mooning over each other and listening to records, until my father opened the door. He told the boy to go home and steered me by the elbow into the kitchen. There, at the table sat my mother and my dear friend, the Random House Dictionary. I sensed I was in deep shit, but didn't know why. Mom had a serious look on her face and Dad seemed kinda pissed.

He said, "Look up the word 'reputation' and read it aloud."

My father, the devout atheist with the photographic memory who knew the Encyclopedia Britannica by heart, had us quote from the dictionary in much the same manner as children in other families were required to quote from the Holy Book.

I read the definition for "reputation":

rep-u-ta-tion (rep ye ta shen), n. 1. the estimation in which a person or thing is held, esp. by the community or the public generally: *a man of good reputation.* 2. favorable repute; good name: *to ruin one's reputation by misconduct.*
3. a favorable and publicly recognized name or standing for merit, achievement, etc.: *to build up a reputation.* 4. the estimation or name of being, having, having done, etc., something specified: *He has the reputation of being a shrewd businessman.*

I was thoroughly mystified, but after reading the definition of "reputation," I felt decidedly ashamed.

Dirty.

My dad looked at me sternly and said, "You must *never* have boys in your room with the door closed."

"But we were listening to records," I argued. "I always close the door when my friends come over and we listen to records."

Mom: "Inga, it's very important not to get a bad reputation. Letting boys in your room and closing the door is one way to get a bad reputation."

Dad: "When your girlfriends come over, you can close the door, but when boys come over, keep it open."

Little did my parents know, it was me and my *girl* friends who engaged in sexual activity. At age ten, I'd *remotely* entertained the notion of kissing boys, while at least three of my girlfriends and I had figured out how to make each other come by the time we were seven.

I've had the satisfaction of clueing my mom in, but I wish my dad were alive so I could say, "Yo, Pops, if you were *really* concerned with my chastity, you shouldn't have let certain friends spend the night with me, ya fool."

This isn't to preface my anger towards my parents for instilling in me shameful associations about my budding sexuality.

They Did the Best They Could.

I quelled any animosity I may have felt towards them the time I saw this real old Japanese print of two people having rapturous sex while their three children peacefully played a game with marbles at their feet. It is the epitome of the family-at-home-together picture. The kids don't care that the parents are fucking because fucking is as much a part of life as playing with marbles. They are completely unconcerned with what their parents are doing because *it's no big deal*. They're just fucking. The parents are playing a game that somebody taught them how to play. By the time those kids got big, they'd know fucking like they knew the soft, glassy chink of marbles colliding.

This was not my reality.

When my mother was pregnant with Nick, the youngest of her brood, she described how sexual intercourse created the magic of a baby in her belly.

"You and Dad have done that *four times*?" I asked, thoroughly disgusted.

People helped me out when it was time for me to walk and ride a two-wheeler. Everyone I knew encouraged me to talk, use the toilet, sing, draw, swim, read, write and make lots of friends.

I am very fortunate and grateful that I got helped out quite a bit.

There was this one—rather crucial—part of my being, however, that was pretty much left to the elements. I didn't get nearly as much encouragement learning how to express myself sexually as I did learning how to pronounce big words.

When I became sexually active with men, sex wasn't what I wanted *at all*. I wanted love and affection. I had fun having sex with my girlfriends, but it was just that: fun. Suddenly, it seems one day, I was supposed to re-enact this with boys and it just wasn't the same, spontaneous, jiveass, wanton fun. It's quite the bummer—not to mention life-threatening reality—that I didn't figure this out 'til after I'd tested sheets with surfers, vatos, punks, nerds and a rather sadistic wrestler-chiropractor.

I didn't even really think about my formal, heterosexual awakening until years after the fact, when two of my hometown friends and I talked about it.

Why did we fuck those boys who never exactly made our clits pound out the Bohemian Rhapsody in the first place? What were we doing? Did we love ourselves at all? We certainly mustn't have, or we would *at the very least,* have practiced safe sex. Why didn't we understand that our quest for love and affection could have easily killed us, and why didn't it? Was the Goddess magnanimously smiling upon the truly ignorant?

Toni Childs sings this really cool song I wish I had heard when I was seventeen. It's called "I Just Want Affection," and it's one of many beautiful songs on the album *The Woman's Boat.* This song taught me about the difference between erotic closeness and fucking.

Lots of girls grow up thinking the way to be loved is to fuck because our culture holds that affection is part and parcel to gettin' down. But in my mind, and in the minds of many, many cuntlovin' women I know, it is dimly related, but not the same thing at all.

Had I been left to my innate feminine wiles, I would've found a much safer and supportive way to procure affection, love and acceptance, starting with myself.

The happy ending is, though, that through trial, error, forgiveness and willingness to accept my ignorance, I learned that I'm the Cuntlovin' Ruler of My Sexual Universe.

Which leads to the story of Mademoiselle Precious, my cousin's daughter.

When Mademoiselle was seven, her parents granted her a premier waltz with independence: a visit to the city to stay with my musical concubine and me for a week one summer.

We were a little nervous. Neither of us had been around kids for long, parentless durations of time. Our home was not designed around the premise of a child's entertainment requirements. We didn't even have a television set. What if she was bored with our lives?

But we needn't have worried. Mlle. Precious loved all our friends. She loved going to the coffee shops, the river, everywhere we took her. She loved the Free Box in our apartment building and insisted on visiting it first thing every morning.

We all got along quite famously.

One day, my musical concubine said, "I've seen Mlle. Precious jiggling under her covers on the couch. Do you think her parents have talked to her about masturbating?"

I said I didn't know.

"Do you think you should talk to her about masturbating?"

I thought about how embarrassed I was that time my sister barged into the bathroom while I was whacking off with the shower massage. I also thought about how I probably wouldn't have had such a baggage-load of negative beliefs to dispel as an adult if just *one measly person* had told me it was fine and dandy to bandy my clit when I was a kid.

But, *jeez,* talking to Mlle. Precious about masturbating? What if it embarrassed her? What if it scarred her for life and it would be all my fault? What would I say?

99

I said I didn't know again.

It was quite the preoccupational quandary in my mind all day long.

We went to the river, played in the mud and the water.

When we came home, my musical concubine made phone calls and Mlle. Precious and I took a bubble bath. We were busy getting clean and shiny and suddenly, it just jumped out of me.

I said, "Hey, Precious. I don't know if you ever do, but if you ever play with your wahchee (that's what her family calls cunts), I just want you to know it's okay."

She turned crimson, looked at me and then down at the water. "I don't do that. I don't play with my wahchee."

Shit.

Goddamn.

I spluttered, "I *know.* I mean, it doesn't matter. I just wanted to tell you that *if* you ever *did,* it's all right. Everybody plays with their wahchee, I swear to god."

She glared at me. "Well, *I* don't."

I hastily changed the subject and we splashed more bubbles to life.

After a few minutes, Mlle. Precious says, "Everybody plays with their wahchee?"

My heart leaped in my chest. Oh, how I smiled inside.

"Yeah. Everybody."

"Do you?"

"Yup."

"Does your musical concubine?"

"Yeah."

"My mom?"

"Probably. I mean, I would *imagine*. Just about everybody does, Precious. And it's *perfectly fine* if you do, too. Even if people tell you it's bad, they're just scared or stupid. It's not bad at all and *everybody* plays with their wahchee."

She laughed crazy, absolutely thrilled, and yelled, "Everybody plays with their wahchee?"

I screamed, "Everybody plays with their wahchee!"

We chanted, yelling at the top of our lungs, "Ev-ree-body plays with their wahh-chee! Ev-ree-body plays with their wahh-chee! Ev-ree-body plays with their wahh-chee!"

My musical concubine, still on the phone: "Jesus Christ! What are you two screaming about? What the hell's a wahchee?"

We laughed and splashed and chanted and flooded the whole bathroom.

I hope this experience has a positive effect on Mademoiselle Precious's sexuality. I hope she remembers all her life that there's not a problem in the world with her jilling off. However, even if our conversation gets lost in her shuffle of growing up, our little talk heartened *me* tremendously. I felt like I'd righted an inadvertent wrong committed against me when I was a little girl.

Felt the cards of karma riffle into place.

In my cosmology, Wilhelm Reich holds the distinction of being the only male psychoanalyst who could knock on my door and be invited in for tea.

Reich's books were banned in America for many years, while he himself was ostracized—even imprisoned—by the U.S. government during McCarthy's scary reign.

He challenged the puritanical ideas about sexuality in our

culture. In laywoman terms, Reich believed humans store emotions in our muscles. During orgasm, muscles in the body contract, then relax, thus releasing emotions. Reich asserted that all aspects of healthy human psychology are dependent upon one's sexual expression.

When you cry, laugh or feel free as a bird after coming, it is partly because you just released a bunch of yucky crap that's been building up inside your body for days, months, years, possibly your entire lifetime.

A moment of epiphany on this subject occurred after six months of Reichian therapy. I was at the beach, thinking and watching the waves. The revelation assailed me quite suddenly, as revelations are wont to do: Each wave is an orgasm. Sometimes they're big. Sometimes they're small. Sometimes they tear faces of cliff from the earth's surface. If the ocean did not have waves, it would be a big, salty lake. A lake is a still pool of water. Personally, I don't venture into water that doesn't move. Bored, malevolent monsters live in bodies of water that do not move.

When women function like the ocean, we live happy, healthy lives. Holding on to stuff that does not serve us in our present situation creates actual, physical blockages within our bodies.

Bored, malevolent monsters.

Which, on the individual level, manifest in bitterness, stifled creativity, sexual perversion and unwillingness to trust, love and/or touch.

Collectively—when an entire society is sexually repressed—phenomena such as war, rape, racism, greed and wholesale shitty behavior are considered acceptable.

It is difficult to strip away cultural thought-patterns and stereotypes to arrive at the pulsating naked core of Woman: Cuntlovin' Fucklove Prophetess. I realized the enormity of this very task on New Year's Day in 1995.

I was walking down the street when a gentleman whose family and tribe have lived in the Pacific Northwest for thousands of years asked me for some spare change.

Due to the rising cost of living, I don't believe in spare change. As I handed him a dollar, he peered into my eyes and smiling, asked, "Hey, did you get Any for New Year's?"

I was just about to say, "That's none of your fucking business, dickhead," but his eyeballs caught me off guard. He didn't have perving eyeballs. He had very nice, open eyeballs with a pretty glint in them. He was just good-naturedly asking me if I rang in the new year with a celebratory tumble in the sack. And, as it happened, I actually did ring in the new year in just such a manner.

So I said, "Yeah."

The gentleman positively *beamed*. He said, "Hey! Me too! Ain't nothin' like gettin' Some on New Year's to humble ya, know what I mean?"

As I walked home, I thought about this man and his message. I thought, sex truly is humbling. I thought, sex, birth, life and death are all humbling. Most of all, I thought how thankful I was to this gentleman for giving me a beautiful message about sex, something seldom resonated in society. I tried to think of all the positive, reinforcing messages about sex

c
u
n
t

I have access to on a general basis whenever I leave my home, or otherwise subject myself to this culture.

The only one I readily managed to summon was the words of a very nice Lummi gentleman on New Year's Day in 1995.

All my life, I've absorbed stimuli about sex from my culture, family, friends and teachers. Most of this information has been hopelessly gnarled all up with violence, racism, power, purity, shame, denial, guilt, humiliation, victimization, objectification, rejection and unimaginative stereotypes of sexual identity.

Probably even more stuff than that.

It all, all, all, all, all, all, all, all, all stems from fear of women and our enormous sexual power.

When we were children, one of my older brother's favorite means of torment was to sit down near me, cut a *foul*, noiseless fart and wait. As soon as he ascertained that I'd detected his gastric horror, he'd restrain my hands so I could neither run nor cover my nose, and diabolically whisper, "Silence is deadly."

While his farts miraculously never threatened my life, I agree with this sentiment wholeheartedly.

Since the early days of the church, women had been barred from speaking in the house of God as well as preaching, teaching, or speaking in public: "As in all the churches of the saints," wrote St. Paul, "wives should keep silence in the churches. They are not permitted to speak, but should be subordinate, as even the law says. If there is anything they desire to know, let them ask their husbands at home. For it is shameful for a woman to speak in church." This prohibition grew out of the synthesis of separate traditions, the Greek, which taught that women were by nature inferior to men and therefore should be their subordinates, and the Biblical, which suggested to many readers that women be perpetually silent as a punishment for the sins of Eve, whose garrulousness brought disaster to all mankind: "The curse of God pronounced on your sex weighs still on the world. Guilty you must bear its hardships," wrote Tertullian in the third century, "You are the devil's gateway . . . you softened up with your cajoling words the man against whom the devil could not prevail by force." Over the centuries these themes hardened until silence became a virtue particularly recommended to women. "By silence, indeed, women achieve the fame of eloquence," wrote one Renaissance commentator. (Brown, 1986, 59)

The enforced silence of women allows men's fear of us and our sexual power to reign unchallenged. Thus the wisdom of brilliant people such as Audre Lorde is not venerated, and we are still sent to schools where idiotic puds like Aristotle are worshipped.

A-hem:

Just as it sometimes happens that deformed offspring are produced by deformed parents, and sometimes not, so the offspring produced by a female are sometimes female, sometimes not, but male. The reason is that the female is as it were a deformed male; and the menstrual charge is semen, though . . . it lacks one constituent, and only one, the principle of Soul. . . . Thus the physical part, the body, comes from the female, and the Soul from the male, since the Soul is the essence of a particular body. . . . females are weaker and colder in their nature, and we should look upon the female state as being as it were a deformity, though one which occurs in the ordinary course of nature. (Aristotle, as quoted in Brown, 1986, 188)

To the best of my knowledge, it wasn't until 1968 when Valerie Solanas published her *S.C.U.M. Manifesto,* that this particular form of intolerance was duplicated with any serious eloquence:

It is now technically possible to reproduce without the aid of males (or, for that matter, females) and to produce only females. We must begin immediately to do so. Retaining the male has not even the dubious purpose of reproduction. The male is a biological accident: the y (male) gene is an incomplete x (female) gene, that is, has an incomplete set of chromosomes. In other words, the male is an incomplete female, a walking abortion, aborted at the gene stage. To be male is to be deficient, emotionally limited; maleness is a deficiency disease and males are emotional cripples.

The male is completely egocentric, trapped inside himself, incapable of empathizing or identifying with others, of love, friendship, affection or tenderness. He is a completely isolated unit, incapable of rapport with anyone. His responses are entirely visceral, not cerebral; his intelligence is a mere tool in the service of his drives and needs, he is incapable of mental passion, mental interaction; he can't relate to anything other than his own physical sensations. He is a half dead, unresponsive lump, incapable of giving or receiving pleasure or happiness; consequently, he is at best an utter bore, an inoffensive blob, since only those capable of absorption in others can be charming. He is trapped in a twilight zone halfway between humans and apes, and is far worse off than apes because, unlike the apes, he is capable of a large array of negative feelings—hate, jealousy, contempt, disgust, guilt, shame, doubt—and moreover he is *aware* of what he is and isn't.

While Aristotle is lauded in our culture, Valerie Solanas is considered—when she's considered at all—to be a terribly unhinged individual who died homeless on the streets of San Francisco in 1988. Whereas, if you changed the pronouns throughout her manifesto, and backdated it a couple of decades, you'd probably have the ramblings of a brilliant, Pulitzer Prize–winning male scholar.

See how that works?

Women and silence have been historically mashed together like potatoes and cheese. Our true erotic nature is not exalted. Rather, it is mutated into some manageable illusion created and sustained by men. Meanwhile, the Washington Monument alone attests to the grandeur with which male erotic nature is glorified.

This same pattern is found in the scant funding for both breast cancer research and the risk of female-to-female transmission of the HIV virus, versus the gazillions of dollars poured into research for prostate cancer, and the risk of male-to-male transmission of the HIV virus.

In an interview in *Bust* #10, the beautiful, genius porn star, Nina Hartley describes what's at stake here.

> I got the first edition of *Our Bodies, Ourselves* for my 13th brithday and it was the most powerful book I'd ever read next to *Sex for One*, which saved my life. Sex is enlightening. The reality is that once a woman knows that the pleasure goddess is at the end of her arm, then she can swing her hand in front of her crotch anytime and woops! there it is, anytime she wants. It's really easy—let's see: teddy bears, washing machines, jacuzzi jets, vibrators, cunnilingus, fucking, ooo, lots of things can do it. Women are denied pleasure because pleasure is very, very powerful, very, very potent. (93)

Women reach orgasm via our clitoris, through contractions of the muscles deep within our cunts or by stimulation of our G-spots. Sometimes all three, or any combination. Women ejaculate. Fingers or other apparati strategically placed up a woman's ass can lead to ten-minute-long multiple orgasms. Women can come just by looking at—or imagining—some major turn-on for a while. Women can come over and over, one orgasm right after the last. Women have orgasms in many, many different ways.

Men, on the other hand, come when their cock is stroked, via a hand, mouth, cunt or anus. Many men can also achieve orgasm through stimulation of their prostate gland, via their asshole. Sadly though, the general feeling among straight men is, "I ain't no fucking faggot, so keep clear of my ass." Thus, a lot of men deprive themselves of this (I've gathered) highly pleasurable sensation.

After a man comes, he's usually spent for at least fifteen minutes, and generally, that's it for the session. This, of course, is in the event that he has not studied any Tantric-type breathing and muscle control practices, which the vast majority of men in our culture don't have the opportunity, inclination or self-discipline to explore.

As a dick is a finite structure, with a visible beginning and end, so too is the potential for a male orgasm.

As a cunt is infinite—how many bloody mysteries and future generations are hiding up there, somewhere?—so too is the potential for female orgasm.

I'm setting my imagination free to roam here, but if I were a man, and had no *biological* idea what it was like to have such a complex orgasm mechanism as a cunt—with *so many* intricate, endless and fascinating possibilities for achieving pleasure—I'd be pretty nervous making love to a woman. And I might find millions and billions of ways to camouflage my nervousness, rather than be like Jesus and just humble myself.

Aristotle opted to obsessively devote his life to the creation of an elaborate belief system based on total cuntfear, rather than simply face reality. That seems like pretty nervous behavior to me. Ditto Sigmund Freud—the Rush Limbaugh our society actually takes seriously.

You might as well throw pretty much all male politicians, military leaders, industrial revolution kings, mafia dons, bankers, artists and executives in there too.

After all, if Rockefeller, for instance, knew how to please a woman, he'd hardly have transferred so much nervous sexual energy to proving his virility—in the guise of Standard Oil—to every woman, child and man on the planet.

In this culture we preserved the words, laws, codices, artwork, religions, music and mergers of a bunch of nervous, insecure lovers. Evidently, there is no shortage of them. Then we went and hailed them as Geniuses of Our Time.

Men have gone to exorbitant lengths to camouflage—rather than reckon with—their cuntfear for thousands of years. The naked female form is idolized, obsessed over and blamed for any maltreatment it meets. There is a veritable surplus of references that state how sinful, impossible, miraculous or wrong it is for women to experience sexual pleasure.

Retarded male sexual power is expressed in maneuvers people have come to look upon with unerring respect, such as warring, ruling or becoming heads of production companies in Hollywood.

In offense to women who positively *refuse* to remain silent, some women are placed on pedestals in poses of righteousness for holding our tongues (no pun intended) in religious, political, artistic, economic and legal arenas. The women on the pedestals, then, provide a twofold service: a) presenting physical evidence that men have no interest in holding us down, and b) serving as a point of reference for other women who want to be "heard" in this society.

This isn't to say there aren't countless numbers of women fighting our hearts raw in all of the aforementioned arenas. If we're vocally pro-woman or speak in favor of healthy human sexuality, our silencing (i.e., the end of our careers, à la the brilliant, courageous, stunning Dr. Jocelyn Elders) is imminent.

Since we are invalidated for speaking our truth, or worse, mute from the get go, men never face how amazing our cunts are, and further, never reckon with the infernal jealousy they have that we can come in so many ways, so many times in succession.

> We young women of Arabia recognized that the men of our land would never pursue social change for our sex, that we would have to force change. As long as Saudi women accepted their authority, men would rule. We surmised that it was the responsibility of each individual woman to ferment desire for control of her life and other female lives within her small circle. Our women are so beaten down by centuries of mistreatment that our movement had to begin with an awakening of the spirit. (Sasson, 1992, 75-6)

Things *are* gonna change, and cuntlovin' ladies all over the world *are* gonna make it happen. Just as soon as we accept the fact that our cunts are the Holiest of Grails, the Hopefulest of Diamonds, the Goldenest of Medals.

Claire Cavanah is one of the owners of Toys in Babeland, a woman-positive sex paraphernalia/erotic multi-media store with branches in Seattle, Washington, and New York City. I interviewed her about women's fears of our own sexuality:

> A lot of straight men come into the store because their partners won't come with them. I guess a lot of women can't imagine a place where there's so much freedom and peace involved with finding out what they want and then getting it. Getting what you want sexually is a huge achievement, and it seems to frighten a lot of women.

They're afraid that if they see how much fun and pleasure they can experience by incorporating a vibrator or dildo into their sexual activities, they won't need their partner anymore. They're afraid to be free. It seems many people have this weird desire to *settle*. It's hard to keep growing, to constantly find out more. For some women, the desire to grow stops even before they learn how to come.

Obstacles such as these would not exist in a society that required students to read Audre Lorde's "Uses of the Erotic: The Erotic as Power" in high school.

The erotic is a measure between the beginnings of our sense of self and the chaos of our strongest feelings. It is an internal sense of satisfaction to which, once we have experienced it, we know we can aspire. For having experienced the fullness of this depth of feeling and recognizing its power, in honor and self-respect we can require no less of ourselves.

It is never easy to demand the most from ourselves, from our lives, from our work. To go beyond the encouraged mediocrity of our society is to encourage excellence. But giving in to the fear of feeling and working to capacity is a luxury only the unintentional can afford, and the unintentional are those who do not wish to guide their own destinies. (Lorde, 1984, 54)

Let's, shall we, go ahead, drop all the bullshit and get down to the nitty-gritty reality that you and your cunt are the Cuntlovin' Rulers of Your Sexual Universe.

Because I have no idea what turns you on, what (if any) sexual hang-ups and/or fetishes you may have, whether you come via penetration, clitoral stimulation, a G-spot massage or by tickling your bellybutton at 1:18 p.m. with a redorangeyellow sunset rose in full bloom, I'm gonna skip all the guesswork and go right to sources. You answer all your own questions, make all your own guesses and explore your own sexual expression.

If you have a really hard time letting go of cultural mindsets you have learned about sex, I highly suggest opening up a dialogue with your women friends or family members. Find out what the women in your immediate community have been taught and how they process and deal with negative shit. Refrain from focusing conversation on your *lover(s)*. Keep everything real nice and personal.

I could underscore the point until profits from the feminine hygiene industry were placed in a college fund for young women and *still*, I don't think I'd do justice to precisely how *profoundly* exchanging stories, fantasies and problems with women has improved the quality of my life.

I know of seven absolutely woman-positive sex stores in America. A woman-positive sex store is *not* a porno shack with twenty-five-cent semen-encrusted peep booths in the back.

I've been in three of the seven: Toys in Babeland in Seattle, Good Vibrations in San Francisco and It's My Pleasure in Portland. All three are owned by women who are *fucken full on dedicated* to redressing sexual stereotypes that keep women down. The atmosphere in each of these stores is: "Come on in and browse at your leisure, ask questions, take a vibrator for a test drive in our private boudoir. Most importantly, enjoy yourself." All three are stocked with state-of-the-art sexual apparati, beautiful, informative and erotic books, videos, calendars, comics, photo-journals. Every staff member is patient, sensitive and totally helpful. *The women who work at these stores are hired for their ability to be fully supportive to women who manage to shove aside their embarrassment and shame to ask, "Where the fuck is my G-spot and why should I care?"*

The five remaining stores are Eve's Garden and Toys in Babeland in New York City, A Woman's Touch in Madison, Wisconsin, Ruby's Pearl in Iowa City, Iowa, and Grand Opening! in Brookline, Massachusetts. Claire Cavanah told me about these stores, and since she and co-owner Rachel Venning are double-handedly responsible for providing many, many women in their community with information and the means to come our brains out, even though I haven't physically investigated these stores, I'm willing to wager they're equally cool.

That covers the Midwest and the east and west coasts. Pile all your girlfriends into a car and barrel ass to one of these stores. Plan a trip! Whee! Spend the weekend contemplating, discovering and achieving your orgasmic potential.

What's that you say? You live in Kansas? You're tied to a job in Tennessee? Well, these ladies got you covered, too. All six stores have mail-order catalogs and/or websites.

The women who work at these stores are warriors in their own right, and have dedicated themselves to freeing women's sexual, erotic nature.

They love you!

They want you to come and come and come.

Write or call and order a catalog. Phone numbers and addresses are listed in the Cuntlovin' Guide to the Universe at the end of this book.

A number of exceptional books and videos are available. They teach everything you could ever want to know about vibrators, dildos, G-spots, female ejaculation, eroticism, Kegel exercises, Ben Wa balls, butt plugs, S&M, pubococcygeal muscles, the clitoris, female erogenous zones and the supportive culture of expressive female sexuality. Some of the more immutably germane include:

Books

A New View of a Woman's Body: A Fully Illustrated Guide [ISBN 0-9629945-0-2], by the Federation of Feminist Women's Health Centers, illustrated by Suzann Gage, photos by Sylvia Morales, Feminist Health Press, 8240 Santa Monica Blvd., Los Angeles, CA 90046, (323) 650-1508. This book is *invaluable*. Did you hear me? *Priceless. You must have this book.* It includes not only a complete list of every woman-positive health center in the country, an awesome glossary, a reference bibliography and breathtaking illustrations and photographs, but it covers every aspect of cunt care imaginable. Explicit descriptions of self-exams, reproductive anatomy, analytic tests, common infections, birth control, menstrual extraction, abortion care, menopause, surgical procedures, home remedies, female ejaculation, the clitoris and universal health problems of women. The full-color photo spread of variations in the cervix

throughout a woman's monthly cycle alone are worth the mere
twenty buck investment. *Buy this book.*

Femalia [ISBN 0-940208-15-6], edited by Joani Blank, Down
There Press, 938 Howard St. #101, San Francisco, CA 94103, (800)
BUY-VIBE, goodvibes.com/dtp/dtp.html. *Femalia* is a collection
of full-color cunt photographs. The ages and races of the subjects
vary tremendously. "[O]utside of 'men's' magazines [writes Ms.
Blank], where the women's genitals were often powdered and
half-hidden, and the images often modified and airbrushed,
women had no resource for photographic representations of
vulvas. . . . Some might wonder how such knowledge benefits
women. My many years of doing sex therapy and leading
women's sexuality workshops have taught me that without such
information a majority of women believe to this day that, in one
way or another, their genitals are not quite normal."

The Playbook for Women About Sex [ISBN 0-940208-04-0], by Joani
Blank, Down There Press (See address above). "This is a sexual
self-awareness book for every woman." Remember those spelling
workbooks from the fourth grade? Well, this is very similar, but
instead of spelling, you learn about what you want sexually, who
you are, what does and does not turn you on. It's very candid,
very fun and highly insightful.

   Down There Press and Good Vibrations are sisters, both
founded by the seemingly tireless sexuality valkyrie Joani
Blank. You can get a free Good Vibrations store catalog (which
contains Down There Press's books as well as videos, toys and
other sexuality products) by calling their toll-free number

(above) or emailing customerservice@goodvibes.com.

Herotica: A Collection of Women's Erotic Fiction. Volume I [ISBN 0-940208-11-3], Volume VI [ISBN 0-940208-25-3] and the forth-coming Volume VII are published by Down There Press (see address above); Volume II [ISBN 0-452-26787-0], Volume III [ISBN 0-452-27180-0], Volume IV [ISBN 0-452-27181-9] and Volume V [ISBN 0-452-27812-0] are published by The Penguin Group, Penguin Books U.S.A., Inc., 375 Hudson St., New York, NY 10014. A collection of erotic short stories written by women, for women. Major, major turn-ons in these books. The only drawback to reading any given volume is it takes a long time to finish because you keep having to put it down to masturbate.

My Gender Workbook: How to Become a Real Woman, a Real Man, the Real You, or Something Else Entirely [ISBN 0-415916-73-9], by Kate Bornstein, Routledge Inc., 29 West 35th Street, New York, NY 10001. According to the publisher, "gender isn't just about 'male' or 'female' anymore . . . if you don't think you are transgendered when you sit down to read this book, you will be by the time you finish it." An amazing resource for discovering your individual gender identity and reaching whatever spot you desire on the *gender continuum*.

Cunt Coloring Book [ISBN 0-86719-371-9], by Tee Corinne, Last Gasp, 777 Florida Street, San Francisco, CA 94110, (415) 824-6636. This Christmas, buy a *Cunt Coloring Book* for every woman on your list. This book is so fucken cool. It was first published in 1975, so there's no excuse for it not being handed out in human sexuality classes in high school. Says the insanely talented Ms. Corinne, "I first published [these] drawings in a coloring book because a major way we learn to understand the world, as children, is by coloring."

Exhibitionism for the Shy: Show-off, Dress Up and Talk Hot [ISBN 0-940208-16-4], by Carol Queen, Down There Press (See address above). A totally awesome, informative and inspiring book. From the back cover: "[D]emonstrates how to turn sexual modesty to your erotic advantage, whether you're single, partnered or in-between. To discover a new world of erotic experience, you don't have to shed your inhibitions, just exploit them creatively." This is yet another cultural gift from the multifaceted goddess we all fell in love with in the "Whores" chapter.

The New Our Right to Love: A Lesbian Resource Book [ISBN 0-684-80682-7], edited by Ginny Vida, Touchstone Publishing, Rockefeller Center, 1230 Avenue of the Americas, New York, NY 10020. I can't bee-leeve this book is only fourteen dollars. It is so packed with information! "The Spectrum of the Lesbian Experience" includes essays from Lakota, Latina, Jewish, Black, Asian Pacific, young, mid-life, old lesbians, incarcerated lesbians and lesbians with disabilities. There is a fully precious directory of national lesbian organizations, a stunning bibliography, and the chapters cover topics ranging from relationship problems specific to lesbian couples, to lesbians and the law. I *highly* recommend this extremely sensitive, forthright book.

Sex for One: The Joy of Selfloving [ISBN 0-517-88607-3], by Betty Dodson, Crown Publishing Group, Inc., 201 East 50th Street, New York, NY 10022. From the back cover: "Confronting one of our last and most deeply rooted taboos—masturbation—noted sex expert and pro-sex feminist Betty Dodson, Ph.D., takes the shame out of selflove by creating a straightforward and appealing guidebook that reveals masturbation as a satisfying, vital form of sexual expression." Chapters cover topics including masturbation stories, sexual fantasies, masturbation as meditation, orgasms beyond reckoning and making love alone. You simply cannot resist a book with a dedication that reads, "This book is dedicated to me. Without my selflove, it could not have been written."

Sacred Pleasure: Sex, Myth and the Politics of the Body—New Paths to Power and Love [ISBN 0-06-250283-2], by Riane T. Eisler, HarperCollins Publishers, 10 East 53rd Street, New York, NY 10022. This book is about sex and culture and it's by one of the biggest geniuses of the 20th Century, Riane Eisler! Here's Gloria Steinem's eloquent blurb: "*Sacred Pleasure* makes the links between sacralizing pain and justifying war, between child abuse and sado-masochism, between patriarchy and the war of the sexes, between the intimate and the political. Only by sacralizing pleasure can new links be forged to peace, equality and sexuality." Fucken ayy. There's only one woman on earth who could *possibly* articulate all of this, without losing sight of the sexuality of the *individual* woman, and that woman is the woman who wrote this book: Riane Eisler.

(I included ISBN numbers because they make it easy to order a title from your local independent bookstore, if for some reason you don't want any of these books delivered to your house.)

Videos

How to Female Ejaculate, Blush Entertainment. Available through Fatale Media, 1537 4th Street, Suite 193, San Rafael, CA 94901, (415) 454-3291. Also, call Fatale Media at (888) 5-FATALE for a free catalog featuring their erotic, woman-made videos. This video taught me how to spew my cuntjuices, and it'll teach you too.

Selfloving: Video Portrait of a Women's Sexuality Seminar, with Betty Dodson, Ph.D., Betty Dodson, Box 1933, Murray Hill, New York, NY 10156. Call (866) 877-9676 to order. In case you haven't gathered, Betty Dodson is the Auto-Eroticism Queen of the Universe.

The Art of Extended Orgasm for Men and Women, by Kathryn Roberts, M.A., NSS Seminars Inc., P. O. Box 620123, Woodside, CA 94062.

Femme Distribution, Inc., 588 Broadway, Suite 1110, New York, NY 10012, (800) 456-LOVE. Erotic videos for couples, but (here's the crucial part) from a woman's perspective. Free catalog, with a self-addressed stamped envelope.

All right! Hop in the car, get on the horn and make all them cuntdreams of yours come to 3-D, pulsating, glorious, sweaty life.

The generally recognized sexual revolution in the '60s was mostly about men justifying their desire to fuck as many women as humanly possible. A common term arising from this era, after all, was not "husband swapping." The sexual revolution that's long overdue is about women loving themselves alone, with another, whenever, however, forever.

Or at least:

Until death do you part.

Acrimony of Cunts

My mind is very logical. Thoughts are a kind of math to me. Well before undertaking the task of writing this book, I understood that certain very specific elements must be present in order to make a whole.

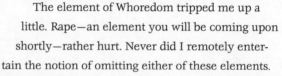

The element of Whoredom tripped me up a little. Rape—an element you will be coming upon shortly—rather hurt. Never did I remotely entertain the notion of omitting either of these elements.

I make this little introduction because I *positively adore* and *consistently seduce* the idea of leaving this chapter—concerning the element of Acrimony—out, out, out. Chills of *ecstasy* shimmy down my spine when I think about putting a big, fat, red X over this chapter.

However, my mind is sometimes just this *very weary* high-school algebra teacher and will not withstand such tomfoolery.

It was very difficult for my sister and I to acknowledge the insidious nature of acrimony that was (and still can be) present in our relationship. Jealousy, cattiness and general shitass vibes were some of the crap-ola emotions we learned to harbor during our socialization in a culture founded upon destruction. It required *months* of conversation focused on total honesty, acceptance and love to even approach overcoming negative patterns we grew up with in our personal relationship.

The idea of acknowledging the presence of acrimony between *all women* is pretty dang-awful daunting to me. It extends far past jealousy, cattiness and general shitass vibes into highly oppressive forms of ageism, classism, homophobia, objectification and racism.

I held my sister in my arms on her ride home from being born at the hospital. My sister and me go way back. You, on the other hand, only met me a few short chapters ago. But in comparison to *my* position, *you're* sittin' tight. I have absolutely no idea who you might be, and I'm about to start talking shit to you about nasty things you may perpetuate.

Big sigh.

Still, I know for a fact that being honest and forgiving about acrimony in my personal relationships has freed me and continues to improve the quality of my life intensely. I am privy to the ways acrimony is manifested between women in our culture, and inevitably conclude this sense of freedom and life-improvement holds true on the much broader cultural level as well.

In an interview, Fiona Apple described a shitty period of her life—which she knows she had to experience in order to survive on her terms—as her "dog years."

In the exact same spirit, I present *Cunt*'s dog chapter.

One time I had an Iranian dance teacher named Jaleh. After
class, we'd often have lengthy discussions about culture. As a
result of these conversations, I developed a new perspective on
the standard by which freedom is defined in my country.

I used to think women in fundamentalist Islamic countries,
or societies where genital mutilation is practiced, have it *way
worse* than us ladies in the West. American women can *generally*
wear what we want, fuck who we want, love how we want and
work where we want.

You know, experience "freedom."

Coupled with her religious and political beliefs, that nagging
inspiration known as survival forced Jaleh to flee Iran. There were
many things about her country she detested with all her might and
mien. Malevolence towards women is one thing that ain't veiled in
Iran. Iranian women are shamed, silenced or killed for many
vagrancies Americans guilelessly take for granted. Iranian women
are very consciously aware of gender-explicit oppression.

Therefore:

with so much more at stake, Iranian women have each other's back:
on the street,
in stores,
at celebrations,
everywhere.

When Jaleh first got here, she *completely freaked* about the
meanspiritedness American women project onto one another in
our day-to-day lives. She eventually learned to live with a dull
thud of longing for the *general*, loving, woman vibe that was
once part of her normal reality. Loss of this closeness truly tore
her heart asunder, and Jaleh wondered about the sacrifices

American women make at the behest of our "freedom." What I learned from Jaleh distressed me greatly because I couldn't *imagine* something so precious as an everyday closeness with women, founded in the common knowledge that we all want to survive and thrive in a patriarchal society.

In my country, women don't seem to like each other much at all.

Sucky, sucky, sucky vibes.

I was offered another profound perspective on the actual reality of American women when I interviewed Soraya Miré, a Somali woman who made *Fire Eyes,* a deeply moving, powerful film about genital mutilation.

> In countries like mine, the law is *blatantly* against women. What we do have, though, is love and *community*. You never think only of yourself, you always think of your neighbors and family, too.
>
> The problem with a lot of Western women is they think they can *help* me, that they *know what's best* for me. Especially feminist women. They come into conversations waving the American flag, forever projecting the idea they are more intelligent than I am. I've learned that American women look at women like me to hide from their own pain. They can't face their pain, and mine is so obvious, they think they can help me without looking at themselves. But many women in this country are empty. They desperately try to find something to fill the empty space inside them—the loneliness deep inside. In my country, this kind of loneliness does not exist.

In America, women pay *the money that is theirs and no one else's* to go to a doctor who cuts them up so they can create or sustain an image men want. Men are the mirror. Western women cut themselves up voluntarily. In my country, a child is woken up at three in the morning, held down and cut with a razor blade. She has no choice. Western women *pay* to get their bodies mutilated.

When you base your whole self-image on a man—on another human being—how can you expect that person— whether it's a man or a woman—to respect you? How can *you* respect yourself when you do not *have* love and respect for yourself?

One of America's finest cultural phenomena is something called *The Jerry Springer Show*. This is an arena akin to the Roman ones where prisoners fought to the death. On *The Jerry Springer Show*, the audience watches people on a stage as they emotionally and physically maul one another. The viewers at home watch both the audience and the people being mauled. It is the pinnacle of voyeurism, where love, American style, is dissected and pinned down in its most caustic glory.

The Jerry Springer Show is one of my all-time favorite contemporary American anthropological studies.

The show titles change from episode to episode:

"I Want My Man to Stop Going to Strip Clubs."

"I'm Pregnant with His Child and Want Him to Leave His Wife and Three Girlfriends Because I'm More of a Woman Than They Are."

"Gee Honey, Your Mom, Sisters and Best Friends Sure Are

Awesome Good Fucks."

The title never matters because it invariably leads to women physically and verbally attacking each other over some ugly-assed schmuck who's main talent in life is pitting women against each other to bolster his sense of manliness and self-worth.

The Jerry Springer Show is a highly charged and concentrated reflection of a much broader, and generally subtler consciousness under which *all* American women—regardless of sexual orientation—exist.

It's easy enough for the viewers and audience members to look at the woman on the stage and really, really wonder if she's ever even *heard* the term "self-esteem." It's even easier for lesbians to pass judgement on the hapless straight ladies who expend so much energy on something of such dubious merit as a man's unsullied attention, but I've yet to encounter a tribe within *any* community that is not similarly rife with cruelty, possessiveness, jealousy, betrayal, power trips and general shitass vibes.

Some say this is inherent to love, but I say it's inherent to socialization in a destructive cultural setting of ageism, classism, homophobia, objectification and racism.

As Soraya Miré points out, American women indeed learn to look at our pain in others, rather than deal with it as a reality in our lives.

America is a collection of many tribes unified under every conceivable banner—from blood and geography to the Selena fanclub and Harley Davidson motorcycles. Within these tribes, women *may* find inner sanctums of cuntlovin' support.

What interests me, though, is the *standard* of how we

the anatomical jewel

127

perceive community, and the ways we judge women based on very negative thought patterns we've adopted in order to survive in this society's environment of out-and-out destructive tendencies. As it stands, American women have no frame of reference for relying on each other—cultivating trust, love, standards of beauty and sexuality, economic power and sisterhood.

The fucked-up elements of destruction we learn to view as acceptable are all founded in the exact same basic consciousness or, rather, lack thereof. Ignorance is the most valued consciousness in America. It rends deep chasms of total distrust and perpetuates meanspiritedness bar none. Education, therefore, is the panacea for undermining all manifestations of acrimony in our society.

Every way we see, hear, feel, taste and smell is a *self-reflection*. Our perception awake and asleep is what we, we, we *choose* to perceive. The way we react to any stimulus is the way we *choose* to react.

For a long time, I had a problem with women I perceived as privileged. Rather than harbor and nurture this negative feeling—which would, ultimately, only constitute a bummer in my personal life—I got into reading biographies. I read books about Imelda Marcos, LaToya Jackson, Princess Diana, the Kennedy women and Marjorie Merriweather Post.

It's not like I'm this massive Imelda Marcos fan now, but I have solid ideas about what her life was like when she ruled the Philippines. (And if you think ol' Ferdinand ruled, you be wrong.) Imelda Marcos is no longer just some greedy, capitalist shoe fetishist to me. She is a woman who developed her own set of survival skills, which I clearly do not identify with. Learning something of her childhood and life, however, has made it very difficult for me to pass judgment.

I never imagined Imelda Marcos would communicate any information I would consider valid in my own life, but she taught me a whole new way of looking at women. Imelda wore makeup twenty-four hours a day, seven days a week, with four complete changes, every six hours. She inspired me to appreciate the intricate cultural art form of presentation. The lengths to which she went to be considered beautiful are astonishing. I have complete respect for dedication, precision and commitment, regardless of the fact that Imelda's particular brand represents an insidious form of cunthatred.

Women choose to be catty, cruel, prejudiced, competitive or jealous of each other partly because we grow up learning that negative behavior towards women is perfectly acceptable, and partly because it is a difficult *task* to see ourselves in our perceptions. Seeing ourselves requires effort and commitment.

This unwillingness to see ourselves is greatly exacerbated by the fact that we, quite often, do not see even a remote semblance of ourselves in the images of women commonly found in our society. The women presented to us in ads, TV shows, movies and music videos are powdered and coiffed under standards set by male associations of what is and isn't beautiful.

As a result, many women are scornful and lay blame on women who work in any of these false-image-creating industries. But women who base identity and economic security on a specific standard of "beauty" exist in an industry that is rife with cuntfear. Women choose to work under self-esteem-corroding conditions such as these because cuntfear is highly valued in our society and corporations are willing to pay women exorbitant sums of money for glorifying illusions of beauty men can deal with.

One of my dearest friends used to be one of them fancy übermodels. This experience psychologically damaged her to the degree that I know she would be terribly hurt if I stated her name. I spent a weekend with her a few years ago and she dug out her modeling portfolio for me to look at. The photographs showed this totally posh babe being either sporty, babyish, scary or spicy. I would never, ever, ever, *never* have recognized my dear friend as the woman presented in her portfolio. "They made me," she said, "That was my 'talent': allowing the people who run companies to make me look the way they wanted me to look." When my friend told photographers at shoots that she was interested in photography, they laughed at her. After she quit modeling—and used all that money she saved up as a tidy little nest egg—she became a successful, award-winning art director, designer and photographer.

It doesn't get anybody anywhere to diss models, actresses, dancers and women in general who identify with this male-made standard of beauty. If real images of powerful women being cuntlovin' and beautiful are what women want, the advertising, television, motion picture and music industries must first be infiltrated and revolutionized from the inside out.

It is less *directly* painful to *ourselves* to respond negatively to women than to honestly figure out what other women represents inside of us that we either dislike, fear, wish we "possessed," or are afraid to love.

Another one of my friends used to be almost pathologically uncool about large women. She was rail thin and readily admitted her own fear of being "fat" was the problem. Once she told me, "I think, in a way, I'm jealous because fat women *potentially* love themselves no matter what society says, and I, obviously, do not."

After this conversation, I bought her a bunch of postcard reproductions of paintings depicting large, voluptuous women in erotic poses. She put some of them up in her bathroom. As time passed, her attitude about women and body image started evolving, and she also gained weight. These positive images of women *aided* her in developing a new, healthier perspective, but it was her own courage to be honest with herself that really spurred along positive change in her life.

It is nice to get in the habit of consciously stopping yourself from wishing ill-tidings to a woman, and ask, "What of myself do I see here?" When you can honestly respond to that question without perpetuating self-judgement or nastiness, you is a cuntlover on high.

Adding to the acrimonious nature of growing up in a society that breeds destructive behavior is the fact that the United States is home to more ethnicities than can be found in any other single country on the entire planet. Most nations have the relative luxury of having a population of a few distinct races. I have a friend who is Chinese and Greek, with smatterings of Swiss, Chicana and East Indian blood. She grew up speaking Mandarin and English. I know Korean-Jews and African-American Irish folk. America's ethnicity is the whole kit 'n caboodle, all mixed up in every imaginable combo.

Our national cultural heritage is gloriously schizophrenic.

The result of living as women in an acrimonious, multiethnic nation is a subconscious negative preoccupation when dealing with each other. It thus quite naturally escapes us that while we are so preoccupied, we forsake our collective power of sheer mass.

This is a bummer for a number of reasons.

American women cannot so much as stand on the same escalator without the presence of discord—much less design and implement cuntlovin' economic and legal systems, run huge cuntlovin' corporations and make sure all of our children are loved, protected, fed, clothed, educated and tucked into bed with a sleepytime story that has a happy, cuntlovin' ending.

A significant portion of the acrimony we honor is rooted in economics.

White people took away the home of Native people who lived on this land since 𝕿𝖍𝖊 𝕭𝖊𝖌𝖎𝖓𝖓𝖎𝖓𝖌. White people said, "Sorry, it's this thing called economics, and your home since 𝕿𝖍𝖊 𝕭𝖊𝖌𝖎𝖓𝖓𝖎𝖓𝖌 is now on our property."

White people stole African people from one place and took them to another, far, far away. White people said, "Sorry, it's this thing called economics and you are not a human being anymore, you are our property."

White people snagged Mexico and named it things like "Southern California," "New Mexico" and "Texas." White people said, "Sorry, it's this thing called economics, and we'll grudgingly let you live here but you hafta remember: It's our property."

White people corralled all the Japanese people who were born in this country same as anybody else. White people said, "Sorry, it's this thing called economics and what was your property yesterday is our property today."

So I figure right off the bat: A lot of women in America
were raised by mothers who have good, solid-assed reasons for
entertaining acrimonious vibrations towards *Las Blancas*.

Good.

Solid-assed.

Reasons.

There is a saying.

It goes, "If you don't face the past, you hafta keep living it."

White women are not readily compelled—much less forced—
to face the past. In a white-dominated society, women of color are
not generally accorded this option. At some point in life, all
children realize skin color plays a major role in one's destiny of
survival in this society. Little white girls learn that skin color is a
non-issue when one is white. Little girls of color, however, must,
at some point, grapple with *why* skin color affects destiny so
dramatically. This often leads to facing the past.

I do not think it is culturally healthy or cuntlovin' that
facing the past is not *everyone's* responsibility.

One day my friend Harper handed me a piece of paper. She
said, "I wrote this at work this morning," as if it might perhaps
be a things-to-do list. But it wasn't a things-to-do list at all, and I
asked her if I could put it in my book.

It is a fascinating Sunday, or at least seems like it should be. I
have been reading *Essence* magazine (the first time in a few
years) and something in it inspired me to think of new
projects to work on. One is the idea of where you come from,

the anatomical jewel

133

and if you can really go far without establishing in truth—or just in any manner—that sense of belonging somewhere. Like when that man from India was so insistent about asking where I am from, and I ended up at slavery, and I think it was the first time I *really felt* slavery. I mean, I recognized that some of my ancestors had been slaves, but until that day I hadn't felt connected to it past the color of my skin and feeling disgust at the mistreatment and the scope of the cruelty that humans have inflicted on each other—and also embittered in that slaves weren't even allowed the consideration to be recognized as human beings by the colonizers or slavery owners. It was like remembering the tiny pieces of scenes, sound bites and music from the mini-series *Roots* that I viewed before my bedtime as a child . . . a sort of far away horror story. In history lessons this story became worse, with descriptions of the tools used for torture, the neckbrace with bells to keep track of slaves who'd tried to escape, the length of the ships, the number of those herded into the holds, the vomit, the smell, the disease, the death and the wounds—and sometimes mentioned, the note of survival, that continual note of survival that is allowing me to write these words. And more than that note of survival—also my denial and my ability to avoid the remembering because of the pre-recognition of how it makes me sick about humanity in general.

I know I do this about many atrocities.

It wasn't until that day, on my way to Seattle, at a gas station with the two East Indian men I barely knew, as my friend pumped gas, that one of the men asked me where I was from, and I said, "Iowa and D.C." And he said, "No,

where are you FROM?" And I said, "Iowa and D.C." And he
said, "No, where are you FROM?" And I said , "Iowa and
D.C." I explained how I was born in Iowa but had grown up
mostly in D.C. "No, ORIGINALLY," he said. Finally understanding that he perhaps made no assumptions that I was a
descendant of black slaves, I started to explain there was
this thing called slavery in this country and . . . But he was
very insistent and interrupted me. "Yes, but YES, WHERE
ARE YOU FROM, *your people?*" And I said, "Africa and
Germany, but *I don't know*, exactly." As my friend—a white
friend—returned to the car, the conversation ended. An
uncomfortable silence surrounded me as the conversation
turned to the tourist sites in Seattle. I felt lost. I realized this
man I had spoken to very likely *knew* what his family was
doing in the 1400s. He knew where he was from and where
he was grounded, all those miles away from his home. I had
just always accepted that I was black in America, and to
me, that meant being of questionable mixed heritage, as
diverse as the skin tones that defined blackness to me. But
this acceptance had never brought me to that question of
where I am FROM. And to come to that question in a car at
a gas station somewhere between Olympia and Seattle on
some random gray day left me silent and lost and feeling
the reality of postcolonialism and the reality of the slave
trade for the first time in my life.

It is a source of great sadness that my friend is forced to identify
with such an ugly treatment of her people in history. If you ever
get into reading history, though, you see how pretty much all

cultures on the planet have pasts filled with bloodshed, rape, war, enslavement, torture and other symptoms of a destructive patriarchy encroaching on and dominating everybody else.

There is much sadness in this world.

If you have the courage to ask, Rigoberta Menchú, Sojourner Truth, Wilma Mankiller, Jacqueline Woodson, Mary Crow Dog and Kathy Acker will tell you:

There is much sadness in this world.

During the '60s and '70s Steve Biko was one of the leaders in South Africa's Black Consciousness movement. In the biography *Biko,* by Donald Woods, I found that Black Consciousness and cuntlove share many of the same basic principles. Biko, as quoted in Woods, writes, "Many would prefer to be color-blind; to them skin pigmentation is merely an accident of creation. To us, it is something much more fundamental. It is a synonym for subjection, an identification for the disinherited." (Woods, 1979, 37)

I can relate to this because the presence of estrogen in my body is a synonym for subjection and identification for the disinherited.

However, America was colonized by male and white people. *All women* experience alienation due to the overwhelming *male* standard based in this history. Women of color experience alienation for the overwhelming *white* standard, too. I consider it perfectly acceptable to expect men of all ethnicities and classes to educate themselves and take responsibility for their individual role in women's oppression. I likewise consider it perfectly acceptable to expect white women of all classes to take responsibility for our individual role in the oppression of women of color. Women of color *have no call* to trust white women until white women take a gander at the world around them, investigate, learn and annihilate ignorance founded in being white in a society where the perspective and voice presented to the general public is white.

Still and too, acrimony between white women and women of color is but one of many pits in our potentially delicious cherry pie. Within each tribe, racial acrimony is present. Acrimony is a way of general socialized American life until you decide you don't want it that way no more. All races of people are divided and isolated from one another.

It is the house that Jack built.

Chinese women might harbor negative stereotypes about Filipina women, who may not think nice things about Jewish women, who might grow up thinking ill of Moslem women, who may think lesbians are the scourge of the earth, who might think women married to Promise Keepers are the incarnation of evil, who may think teenagers who get abortions should be sentenced to hard labor at juvey.

And on and on.

In school we learn that one of the best survival strategies is being part of a clique. With our friends, we create a little, tiny world with codes for conduct, morality, dress, communication, ethnicity and sexuality. We then learn to judge everyone else who is not part of our little world by the standards that are acceptable to us. This is called "divide and conquer," and happens to be exactly how male, white patriarchal society operates. When you choose not to see how you, yourself, perpetuate this social model, your world assuredly becomes—or remains—small, "safe," persnickety, judgemental and uninspiring.

How else could Bill Gates decide it was a good idea to build such a temporal item as a sprawling multimillion-dollar house for his one-child nuclear family, in a society where kids in schools hafta *share* textbooks published in 1987? In his little, tiny world, it is acceptable to squander money and responsibility in this manner. I consider it an embarrassing display of karmic retardation when someone invests so much money in something that could *burn to ashes in a fire,* while human beings continue to starve and go insane on the streets.

We learn to justify many preposterous actions within the small worlds we are encouraged to create throughout life.

> You can't be a solitary human being. [We're] all linked. . . . Because of this deep sense of community, the harmony of the group is a prime attribute. And so you realize that anything that undermines the harmony is to be avoided as much as possible. Anger and jealousy and revenge are particularly corrosive, so you try . . . to enhance the humanity of the other, because in that process, you enhance your own. (*The Progressive,* February 1998, 19)

We are *all* raised under the influences of negative standards set by our culture. We naturally fail to note that all the women around us are dealing with the exact same things, in entirely different ways.

If you want to find out how your oppression infringes on your freedom, walk into the bathroom, stare deeply into your eyes, and face your pain without blame. Don't go feeling sorry for them ladies in Saudi Arabia and Pakistan until you do this first. Don't be dissin' on übermodel-types with silicone titties until you do this first. Don't sneer at women from a class or ethnicity different from your own, at lesbians, bi-women, straight women, fat women, skinny women, old women or young women until you do this first.

There will remain much sadness in the world until people are willing to rise to the task of facing the world's pain in the bathroom mirror.

American culture is very, very, very, very, very beautiful.

I am thankful and happy to live in a society where so many perspectives and bounties of educational resources are available. My society honors the public library system. I have *every* opportunity to learn about things of which I was raised to be ignorant.

Wheee!

In one American afternoon, I might encounter Cibo Matto sounding out from a used bookstore, a Peruvian band attracting a crowd on the street corner, Missy Elliott pulsating from one of those cars that are really state-of-the-art sound systems on wheels, while a queer Lithuanian-Basque Vietnam vet caterwauls Barbra Streisand songs in the doorway of an office building.

Wheee!

I believe it is possible for women who live in this beautiful culture to access a forsaken—but still inherent—love and respect for each other based on the sole criteria of what our cunts have been through for the past few thousand years.

Which segues into a commandment the bible, koran and torah writers plumb done forgot to include . . .

Rape not Cunts

While writing about orgasms at four o'clock in the morning, I
ran out of soymilk for my coffee. I was tired. I
needed a bike ride and coffee to keep da pace.

At 10 a.m., I would've encountered no internal
deliberation. The wee-dawn hours, however,
are definitely past curfew time for women on
solo ventures.
Still.

I didn't want to drink my coffee black. I didn't want to be
afraid of going to the grocery store just because I have a cunt.

So I:

1. Put a beanie on my head to camouflage my female-
   ness, at least from a distance.

2. Did the ol' once over in the mirror to ascertain that my
   sweats were baggy enough to hide the contours of my
   fine, round, womanly ass.

3. Tied my running shoes nice and tight, in case I might
   have to kick or bolt.

4. Donned a loose, black, butchy-poo jacket.

5. Stuffed the five medium-sized rocks I keep on hand for excursions such as this into the pockets of said jacket.

6. Made sure the tires on my bike had enough air in them, in the event that I'd have to race to safety.

All six of these steps are part of a survival tactic I have incorporated into my lifestyle because: *I can't stand the fact that the danger of having a cunt is threatening enough to keep me from doing as I please.*

Though I've lived away from home for over a decade, my mother still has a tizz when I go out by myself after 11 p.m. So I don't tell her it drives me insane to allow the possibility of being raped to dictate my will.

I Do the Best I Can.

My friend Esther, who lives in the same apartment building, gets off work at three in the morning. She rarely goes to bed before eight. The last step in this particular survival tactic is calling her.

"Esther, I'm going to the store. If I'm not home safe and sound in fourteen minutes (we have it timed), come find me. I'll be riding up Olive and down Broadway."

"Okey-dokey. It's 4:18. Go. Oh, wait. Pick me up a pack of smokes, will ya? Go."

Esther and I have never discussed my motive for calling and letting her know I'm going to the grocery store. One night, the need simply arose. How telling it is that *not once* did it occur to Esther to question me. As women raised in a violent, patriarchal culture we inherently understand the risks one may encounter when one has a cunt.

I ride my bike to the grocery store. The cashiers are used to seeing me at unseemly hours. They let me park my bike inside, by the greeting cards. I feel safe in the grocery store, but at the same time, I know not to assume this to be a fact.

I go to great lengths to make it seem like I'm not fettered to the violence—and subsequent injustice of the American legal system—that my cunt can potentially inspire.

But I ain't foolin' nobody.

Certainly not myself.

I'm fully privy to the reality that my cunt's presence on my body can inspire people with cocks to attempt to exert their power by attempting to humiliate me. I have no illusions about what happens to women in "the wrong place at the wrong time." I have seen too many movies, read too many news-papers, watched too many episodes of *Unsolved Mysteries*.

I know too many women who have been raped.

I do not pretend too realistically that I am free to go where I please. At least, not without taking extreme precautionary measures.

Purchasing soymilk for my coffee at four o'clock in the morning, then, is an act of rebellion.

A foolhardy and mundane one, perhaps.

Like I said, I Do the Best I Can.

When I was twenty, my mother told me she had been raped. Five years passed before I mustered the courage to write about it.

It is highly distressing to learn the sacred, holy place where you lived during your first nine months on this planet was ruthlessly pillaged long before you were conceived.

It makes you wonder if there exists a safe place.

She was nine.

She was nine.

My mother was nine.

Over a Christmas holiday, Mom and I were talking in the kitchen. I don't remember that we were discussing anything in particular. Liz popped her head in to say goodbye. She was going to a party, dressed to the nines in a satin slipdress.

Our mother stopped in mid-innocuous-sentence and stared. Liz and I stared back. Mom looked down at her hands. (Momspeak interpretation: **Something Is Up.**)

Big sigh.

"I really wish you wouldn't go out dressed like that."

In the past, my sister and I would have rolled our eyes at each other and made light of it. Mom said things like this pretty much whenever she saw us dressed scantily for a party. This exchange had taken place hundreds of times.

But we could tell from her voice that tears were welling up in her eyes. This wasn't something we could shrug off as Mom's "overprotectiveness." There was suddenly a **Big Problem** in the kitchen.

Liz put her purse on the table and felt for a chair.

Neither of us could tear our eyes from our mother.

"Mom . . . " my sister spluttered.

I whispered, "Mom, what's wrong?"

Both of us were crying, but we had no idea why.

Nobody went to any party that night.

Two men saw her walking home from school in her Catholic girls' school uniform. The temptation was too much for them. The men pulled her into some bushes in Hyde Park and raped her.

Our mother, our, our, our beautiful mother.

Two men did that to her.

She was nine, she was nine.

She had no words to correspond with the defilement. She didn't come across sufficient vocabulary for an entire decade. She walked home, changed her clothes and never breathed a word to anyone until she was in college. In the meantime—that is, throughout her adolescence—my mother relied solely on rape's best pal, silence, to help her survive this experience. She buried her silence deep because what else could she do.

When the Goddess eventually blessed her with two daughters, oh, how she watched us.

She said, "You two always thought I was paranoid, but how could I tell you why I was like that, how could I hurt you when you were so little and free? Then as you got older, I didn't know *when* to tell you. I knew it would make you cry like this."

We sobbed from the pits of our guts.

The whole time we were growing up, she attended seminars and clinics focused on rape to help her deal with the pain she sequestered in a dark region of her heart when she was a child. She had to learn how to control her fear that "something would happen" to my sister or me.

Hawk, mother hawk.

A new panorama slammed into my heart. I remembered years and years of relentless warnings: "Don't take short-cuts," "Come straight home from school," "Never walk past vans," "If a car is following you, cross the street and run to a neighbor's house. If you aren't near a neighbor's house, run into the middle of the street and scream 'FIRE!' at the top of your lungs."

A childhood memory assailed me.

I was eight. One morning, my friend Kit and I went to the mall to buy our moms' gifts for Mother's Day. We ended up dawdling awfully long, and I didn't get home until dinnertime. My mother was standing in front of our house. There was no color in her face. Her eyes were blind terror. She swept me into her arms and hugged all of the breath out of me. Then she slapped me across the face.

It stung.

My father was cruising the neighborhood in a cop car. He came home and immediately grounded me to my room for a week.

My mother didn't utter a word.

That week I brooded in my room.

I thought they were overreacting.

In other words:

Because of the action of two completely unknown males in the year 1948, I was slapped across the face and grounded to my room for a week in 1974.

A different way of looking at this is:

I was raised by a woman who was held down in a park and raped when she was a little girl. While the consequences of this event became, for Liz and me, a Grand Duchess Overtone in our upbringing, the two men who raped our mother have no idea either of us exist on the planet to have been raised under the shadow of their action.

A further perspective might be:

A man could, feasibly, sacrifice his coffee break raping a woman.

That woman would then spend her entire life dealing with it.

So would her daughters.

So would theirs.

This distribution of power is not acceptable.

The Lakota believe a people cannot be vanquished unless the spirit of woman is broken.

Though rape is viewed merely as a crime, it is the fundamental, primal, most destructive way to seize and maintain control in a patriarchal society.

When wars are declared, everyone involved in the declaration assumes women will be raped. Invading soldiers do not necessarily rape women to hurt us, per se. Women are raped to stymie the morale of husbands, fathers and sons. Women's bodies are considered solely in regard to how they affect men. In the context of war, rape literally plants the seed of the invader in the body of a people. The secret weapon of war is spiritually crippling an entire nation of human beings and generations to come by sexually assaulting as many women and girls as possible.

Men use our bodies to bear witness to their power.

America was founded on the bodies of women: African women, Jewish women, Native women, Latina women, Chicana women, Asian women, European women. Grandmother, grandmother, grandmother, grandmother, grandmother, grandmother.

Guatemalan, Bosnian, Vietnamese women know war.

Pretty much every nation in this world was established by war.

How many women do you think that is?

In 1993, a woman named Mia Zapata, the lead singer of a rock band called the Gits, was found dead in Seattle, Washington. I lived in Seattle and wrote for a local weekly newspaper at the time.

It sucked very hard.

I clung to the fact that newspaper and word-of-mouth accounts did not mention the word "rape." Strangled, murdered, killed. Those words were already quite unbearable. No sooner would the word "rape" flit through my mind than I'd remind myself none of the newscasters mentioned it.

I felt the world could still seem a halfway decent place, so long as Mia Zapata wasn't raped.

I never knew her, never went and saw her band. Never listened to her music, not even after she died. But Seattle's a small city, and we shared a number of friends. She was generally associated with things like outspokeness, creativity, powerful expression, talent and loving inspiration.

She was strong.

A Whore found
her body
in
an
alley.

I knew no woman who was not profoundly grief-stricken by her death. This was the feeling *before* the word "rape" was associated with Mia Zapata's death.

In the autumn following Mia's death, I interviewed the band 7 Year Bitch in the very tavern where Mia spent her last night. That is when I learned, once and for all, beyond a shadow of a doubt, yes, Mia Zapata was raped.

Even though women are raped and murdered every day, I tried really, really hard to pretend it didn't happen in my world, where I live, to women I see when I'm walking down the street each day.

I don't do that anymore.

In the final analysis, it took far more negative energy to live in denial than to face my fear and acknowledge the astounding prevalence of rape in my culture.

Now, I routinely assume that if the cancer of a man's soul condones the murder of a living, breathing, hoping, loving, fighting, singing, dancing, searching, yearning human being, the chances are pretty slim his cancer has spared his cock.

Now, when I hear of a man murdering a woman, I assume that he raped her unless I read the fucken coroner's report myself.

A definition for "martyr" according to my trusty 1965 Random House Dictionary is: "One who is put to death or endures great suffering on behalf of any belief, principle or cause."

The greatest purposes martyrs serve are teaching, inspiring and giving strength to those who live on after their death.

In contrast to the killing of Dr. King or Malcolm X, there is little to support the idea that Mia Zapata was raped and murdered because of her personal (that is, political) actions as a woman. Nevertheless, her unspeakably tragic death is symbolic in that very mien. Ms. Zapata was a pillar of strength—a living, thriving, raging testimony of the power of unleashed artistic expression.

That she was killed in a horrible way psychologically tortured an entire community of women. Mia Zapata's life and death moshed into a collective consciousness.

Being part of a community that was grieving the brutal murder of one of its priestesses had a massive impact on my life. I could no longer contain my fear and rage. This was sickeningly exacerbated by another incident, which took place a few months later.

A woman parked near her apartment building late at night. As she was getting out of her car, she noticed two men up to some kind of mischief. She judged the distance to safety and thought she could negotiate it.

She was wrong.

The two men grabbed her, put her in her car and drove away. They cruised 'round the city for hours, taking turns raping the woman in the back seat of her car. When they were done, they took her to a high-school field, stabbed her in the head repeatedly with a Phillips screwdriver, and left her for dead.

She did not die.

She had to learn everything all over again. She will probably never function in the way she had once always assumed she would.

One kinda takes it for granted that since one learned to read in first grade, one probably won't ever have to learn to read again.

For many, many women in the Pacific Northwest, it grew increasingly unavoidable to confront the issue of rape in our culture.

Directly after Ms. Zapata's death, the organization Home Alive was founded. Their mission statement reads:

Home Alive is a collective of performance and visual artists (and other freaks) hell bent on fighting all forms of violence and oppression including rape, domestic abuse, gay/lesbian bashing, racism, etc. We support people choosing any form of self defense that is necessary to survive in any given situation. Examples of self defense are verbal boundary setting, walking friends to cars or houses, locking doors, planning escape routes, de-escalation techniques, using pepper spray, physical striking techniques, fighting, yelling, martial arts, knives, guns, other weapons—ANYTHING that keeps us alive.

Since the brutal rape and murder of Mia Zapata on July 7, 1993, we are dedicated to presenting an on-going series of high intensity music, art, spoken word, theater, film and video events that raise money to provide our community with free and affordable self defense workshops, educational material, resource information and a nagging reminder that none of us are safe.

In Seattle, Olympia and Portland, self-protection classes became *de rigueur*. In Portland, a beautiful compilation album called *Free to Fight* was released. Home Alive later released a compilation album, *The Art of Self-Defense*, featuring the work of many regional and national artists. Creative expression rolled to a boil, and women performed en masse. Rage crested at the forefront of songs, words, movements.

A lot of brilliant women all thinking about the same thing at the same time is very powerful. This is how change happens. Rather than underscore this to queendom come, I dedicate the next few pages to the voices of some of the women who lived in the area at the time.

Because I didn't know Mia, I didn't feel the intensity of grief a lot of people around here felt, but it made me really paranoid to the point where I felt I was losing my mind. For about three months, I lived in a state of terror, where I became afraid of everyone I knew, everyone I met, everyone I saw. I even became afraid of myself. I felt this vast rage, like I wanted to kill someone, but I didn't know who. That was very frightening. I'd never felt like that before.

But what I did was, I wrote a play called *Again*. It was all about sexual violence and abuse and the fact that your own sexuality seems to invite danger. I spent a lot of time asking myself how I can still be a sexual person, while at the same time warding off dangerous situations. Having my sexuality at the surface is very important to me, and I'm not willing to give it up. Somewhere inside myself, I suddenly believed that in order to get through this life without being raped, I had to give up my sexuality.

So, I wrote *Again*. I didn't pursue having it produced because I wasn't sure that it wouldn't make people feel more afraid and disempowered, which is not what I'm trying to do with my work at all.

Recently, my friend was telling me he was reading this book about serial killers. When he'd read about half of it, he threw the book out the eleventh-story window of his apartment because he felt it was some kind of evil totem. He wasn't learning anything from it, it was only exacerbating a fear he already had, and the book was debilitating him.

The way he described it to me sounded like that terror I felt after Mia's death, but also what I felt like when I was finished writing *Again*. It helped me, the individual, deal with my fear, but as a piece of art, I felt more like it would debilitate society in general.

There wasn't enough hope in it.

I still have so much fear of my sexuality. I hope to someday produce something to honor my sexuality, but right now, my relationship with my sexuality is colored by how other people respond to it, which I distrust greatly.

People seem to have a hard time responding to a woman's sexuality without having the desire to literally touch it. I guess in some ways, sexuality implies that, but I don't think sexuality necessarily invites someone else to participate. I don't want people to interpret my work as an invitation to fuck me.

I did read *Again* a few times, at a couple small theaters and a nightclub. There's one part where the woman character is describing what she finds erotic to a man who wants to have sex with her, but she does not want to have sex with him. She talks about listening to the rain gush into a gutter, watching a woman dip her finger in her latté and lick the foam off her finger, and someone taking their shirt off and having another one on underneath. She's telling him all these things that have nothing to do with intercourse, and often nothing to do with other people, in an effort to explain her idea of sexual eroticism to him.

After I read this at the nightclub, a friend of mine told me an acquaintance of his came up after my performance and said, "Who's that? I'd like to bone her." I was amazed. Was this guy listening to what I was saying? The character was telling a man exactly what she did not want from him and this guy thought I, the writer, would want that? That I'd want to be "boned"?

In *Letters to a Young Poet*, Rilke says, "The highest form of love is to be the protector of another person's solitude." That's what I want. For other people to love each other without having to *partake* in them, to *possess* them, to allow them to be their own inside their solitude, to protect that. I wish people respected each other's aloneness. I wish I could write something very beautiful and erotic without worrying about people wanting to use me to fulfill some fantasy—which I have no control over, and often, has nothing to do with me—inside themselves. (Kristen Kosmas, writer and performer)

When Mia died, it was like, "This is something that happens to *other people*." I mean, it happens all the time. A woman is raped in this country every four minutes, but for someone you know to be raped and murdered, someone so strong . . . . It's hard to talk about the effect Mia's death had on other women in the community. Mia's rape and murder wasn't just one isolated event, unto to itself. It happened in a really vocal, outspoken community of women, who were already trying to find their voice. A lot of people say, "I didn't know her, but I felt moved to do something about her dying the way she did."

There's also a general, unifying feeling of rage in the community. Rape and murder will inspire that, regardless. Like [the young woman mentioned earlier who was abducted by two men]. She's still alive, and there was a huge response to her attack.

I teach self-defense in the community to instill in women the idea that no one has any more or less power than anyone else. What happened to [the young woman mentioned earlier], to Zolah Lippe [a Seattle writer who committed suicide in 1995], Kristin Pfaff [Hole's bass player, who overdosed on heroin] and Stephanie Sargent [7 Year Bitch's guitar player, who also overdosed on heroin]—it's all related in the sense that within the span of every minute, a woman dies in some fucked-up way, based upon her belief that she is powerless.

I started performing because I had to. It was a natural progression of what I was already doing. I make a difference and have an effect—it's not that I think people will see me perform and view violence against women in a completely different way, but I am definitely part of a larger thing which effects change. Often people either don't want to, or aren't used to seeing women angry. Not emotional, not upset, just angry. Not reactionary anger, necessarily, the anger of just being a woman. My anger serves me. It gives me a lot of energy. Sometimes, it hurts, which is the flip side of the same coin. But, I'm happy. I like my life. I like being free to express my rage. (Cristien Storm, spoken word performer, self-protection instructor, co-founder of Home Alive)

My life profoundly changed [after Mia Zapata's death] because Home Alive started out of that, and it's been one of the major focuses of my life.

My personal habits have changed dramatically as well. I used to hop on the bus alone late at night, walk around late at night. I don't do that at all anymore. I always ask my female friends how they're getting home at night and if they don't have a ride, I'll drive them. I never leave my friends without asking them if they need a ride home and they do the same for me. The whole "Okay, see you later, bye!" thing just does not happen in my life anymore.

Self-defense is something you have to work on consistently and practice. Cristien [Storm] is a fine example of a woman who practices self-defense. I never took self-defense before Home Alive started.

I've still never shot a loaded gun, but I've taken gun classes. I respect other people's choices to have a gun in their life and use it as a form of self-defense. I know a lot of women who have guns and that's their business. I don't feel comfortable with guns. However, we live in a society where guns are quite prevalent. You never know when there's gonna be a situation where a gun might be present, so you might want to know how to use one.

A big part of the philosophy of Home Alive is that people have to make their own choices about self-defense. Anything they're comfortable with, that makes them feel safe and keeps them alive is the right choice. (Gretta Harley, musician, co-founder of Home Alive)

A couple of years ago, I woke up at three in the morning to this knock on my door. My friend was standing there, scared and crying. She hadn't been feeling well and couldn't sleep, so she had gone for a walk. She was walking by the park a few blocks from here and this car started stalking her. Later she didn't know why, but she thought she'd be safe if she hid in the women's bathroom. He found her and went into the bathroom. They struggled for a while and I think she did the "I could be your sister" thing and he finally went away. That's when she came to my house. I imagine her walking those three short blocks and how frightened she must have been. Later on, we had to go back to the bathroom to find her glasses, which she lost when she was struggling with the man. That was very terrifying, even though there were three of us.

The next night was the Olympia Art Walk and the streets were full of people walking around town. I'd been projecting images on the Arts Center's wall across the street from my apartment building, so we worked feverishly all that afternoon making a slide show to let people know what had happened the night before. We projected a description of the man and his car, when and where he tried to attack my friend. It was really strange to see people's reactions to it because since we didn't have much time, the images were really cartoony so people kinda laughed until they understood we made this because our friend almost got raped the night before, three blocks away from where they were standing. Then they were like, "Oh, that's right over there."

No matter how strong you are, no matter how safe you are, no matter how lucky or crafty you are, you still might be put in a position where you could get hurt. That kinda might be depressing to some people, but I think as long as you're aware of that reality, you might actually make it to the moon if you're a rocket scientist. [Laughs.] You might survive.

Also, realizing that you might not have everything you need to survive makes it more likely that you'll seek out other people to help you. Like when my friend came to my door that night. She could've run up to the park and screamed, knowing someone would've opened their window and helped her, but she knew we'd hold her instead of just providing her with a place to be removed from the danger.

I thought about that a lot when I was working on the *Free to Fight* album, which is this really great collaboration project Candyass Records put together. It was so cool when I got this lovely letter from Donna Dresch, saying they were gonna be putting out this record and asking me to contribute. I was like, "Oh, wow!" I don't really know how the whole thing came about, but it seemed like a great idea to me, an amazing thing to be a part of.

Anyway, during the *Free to Fight* tour, there were self-defense workshops before each show. Self-defense is something I've never taken the time out to learn, but this was really cool because it was right there. It was very beautiful. Everybody lined up in three rows, the whole room was shouting in unison. Three girls would go up at the same time and do the move while everyone else yelled and cheered them on. So many voices. It made me so happy. The workshops made people feel good about themselves, like, "I can do this!" It wasn't like, "You better do this because the world's scary and people are out to get you." It wasn't inspired by paranoia or anything. It taught me that I already do a lot of these things, I just never thought of it as self-defense before. Everybody has their own way of defending themselves, they just never think of it as such. Simple things like walking tall, talking loudly, crossing the street.

Last night I was at a show in Seattle. I went outside to get some fresh air and there was a girl standing there near me. These two guys walked up and asked her what was going on inside and all these other questions. They weren't being assholes or anything, but I stayed near, even though I'd gotten enough fresh air. I didn't want to leave her alone outside with these two guys. I stood there until they left and then I went back inside. That was self-defense. (Nikki McClure, performance artist)

If the violent rape and murder of one woman has an impact on the lives of thousands of her sisters, then at the very, very least, she did not die in vain. Unfortunately, for every solitary woman whose death inspires something other than cavernous silence, millions of women are raped, maimed, mutilated and murdered without garnering so much as a paragraph in the local newspaper.

There is no Howardina Stern on the airwaves every morning instigating passionate, pro-active, cuntlovin' dialogues about rape in our culture. News helicopters hover over the scenes of bank robberies and traffic accidents, not parks where a woman was raped. Cities bestow awards of valor to fire fighters and good samaritans, not women who elude, maul or successfully prosecute would-be rapists.

On the back cover of Migael Scherer's courageous and brilliant book, *Still Loved by the Sun: A Rape Survivor's Journal*, Ursula K. Le Guin says, "The power of the harasser, the abuser, the rapist depends above all on the silence of women."

Contemplate the simplicity, depth and truth of this statement:

The power

depends

on the silence.

Silence is our focal point of attack.

Silence is the unlocked door through which intruders enter and pillage the sacred temple of womankind.

The threat of rape lurked around my childhood in relentless warnings and admonishments. When my mother told me she had been raped, I understood the source of the fear I grew up with.

Like many women, it saddened me to feel "lucky" that rape remained a threat, but not an actual occurrence, in my personal life. I was further saddened by the fact that the very reason, I believe, neither my sister nor I has been raped is in part due to our mother's experience. She actively, consciously, ferociously protected us. Long before we knew our mother had been raped, Liz and I developed a sixth sense for dangerous situations. I am thankful for that. I believe it has aided me on a number of occasions. I wish, however, it was not initially inspired by fear and feelings of powerlessness.

Fear and powerlessess.

Silence.

Rape.

Cunthatred.

It's time for this to end.

When I started this chapter, I was re-studying Pippi Longstocking. Partly because of my childhood, I would like to formally invoke Ms. Longstocking's attitude to serve as the Grand Duchess Overtone for the duration of this book:

"Have you ever seen hair like hers? Red as fire! And such shoes," Bengt continued. "Can I borrow one? I'd like to go out rowing and I haven't any boat." He took hold of one of Pippi's braids but dropped it instantly and cried, "Ouch, I burned myself."

Then all five boys joined hands around Pippi, jumping up and down and screaming, "Redhead! Redhead!"

Pippi stood in the middle of the ring and smiled in the friendliest way. Bengt had hoped she would get mad and begin to cry. At least she ought to have looked scared. When nothing happened he gave her a push.

"I don't think you have a very nice way with ladies," said Pippi. And she lifted him in her strong arms—high in the air—and carried him to a birch tree and hung him over a branch. Then she took the next boy and hung him over another branch. The next one she set on a gatepost outside a cottage, and the next she threw right over the fence so that he landed in a flower bed. The last of the fighters she put in a tiny toy cart that stood by the side of the road. . . . The boys were absolutely speechless with fright. (Lindgren, 1950, 32-33)

There are two things women can do to facilitate the end of rape as an inevitable—even acceptable—aspect of our culture. The first is relatively easy, but the second will take a bit of serious cuntlove to come to fruition.

One out of eight movies produced in Hollywood contains a rape scene. In American cinema, rape scenes tend to be violently eroticized, and often have nothing to do with the main plot of the film. When viewing a rape scene, scads of men feel confused and disgusted with themselves if it turns them on.

Eugene Chadbourne, a columnist for *MAXIMUMROCKNROLL* eloquently discussed a male perspective on Hollywood rape scenes. In response to *The Accused*, he stated:

c
u
n
t

After more than an hour of the film, the audience is shown the rape. There she was, Jodie Foster, stretched out on top of a pinball machine with a bunch of assholes holding her down. The first few shots of her breasts and the man kissing her and slurping around were undeniably erotic. . . . I kept wondering why I was turned on. I explained it to myself that I just knew it wasn't a real rape, [but] . . . if the whole center of the film, a supposedly brutal and disgusting rape, turns on even one person in the audience just a little bit, then the film has completely missed its mark.

A few weeks later, I saw an Australian film entitled *Shame*. This was also about rape . . . the differences between these two films were many, but one basic thing was that the makers of *Shame* chose not to show the rape, the makers of *The Accused* made it their climactic scene. *(MAXIMUMROCKNROLL,* March 1990)

Another non-Hollywood film that deals with rape in a responsible way is *The Bandit Queen*, which is based on a true story. The protagonist, Phoolan Devi, was raped for a number of days by high-caste men in an Indian village. The camera focused on the door of the room she was kept in, with images of man after man entering and exiting. The point of her assault was clearly, horrifically made, and there was absolutely nothing erotic about it. (Her gang was allegedly responsible for later assassinating all of these men.)

On July 25, 2001, Phoolan Devi was murdered outside her home in New Delhi. A moment of silence, please.

In general, with the exception of a few films—*Thelma and Louise* comes to mind—rape scenes found in American cinema are filmed from the p.o.v. of men, who evidently experience some kind of personal gain by humiliating women. I do not know if the men who make movies enjoy humiliating individual actresses, or if it is a symbolic show of power over women in general. I do know that too many movies contain scenes that deal with rape in an unrealistic, male-fantasy-based manner.

Women viewers subjected to such scenes may experience any emotion between utter indifference and profound grief. It is safe to assume, however, that underneath any emotional response is a basic assumption of powerlessness. We are powerless to help the woman on the screen, unable to change her destiny, we cannot kill the piece of shit who violates her. We are forced to watch the pillage of one of our sisters unfold, under the charmed auspices of something executives in Hollywood refer to as a plot.

Perhaps also, we are unwilling to take responsibility for something we are brought up to think of as inevitable.

The last rape scene I ever saw was in *Last Exit to Brooklyn*. The gang-rape of Jennifer Jason Leigh's character physically sickened me. When someone tells me about a great new movie, I almost always asks if there's a rape scene in it. Once this information is obtained, I can gauge whether or not this might, indeed, be a great new movie. Boycotting movies with rape scenes has enriched the quality of my life.

I don't need to see that shit.

And so, I don't.

We do not need to see our sisters up there on the screen

being overpowered and assaulted by bad, scary men. We do not need to see good, righteous men saving our sisters in the knick of time, or achieving "justice" for us in the courtroom.

It does not serve us.

There are a couple of options here.

Option #1:

If you know a movie will contain a rape scene, forego seeing it altogether. If you unwittingly go to a movie that contains a rape scene, leave the theater and demand your money back from the manager. Let the manager know you will not pay to see women raped. Write a letter to the president of the movie theater's distribution company. Feel free to incite your friends. Especially if you're a teenager and you organize a huge protest. The ten o'clock news likes nothing more than high-school girls causing a ruckus in the name of social change. Even though it may seem like a faraway, remote place, Hollywood is a very small town with very big ears.

Movies featuring women who are strong, ass-kicking controllers of destiny are not so hard to come by these days, so it's not like such a boycott would encumber our movie-going habits. There are plenty of wonderful films to choose from. It's far healthier to watch *The Long Kiss Goodnight* five times than to bother yourself with *Showgirls* or *Kids* once. *La Femme Nikita* and *Gloria* are excellent classics. *Set it Off, Freeway, Girls Town* and *Bound* are part of a very welcome influx of excellent, cuntlovin' movies produced in the 1990s.

Option #2:

Plan to attend movies that you know contain rape scenes. Go with a bunch of your friends. Once the rape scene is underway, stand up and scream. Freak. Loudly narrate your own version of what is happening on the screen:

"Now she is pounding his face into the metal stairs of the fire escape. Her shoe is off. Ooo! Spiked heel to the temple!!! Look at all that blood oozing from his head!" Etc. . . .

When the scene is over, march to the manager. Demand your money back based on the affront to women you were forced to witness. Continue making a huge, articulate scene in the lobby. When all your friends get their refunds, leave quietly, but continue to be cranky about it.

If our buying dollars are not squandered on that which does not serve us, sooner or later, the gentlemen in Hollywood may see the light. However, in the not too unrealistic event that gentlemen in Hollywood never see the light, our money can be used to generate more movies that serve us. There is an *entire regiment* of women in the motion picture industry struggling very hard to deliver such products to us. Let us, shall we, constructively focus on this branch of American cinema. At the same time, we also can choose to offer constructive and loud criticism to the present movie machine that makes billions of dollars off us each year.

You may have already figured this out, but the whole reason I ever felt inspired to sit down and write this book originated with the rape of my mother. I couldn't think of any other way to exact vengeance on the men who hurt her, my sister and me so deeply.

I have thought long and hard about why women are objects of violence.

I've been through the Blaming Men phase and then I passed on to the Blaming Women Phase. Neither phase did me, as an individual, much good. So then, I guess for sheer lack of imagination, I blamed myself. That didn't last long though, 'cause one night I was falling asleep and this cherry '68 Impala Lowrider cruised around in my head, and it had a bumper sticker that said:

Blame is lame with a "b"

So I thought to explore an option I hadn't considered before. I decided to love myself. To love my cunt. To love everything it does and represents.

That seemed to do a lot of good, and led me to ask myself: What is the result of women loving our cunts, en masse?

There is no place for rape in a society filled with women who love our cunts. Women can be kicked when we are down, but no one is stupid or strong enough to kick us when we are standing up, all, together.

This may sound idealistic in some regards, but cuntlove envisions no mass utopia. Cuntlove is about the individual and her community. Cuntlove is about the power of you, your sisters, cousins, daughters and intimate friends. Cuntlove is not distant rhetoric found in books and debate halls. Cuntlove is in your head, on your heart, between your legs.

Aldous Huxley, a white male writer with the ensuing sense of entitlement for which white males are famous, said, "Liberties are not given, they're taken."

In the past, women have relied on individual men and patriarchal judicial systems to fight rape.

Unfortunately, this nets exactly the same result as when I got my brothers and sister to lean towards the Baskin Robbins as our family car approached that big, gorgeous pink-'n-white "31 Flavors" sign.

At the time, I thought the sudden redistribution of our body weight would affect the momentum of our Volkswagen van, forcing the parent driving to involuntarily swerve into the parking lot. Sometimes our parents stopped in and we all got ice cream cones, and sometimes they did not. Even though I once believed my siblings and I contributed to the former destiny by leaning towards the Baskin Robbins, I'm willing to face the fact now that it was, ultimately, always Mom and Pop's call.

Women can continue to sit in the car and lean, or we can climb over into the front seat, yank the person controlling the vehicle out of the way and make a sharp-assed left into the Baskin Robbins parking lot.

This involves something I warmly refer to as:

Cuntlovin' Public Retaliation
(C.P.R. for short)

In a climate of cuntlove, if a woman in the community is raped, other women react.

We understand there is no such thing as an isolated attack on an individual woman. We understand that a Haitian-American sorority girl, a Norwegian-Filipina construction worker, a Chumash/Cree librarian or a Jewish Whore is *us*. **C.P.R.** is not at all dissimilar to a mafia philosophy in which a sister's rape is a rape of the family and cannot go unpunished. Someone has offended the honor of our family. Naturally, then, we do something about it.

In a climate of cuntlove, no one feels "lucky" it was "some other woman" who got raped. There is no such thing as "some other woman" when you have compassion and cuntlove for yourself.

The basic premise of **C.P.R.** is publicly humiliating rapists. Since rapists count on a women's shame and silence to keep them safe and on the streets, it seems to me that an undue amount of attention focused on rapists would seriously counter this assumption.

C.P.R. can be employed when a woman is sure of her attacker's identity. Since most attacks are *not* perpetrated by strangers, this is a highly relevant factor.

There is safety and power in numbers.

A group of two hundred women walking into the place of employment of a known rapist would have an effect. If each of these women were in possession of a dozen rotting eggs which were deposited onto the rapist's person, the rapist might well come to the conclusion that he had committed a very unpopular act, one that was not appreciated by the community. If a rapist had to walk through a crowd of angry, staring, silent or quietly and deadly chanting women to get to his car in the grocery store parking lot, he might feel pretty uncomfortable.

Cuntlovin' Public Retaliation has limitless possibilities.

C.P.R. actions can be executed without breaking too terribly many laws and without becoming violent—the latter being true especially if women only are present. Unnecessary violence is for stupid, unimaginative people. There are far more damaging ways to punish someone without invoking violence.

Cuntlovin' Public Retaliation serves history as well as the future. Women who have been raped may find enormous satisfaction and healing by acting out in a setting with other women who are present in total support, rage and love. In this context, we are offered a liberation from silence, self-blame, quiet acceptance or any other negative reaction we have—in the past—believed we needed for survival.

Men should not be included in **C.P.R.** actions. Excepting situations where men have been raped, the general male response towards the rape of a friend, relative or lover is outraged, self-righteous indignation. I've seen this reaction a number of times, and believe men react this way because it gives them a chance to prove to themselves what good non-raping men they are. If men really and truly want to be "good," they can stand in the background and quietly support their women friends and relatives while we stand up for ourselves. They can chip in money to charter the busses we may need to transport everyone to the **C.P.R.** site.

We don't need men to protect us.

This is between women and rapists.

More to the point, this is between women and ourselves.

Here is physics: A positive action yields a positive reaction.

At present, the cultural reaction to rape is generally a negative, shame-filled silence.

Fine, let the culture react that way.

We have the power to put something else there. Women can react in our own poetic, imaginative way, utilizing the resources in our community. We have power in numbers, and many, many means of communication.

Yes, indeedy.

It's time for a cool change.

Any rapist would feel pretty dang upset to see his car packed full with rotting fish heads and limburger cheese. Especially if it was a Jaguar XJS. Also, especially if the 542 women responsible were crowded onto the street where he lived, insisting that he move himself and his stinky car to another locale.

Nobody likes to be pelted with 2060 bloody tampons.

Wouldn't you just hate like the devil to be pilloried, smeared with dogshit, forced to kneel in front of a high-powered microphone on a raised platform and apologize to the ten thousand women who solemnly marched by you? Boy, that would be an unpleasant day that you might not forget right away, huh.

Perhaps some communities of women would be interested in constructing huge severed penises and burning them on a rapist's front lawn.

Cuntlovin' Public Retaliation is a valid cultural custom. Different tribes decide how to implement this custom in the community.

It could be highly effective.

Most importantly, with a little love, communication, temporary organization and networking, **Cuntlovin' Public Retaliation** is very, very possible.

It's also very, very up to you.

Part III
Reconciliation
(rē′kən-sĭl′ē-ā′shən) n.

a dab of religion

Recently, I saw a lady wearing a T-shirt that read, "In the post-patriarchy, I'll be a post-feminist." I realized that just a few short years ago, our vocabulary had no need for either of these terms, and I smiled.

It was the same week nuestra Virgin Mary was on the cover of *Newsweek*. The pope is evidently receiving thousands of petitions daily from Catholics all over the globe, asking him to indoctrinate nuestra Virgin as co-redemptrix—Jesus' "equal."

Each passing day heralds the emergence of yet another athlete, rock star, activist, artist or politician who reminds women we can do pretty much whatever the fuck we want.

Signs of the dawning post-patriarchal age are positively rampant.

My 1965 Random House Dictionary reveals the following about the word "reconcile":

1. to render no longer opposed; bring to acquiescence or acceptance (usually fol. by *to*): *to reconcile someone to his* [sic] *fate*. 2. to win over to friendliness; cause to become amicable: *to reconcile hostile persons*. 3. to compose or settle (a quarrel, dispute, etc.). 4. to bring into agreement or harmony; make compatible or consistent: *to reconcile*

differing statements. 5. to reconsecrate (a desecrated church, cemetery, etc.). 6. to restore (an excommunicate or penitent) to communion in a church.

The definition most pertinent to this book is number five: "to reconsecrate a desecrated church."

The religious ritual of submerging a newborn child in a bowl of water inside a house of god is an attempt to simulate the power all women are potentially born with. If it is reasonable for the patriarchy to call these houses of god "churches," then it is reasonable for me to believe that both the individual female body and the body of womankind are churches too. *And I do.*

Fixing up our church, as well as the reference point of worship inside our hearts, is therefore a timely thing to do.

The following items comprise a church:

1. Protection from potential hostilities represented by opposing belief systems. Our mission to educate ourselves and children the way we want.

2. All mediums of art and literature depicting a corresponding creed and collective consciousness. Our immolationless stained glasses and holy scriptures that we design to our specifications.

3. Resources. Cashflow. Passing around our tithe baskets that fill our coffers with our money, honey.

For the reconciliation of our church, we will be utilizing cuntlovin' perspectives on protection, representational art and money. I start with protection because it flows nicest after the subject of rape.

Aggro Beyond Your Wildest Dreams

I will kick your fucking ass. —Ancient Goddess Mantra

Mapping Out a Belief System

The first thing you need in order to protect yourself is a womanifesto. My friend Panacea turned me on to the importance of womanifestoes when she said:

"I like them because they tell me what I think."

Defining and articulating your beliefs serves you in any context. By taking that a step further and causing those beliefs to exist in the material world, you contribute to a social climate of cuntlovin' evolution.

I offer my womanifesto on self-protection to perhaps give you some ideas about how you might write yours. A womanifesto does not have to be written. It can be a song, dance, painting or whatever medium stirs passion in your heart. I strongly suggest

creating your own womanifesto before moving on to the next
section, "Kickin' Ass Like There Ain't No Tomorrow."

The Womanifesto for the Categorical
New Freedom Lady

**when you see a really drunk girl leave a bar alone late at
night and you follow her and make sure she gets into her
taxi all right,
that's self-protection.
when you aren't afraid of looking like a supreme
chickenshit and ask your friend to go into a public bathroom with you because it creeps you out, but not for any
tangible reason,
that's self-protection.
when you are in the music store and you pick a CD by
women musicians who have your back instead of by a
bunch of boys who hog all the air time on the radio,
that's self-protection.
when you are sitting on the bus and the man who sits next
to you gives you a bad vibe and you get up and move to
another seat without giving a rats ass about feeling like
you're being rude,
that's self-protection.
when you find out which politician is supportive of women,
lesbians and motherhood and vote for her,
that's self-protection.
when you look at all the beautiful women on TV and in
magazines in the grocery store and think they are part of a**

weird industry run by men with major, major

dick complexes,

that's self-protection.

when you boycott all media not responsive in every way,

shape and freudian slip to women's rights,

that's self-protection.

when you make a conscious effort to spend your money in

establishments owned by women,

that's self-protection.

when you tell your dude if he can't hold his wad until you're

damn well ready to come then he's gonna hafta invest in a

strap-on dildo of your choosing,

that's self-protection.

when you ask for a raise,

that's self-protection.

when you insist everyone re-read Pippi Longstocking

again,

that's self-protection.

when you and your friends concoct plans of poetic guerrilla

terrorism against a teacher, fellow student, co-worker or

boss who sexually harasses women,

that's self-protection.

when you decide it's in your best interest to worship a

goddess who innately respects women,

that's self-protection.

when you cook a gourmet, five-course meal no one but you

will partake in,

that's self-protection.

when you "accidentally" spill your drink on a man at a

179

c
u
n
t

party who looks at your body rather vulpinely, and you don't
in the least appreciate it,
that's self-protection.
when you educate yourself about clitoridectomies, infibulation, forced prostitution, rape as a war tactic and a way of
controlling women, the Nation of Islam, Judaism, Chris-
tianity and prepatriarchal religions, the Inquisition,
women painters, photographers, filmmakers, poets,
writers, activists, politicians, sex-industry workers,
historians, archeologists and musicians,
that's self-protection.
when you read, then watch *The Bandit Queen*,
that's self-protection.
when you massage your friend because she's PMSing hard,
that's self-protection.
when you keep a tire iron by your front door,
that's self-protection.
when you buy a pull-up bar and install it in a doorway you
pass constantly so you end up doing pull-ups all the time,
even though you used to think you couldn't do pull-ups,
that's self-protection.
when you dance, run, jump, buy yourself a birthday cake
even though your birthday's five months away, cavort, kiss
all the girls you love to love, laugh, sing, shout, jump rope,
ding-dong ditch the house of someone who gets on your
nerves, swing, climb trees, pick your nose in public,
daydream, eat with your fingers, break something on
purpose, fart loud, skip and pin your friends to the ground
and tickle them,

that's self-protection.
every time you look in the mirror and your heart races
because you think,
"i'm so fucking rad,"
that's self-protection.
protect your self.

I wrote that when I was twenty-eight. I went through a lot of reconditioning on my own terms before I had the knowledge to sit down and compose those thoughts off the top of my head.

I grew up in a relatively small town in the Central Coast region of California. The *president of the Elks* spoke at the high school graduation ceremony I boycotted. Cruising up and down the main street in a car, going to the mall and attending drunken date-rape festivals called "parties" were the culminations of social interaction.

I was never entirely comfortable in this setting.

Until I was eighteen and left "home," I was constantly at odds with this culture I grew up in. The older I got, the more clearly I saw what was supposed to be looming ahead for me as a woman.

I wanted nothing to do with any of it.

This conflict became increasingly unsettling with each passing year. I did not want to keep my mouth shut and act ladylike, stop having sex with my girlfriends or respect the idea that all of my teachers were smarter than me. Dealing with such opposition on a day-to-day basis disrupted the momentum of womanpower I was born with. I struggled to keep my power somewhat apace with my life. This proved difficult, as I expended a large amount of energy defending my own concept of the woman I wanted to be. Furthermore, deprived of the experience I needed in order to *know* exactly what "the woman I wanted to be" *meant*, things were not only difficult, but mind-bogglingly complex as well.

At one point in my life, I detested the adage, "What does not kill me will only make me stronger."

But it is true.

When I was a kid, I was on the swim team, played tackle football and moto-mud bicycled. My friends and I endlessly plotted live-action *Charlie's Angels* episodes, including our edited-in couplings between 'Bri and Jill. Underwater Tea 'n Smash Party in the ocean always ruled. I loved the "Heidi" look and wore dresses with my waffle stompers. I was a late bloomer in terms of clearly established gender roles.

Largely through the teachings of my philandering, sexist father, who did not want me to grow up prey to men like himself, I became a premature and great advocate of vigilante-type behavior. I heartily beat the shit out of any mean boy who made the sorry mistake of pulling my pigtails or pushing any girl's face into the water fountain at school.

My mother, for obvious reasons we've already discussed, had no qualms about this sort of behavior. Fighting with girls was not cool (and seldom occurred), but she didn't give a rat's ass if I beat the shit out of a boy.

My older brother was not only bigger than all the boys at

my school, but acted in the role of sparring partner in our perpetual sibling battle for turf, rights and privileges. Childhood with my brother provided an ongoing study in the velocity of a strategically placed kick, the rhythm of a punch in the gut and the mother lode of reactions illicited from a well-timed, ear-splitting scream.

Between the (albeit dubiously inspired) sense of entitle-ment fostered by my parents' philosophies and the practical, tactical skills I derived from life with my brother—not to mention the wolf-pack mother mentality I found in such sister bad-asses as Deanna Alvarado and Hannah Class—the mean boys at my school were resoundingly pummelled whenever a girl reported untoward behavior to one of us.

A most satisfactory arrangement, as far as I was concerned.

Then I grew up.

The mean little boys who taunted and teased and harassed little girls also grew up.

We all grew up.

The taunting, teasing and harassing evolved into rape, passive-aggressive control lurking behind proclamations of "egalitarianism," sexual harassment and collective beliefs of male superiority.

I experienced damnable levels of confusion going from a little girl who accepted highly suspect gender roles to a young lady suddenly in possession of a very specific set of restrictions and scriptures.

One of the many, many, many scriptures imposed upon me once I got big, was: "It is your duty to ignore mean boys and their games."

And see, given the latitude I enjoyed throughout my early years, I just had a very difficult time ignoring this kind of stuff. But now that I was big, even if I tattled (a wimpy manipulation I rarely resorted to as a child), no one listened or cared. If I retaliated, I got in trouble, lost jobs, made enemies.

Oh, how I sometimes longed for those days on the playground when kicking a mean boy's ass was a mundane occurrence in any given school week.

It became my reality to let mean boys slide. Though I did not like it, I also didn't see much in the way of options. The operative words here are *I didn't see*. Before any option-seeing went down, I had to *really see* my own fears.

It was a *struggle* to see options.

I looked very, very painstakingly.

I came to terms with the reality that in the eyes of an overwhelming percentage of the population, my sole purpose on the planet is to make dicks ejaculate, either for procreation or recreation. Being reduced to this identity every time I venture out in public is an affront I chose to ignore for a long time. It is still a drag to see men looking at me in terms of their dicks, and to know that no matter what I accomplish as a person, or how I live my life, this will probably not change significantly in my lifetime.

If I had not avidly, passionately, relentlessly sought options, I am sure I would have gone insane. Regardless of whether or not *I* ever recognized the existence of options, they were always there. Like a faithful old family dog, my options waited for me to recover the survival skills I relinquished in adolescence.

Kicking Ass Like There Ain't No Tomorrow

It got to a point when I reasoned, if I take my survival into consideration every time I leave the sanctity of my home—if indeed, my home sometimes seems to be a fortress that deters enemy forces—then aren't I kind of like a soldier, and isn't my life kind of like a war?

It plain and simple dawned on me: Somebody here was seriously out of the loop. There was no circumventing the fact that I had allowed my nice wolf-pack mama girlhood survival skills to languish.

A sad—but certainly not irrevocable—mistake I made in order to survive into adulthood.

So let's see.

The first thing a soldier does is train. In boot camp she learns physical tactics and the psychology of her enemy. She meditates upon all the nuances that come into play in the battle of how a life lived in fear is a life half lived.

In the Army of Me, self-protection class was appointment number one, dee-dee-dun.

After I published an article about rape, a cartoonist named Ellen Forney wrote a letter to my editor. Ms. Forney eloquently pointed out my responsibility to urge women to learn how to protect ourselves, rather than merely publish essays about all the things we had to fear in this world. In the letter, Ellen described her pivotal experiences, learning and then teaching self-protection. Her letter fully inspired me. I asked if she'd be interested in teaching a class if I organized it, and she graciously agreed.

Ms. Forney taught us about using our voices and deflecting

verbal assaults before venturing into physical maneuvers. I was all geared up to kick me some ass; it was surprising to discover such a fount of strength and release simply by listening to women talk about how we deal with everyday situations that rankle the psyche in a slow and eroding process.

I learned a lot of physical tactics in this first self-protection class. More importantly, it became clear that these skills exist as part of a larger philosophy of self-protection that is explored and practiced by each individual woman, on our terms, at our pace.

Ellen's class ruled, and my second self-protection class kept the ol' synapse pulsations spurring along.

The next course I took was Model Mugging. It's a form of self-protection developed by a group of martial arts experts. A woman in this group had been raped. This, in itself, is not terribly unique. However, she was an eighth-degree karate black belt. She knew a martial art very, very well, but she did not know how to protect herself in the specific context of sexual assault. The group decided to pool their expertise and design a way to teach any woman, regardless of agility, prowess or strength, to protect herself.

They did an awesome, good job.

Model Mugging was intensive and expensive, and all my ass-kickin' dreams came true because there were *actual, live human men* in padded outfits that I got to pound on. My job in this class was to use my power to change the physical course of another human being who, for all intents and purposes, meant me harm. Even though I was in a room with nineteen other women and rubber mats were spread out all over the floor, the reality was daunting. *These men were present to attack and react.*

Us twenty women were present to react and attack.

Attack, attack, react, react over and over and over.

Certainly on par with the joy of actually downing the big, burly, padded dudes was watching other women negotiate power against them. This was when I *really understood* there are as many different definitions for self-protection as there are cerebral filing systems. No one reacted to the exact same situation in the exact same way, even though we were all being taught the exact same tactics.

A womanifesto and self-protection classes (note the plural form of "class") are fantastic starting points for powerful reconditioning. Define what you believe. Train your mind and body to react to detrimental situations in a powerful, assertive way. These two survival tactics are, however, just that: *tactics*. They *help* your brain to think differently.

Remember back yonder when I induced an abortion without going to the vacuum cleaner? Remember how the herbs I took aided me in directing *my own focus?* The same concept holds true here (and at many other outposts in a cuntlovin' lady's life). Training requirements aren't fulfilled by attending a course every Wednesday night for eight weeks. Self-protection is a *way of thinking, constantly*, each and every moment of your life. Classes help. Entertaining pro-active dialogues with the women you love helps. Womanifestoes help. Lotsa stuff helps. *Nothing* is as valuable as implementing new learning tools and committing to your focus for *the rest of your life*.

I advocate self-protection as a lifestyle philosophy-modus operandi. I don't believe that wielding a can of pepper spray, a

switchblade or a gun is on par with existing on the planet with a
self-protection lifestyle at the forefront of one's being.

Neither do I in any way oppose the use of weapons as self-
protection. When one chooses weapons to protect oneself in this
world, it is of *utmost importance* to learn *formal, rigorous safety
and precision in the specific context of protection from physical and/
or sexual assault.* Deer hunting and gang banging are probably
not gonna prepare your spirit, mind or body for a potential
sexual assault.

The most reliable weapon is your mind. When women
relinquish the power of our minds to objects that can inflict
debilitating pain or death, we weaken our position. A quick,
resourceful, well-trained thinker is a *much deadlier opponent*
than someone who projects power into a deadly instrument.

A quick, resourceful, well-trained thinker with a deadly
instrument in hand is then Warrior Goddess incarnate.

Hee fucken hawww.

Cross that bridge when you get to it.

In the meantime, the most wonderful way I have found to
train my mind for assessing situations and reacting with the
resources I have available to me is on a checkered playing board
that has two sets of sixteen figurines carved to represent
different qualities and nuances of power.

Chess Is Our Friend

I am thankful to Boaz Yakim, a gentleman who made a movie I
will watch any time, any place. It's called *Fresh.* In light of its
phenomenal importance, the injustice of *Fresh*'s poor distribution
makes me almost pass out.

Fresh is an adolescent young man growing up in a situation rife with predators. His environment is predatory, his inherited socioeconomic latitude is a predator and all but one of his role models are predators. Fresh's sole nonpredatory role model is his father, played by the incomparable Mr. Samuel L. Jackson.

Fresh lives in a foster home. He isn't supposed to see his father, but he does. Every week, they play chess together in a park. I said Fresh's father is not a predator, but that's not altogether true. He manifests his predatory traits on the chessboard, in the game he lives and breathes by.

The story of Fresh unfolds around these weekly chess games with his father. Territory being what it is, both on the chess board and in life, Fresh's father routinely wins the game. Meanwhile, in his day-to-day life (of which his father is completely ignorant), Fresh faces responsibilites and situations that would cause chronic intestinal complications to the heartiest CEO at IBM.

Fresh meets his father in the park every week and plays this very old game. It is kind of a ritual. His father says things like, "What kind of player am I? Am I an offensive player or a defensive player? Right, I'm neither. *I play my opponent.*"

With all his heart, Fresh listens, looks, learns. The gift of chess and its lessons in strategy may be all his estranged, alcoholic father has to offer him. It is also more valuable than an eight-digit trust fund.

Fortified with nothing more than a psychology that assesses and undermines their *individual* ways of operating, Fresh pretty much mauls every predator in his life—without personally committing a single act of violence. He learns how to *think like the predators*. You know who reigns supreme, or the movie wouldn't be called *Fresh*.

Fresh has become one of the biggest role models in my life. I constantly ask myself, "How would Fresh deal with this situation?" When I'm reacting like a dork in response to some damn stimuli or another, I say, "Fresh wouldn't do that in a million years." Perhaps most significantly, Fresh reminds me to get off my ass and play chess every chance I get.

My father taught me how to play chess when I was five. I played quite often with my sparring partner—er, brother. Just as I had grown up and left my survival skills in the hinterland, I likewise stopped playing chess at some obscure point in adolescence. Whenever I had the opportunity to play chess as an adult, I met a fierce resistance inside myself. I didn't like the competetion, the cutthroat vibe.

After Fresh came into my life, I managed to shred this resistance asunder. However, it turned out most of my opponents were of the male persuasion. With precious few exceptions, my girl friends either never learned how to play or said the same thing I always said, "I used to play when I was younger, but I haven't played in a long time." As if not having played "in a long time" is somehow grounds for continuing this trend. Throughout my non-chess-playing rehabilitation, this response started sounding like, "I used to enjoy honing my strategy and getting what I want by employing my vast intelligence, but that stuff just doesn't interest me anymore."

Chess is a psychological exercise. It whets the brain for every conceivable means of self-protection.

When my pieces are threatened, my brain is presented with a puzzle. I must come up with a way to counter—with a ruse, sacrifice or threat of my own. No apologies. My A-1 priority is devising any plan in the whole wide world that does not involve retreat. Unless it diverts my opponent's attention from how devastatingly I plan to fuck them over on my next coupla moves, retreat is an absolute anathema.

Each person I play chess with tells me about their way of surviving in the world. If I piece together an overall view of their modus operandi, I win. When I sit across the board from someone, I'm engaged in more than a game. I silently beseech, "Tell me how you survive." Each opponent I play offers yet another survival strategy for my cerebral filing system.

Chess teaches how to deal with threatening situations and individuals *in the midst* of taking territory for oneself. The chances of being caught off guard have discernable boundaries. Predators become opponents instead of scary monsters over whom one has no control. When played on a regular basis, chess melds into one's consciousness. It becomes evident that one is never not playing this game.

Chess fortifies the psyche. When interwoven with physical and psychological training, it keeps a lady on her self-protective toes.

This game matters.

Get good at it and then get better.

Play chess with your friends instead of watching the M TeeVee. Organize all-girl tournaments at your school and all-women tournaments at your work. If you're not kickin' everybody's butt, then put a lot of thought into why they're kickin' yours. Play yourself. Play your mom. Invite a woman you think you can't stand to play a game with you. Play chess at a coffee house with someone you would never otherwise interact with. Have e-mail chess challenges. Tell your boss if you beat her at chess she hasta give you a raise.

Get on down and get back up again.

Play chess every day.

Predators Are Our Friends

I founded a direct-action anti-rape warfare group called Mobilizing Our Neighbors and Sisters To Eradicate Rape (M.O.N.S.T.E.R.). More accurately, I thought up a clever acronym and organized a space for women to come together and address the issue of rape as a cultural oppression tactic used to control women. The group of women involved did all the founding.

M.O.N.S.T.E.R.'s objective, decided upon after much discussion and debate, was to be a primarily nonviolent vigilante group that (more or less poetically) terrorized known sexual predators in our community, educated people about rape and provided a safe, supportive environment for women to devise and carry out nefarious plans of poetic attack.

As with every activist group on the planet, M.O.N.S.T.E.R. consisted of a balance of two creeds. One was of the passive leaflet-plastering, networking persuasion, while the other had a much more aggressive, predatory nature.

For many weeks, I interacted with this group of bright, imaginative, angry women and listened carefully to both systems of belief. While I was a subscriber to the predatory creed, I came to have a deep understanding of the women who wanted to act out in a more genteel manner. The argument ran along the lines of "We don't want to act like predators because then we are lowering ourselves to the level of a rapist," which is as valid an argument as can possibly be. This would invariably provoke the "nature vs. nuture" argument and someone would cite the ferocity of a mother serengeti lion or an arctic mama polar bear.

As is evidenced by M.O.N.S.T.E.R.'s eventual objectives, compromises were reached, leaning towards the predatory.

What I learned from this experience was a pretty solid foundation for *Cunt:* When women 100 percent define any-thing—from simple words to complex institutions—the meaning or outcome inherently serves us *most* satisfactorily. Period.

It is very simple, but a lot of work.

A predator, as defined by our society, is a bad man who will hurt you.

Ouch.

A predator, as defined by M.O.N.S.T.E.R., is a nice lady who pro-actively protects herself and the women in her community.

Whee!

Both definitions are sound.

M.O.N.S.T.E.R.'s cuntlovin' definition doesn't attempt to make the former one null and void. It sits right along next to it, happy as the day is long. Practically *the instant* we actually defined "predator" for ourselves, the group's Kali the Destroyers piped down a few notches, while nuestra Virgens de Guadalupe started baring teeth.

Fucken refreshing, you know?

✳

Predators are important people. Why else would there be one in almost every movie and story throughout history. Take away the predator, and where does that leave the koran, bible, torah?

Nowhere, that's where.

Predators are not the problem.

I, for one, don't *feel* like going out into the world and making sure all the predators who focus on women are put behind bars or executed or whatever. In this cuntfearing society, there's plenty more where that came from. Some Sisyphean tasks can be fun, but that's not one of them.

It is impossible to change the fact that sexual predators are a product of our society, whether they are incarcerated or free to roam. And *damn,* it sucks that no incantation from heaven and hell combined will undo the deeply rooted damage rape has already done to the collective consciousness of womankind.

Dang, that's all impossible, so forget it.

Say goodbye to the impossible: toodle doo.

It *is* possible to change our way of reacting and dealing. Without silence, the *cycle*, the *livelihood* of violence towards women goes hectic. Women break the cycle and the situation then belongs to us.

Our ball, our court, our move.

As I see it, the major problem facing us ladies is not all the horrible shit that's been happening to us for the past two thousand–odd years.

Nor is it the perpetrators of the horrible shit.

The problem is we don't seem to think we have much of a

predatory disposition. This is heartily reinforced by our culture, which unduly punishes women who are caught acting out in a violent, predatory way. It frightens people very, very much when women do violent things. The United States legal and judicial systems are hardly exempt from this fear. Jails are populated with women who murdered the lovers, friends or male relatives who assaulted us or our children for years. If it is at all possible to completely avoid contact with this sector of society, I suggest doing so with vigor.

Physical violence is something one resorts to only when it is the very, very, very best way to safety. Violence is not a defining trait of a lady predator. It is certainly imperative to know how, when, why and where to be violent. It is also imperative to know how, when, why and where to get away before a situation has the chance to escalate.

Lady predators are cuntlovin', imaginative women. We therefore manifest our predatory stance in just such a manner. We're not too shy to be highly visible. We'll scream "My Country 'Tis of Thee" to drown the voice of Loudmouth Asshole who is trying to impress his friends by telling everyone on the street the effect we do/do not have on his dick. We're not too proud to be invisible, either. We know that for Mr. Obviously Fucked Up in the Head, "Amazing Grace" sung soft 'n low under our breath miraculously makes him forget we're crossing his path.

Lady predators get all our friends to confront the dickwad who bugs us at work or school. We ensure employers know which of their employees is a date rapist and picket the place if

c
u
n
t

the boss does not respond accordingly. We publicly humiliate the man who rapes our daughter, sister, lover, mother. We organize into mama wolf packs with a rabid sense of humor. We have Abusive Husband Treasure Hunts on Super Bowl Sunday.

We interrupt the game.

It

is

funner 'n shit.

Who Remedios Varo Is

*If you would understand a people, look at them through the eyes of
the poet, the musician and the artist.*
—Cynthia Pearl Maus, *The World's Great
Madonnas*

When I was ten, the Fam took a trip to L.A. to
see the Treasures of King Tut exhibit. At this
time, my art world consisted of paintings, pictures,
books, records and the radio. (My father's tyranny is in evidence
here. We didn't have a television set in our house for *simply
ages.*) Art was furthermore associated with making a huge mess
that was magically sanctioned by most all authority figures.

Art was a wonder to perceive, and I percieved it at complete and utter face value. This is to say, I very much enjoyed
art, but did not attach a symbolic interpretation to either my
own or other people's.

The King Tut exhibit forever altered this tabula rasa.

I remember gold.

I remember gold, and I remember four women who

guarded the box where King Tut's body lay. They were gold, of course, and stood with arms to their sides, hands outstretched hip high, palms perfectly at my eye level, staring me down. Their eyes never left anyone in the room. They saw all. They were impassable. Their gaze was searing and irresistible, like licking a nine-volt battery.

My parents and siblings wandered off. I was not interested in anything else the King Tut exhibit had to offer, and installed myself with the sentinels until it was time to go.

I knew little of Christ, much less anything that went on Before Christ, but it was quite obvious those sentinels were *obscenely* out of their element in a museum in Los Angeles, California, circa One Thousand Nine Hundred and Seventy Whatever A.D. And yet—through what I later recognized as the wanton pillage mentality of my culture—in this context, innocuously referred to as "archeology"—there they irrefutably stood.

Magnificent overseers of an entire civilization, brought across oceans on a boat driven by the victors of history's present telling.

I felt incredibly minute and *of the flesh* in their presence. It was important to remain in contact with what was in the pocket of my shorts: half a bag of M&M's and two green plastic army men I'd fished out my little brother's mouth on the drive to L.A. I think the contents of my pockets comforted me, because fear was certainly present.

The sentinels possessed incomprehensible powers for thousands upon thousands of years. They were *alive* under the desert sands of Egypt long before even my *grammy* was born. And now, standing in this weird museum room, they were not only alive, but *pissed as hell* to be taken from their place.

I could not stop digging the amazement of this whole situation.

I was too young and impatient to understand what compelled people to create all that gold stuff, and too uninterested in the museum itself to put much thought into the little explanatory plaques affixed near each piece, but I knew God when I saw Her.

This, I understood.

This, I respected.

This was a whole new slant on art.

I grew up and found out three more things about art:

1. The individual artist is a *medium* for making representational and deeply meaningful symbols of the community's collective consiousness, whether they are symbols of the community's religion, love, hurt, power, hate, hope, dreams, fables, foibles or on and on and on.

2. Some cultures know this, think it's divine, and respect the importance of art and artists as perfectly natural manifestations of innate human life, growth and expression—without insanely glorifying huge, corporate-induced false images of individual superstars.

3. American culture is not one of them.

One kind of art occurs naturally in the course of everyday life, and does not generally involve widespread cultural glorification. My mother's Thanksgiving dinner is art. The one Aunt Genie creates is of a completely different genre, though she utilizes the same basic components. The dashboard of Liz's car is art. Shells and goddesses and pretty rocks are arranged in a specific way that holds meaning for anyone who is privy to the need for protection when navigating an automobile. Grammy's wild-flower and bird sanctuary garden is art. She designed it. It is a reflection of her and her community. It is symbolic of the culture she lives in.

Another kind of art is the art people make and *intend* to be considered art as symbolic representation. Art such as this moves you for certain very specific reasons directly related to your history and experiences, and moves your girlfriend in a thousand and one absolutely different ways.

This art includes paintings, metal work, sculptures, murals, photographs, dances, poems, stories, storytelling, essays, plays, screenplays, movies, videos, ads, buildings, fashion designs, performances, puppet shows, monuments, pornography, erotica, music, spoken word and so on.

Both kinds of art represent a culture, a collective conscious-ness and the passions of an individual. Grammy's wildflower and bird sanctuary garden is as monumental as Toni Morrison's epic, *Beloved*.

On a scale that measured love and pain,

they'd proportionately weigh the same.

The difference between these two kinds of art is:

I know my grammy's story and the average onlooker does not. I've developed an emotional bond with my grammy since I was born. Therefore, I walk into her garden equipped with a lifelong perception which is in continual evolution. I am thus able to identify with her garden utilizing symbolism unavailable to most everyone else.

Beloved directly, out and out tells a story. The words of the

story are arranged with high regard for the common bond of
human-ness that each and every reader shares. Everyone who
can read is equipped to identify with *Beloved*.

Beloved taps into the collective consciousness of a community that spans the entire planet.

Grammy's garden doesn't echo out much farther than
Sweet Home, Oregon.

Art imitates life as life imitates art. Art and the community are
whirling dervishes unto one other. Takes two to tango. It doesn't
matter which one causes and affects the other, or when, or why,
or how. This came first: the chicken or the egg.

There is, of course, a huge problem here.

Throughout the history of Western civilization—and by this
term, I mean the destructive, competitive, capitalist, patriarchal,
filthy-rich, white, male social system which threatens to
consume every other culture on the planet—what is considered
"art" has been presented by and for far less than half of the
human community: the white, male portion. Art that our
culture takes seriously, invests in and reflects upon was created
by men. Women do not belong to the "art" community, as it
presently exists.

In what is considered the art community, the enormous
contributions of artists such as Yoko Ono and Octavia Butler are
methodically and unquestionably overshadowed by those of the
Andy Warhol/Stephen King ilk.

In the early '90s, I attended college at one of America's most
liberal, progressive institutions. There, my friend Panacea turned

me on to the surrealist painter, Remedios Varo.

One quarter, Panacea took a course in "art history." She asked her teacher numerous times throughout the quarter to include Ms. Varo's totally brilliant, fabulous and inspiring work in the program. The teacher resolutely overruled this motion, time and again. His argument was that there must be a solid reason why Ms. Varo's work was not "good enough" to be included in any of the art history books he had ever seen. Since none of the sources this teacher deemed reputable recognized Remedios Varo, why on earth should he?

Catch-22, deedle dee-doo.

In her second autobiography, *Beyond the Flower*, Judy Chicago provides a simple, astute answer:

> Historically, women have either been excluded from the process of creating the definitions of what is considered art or allowed to participate only if we accept and work within existing mainstream designations. If women have no real role *as women* in the process of defining art, then we are essentially prevented from helping to shape cultural symbols. (Chicago, 1996, 72)

As I learned in a beautiful book entitled *Spider Woman's Granddaughters*, there is a name for this: intellectual apartheid. In her brilliant introduction to *Spider Woman's Granddaughters*, Paula Gunn Allen speaks as a Native artist working in the white-American literary world, but her profound truth is applicable to many artists existing in many worlds:

Intellectual apartheid . . . helps create and maintain political apartheid; it tends to manifest itself in the practical affairs of all societies that subscribe to it. Contrary to popular and much scholarly opinion in Western intellectual circles, aesthetics are not extraneous to politics. And because political conquest necessarily involves intellectual conquest, educational institutions in this country have prevented people from studying the great works of minority cultures in light of critical structures that could illuminate and clarify those materials in their own contexts. The literatures and arts of non-Western peoples have thus remained obscure to people educated in Western intellectual modes. Moreover, non-Western literature and art appear quaint, primitive, confused, and unworthy of serious critical attention largely because they are presented that way. (Allen, 1989, 3)

Men forge merrily along, continuing to get 99.9 percent of the credit for doing pretty much everything. When the glaringly obvious retardation of this situation is pointed out, the ensuing rebuttal tends to be that men just unanimously happen to be the most fabulously talented creators on earth. Thus, everyone who is not a man fails to get due credit.

In order for women painters, for instance, to be included in the history of art in modern civilization, it must first of all be established that we *exist*. This places the art work *in the hinterland* of the artist's gender. Women artists are required to explain our presence, to defend our identity, to speak for our multitudes, and men are not.

Meanwhile, reproduction upon reproduction of women in various stages of undress litters "art history." Women artists are airbrushed out of art history and still endure alienation and invalidation, yet images of women positively abound as the focal point of men's art work.

In this kind of setting, one learns that Salvador Dali is deemed an uncontested surrealist Master (though he readily admitted his obsessive reliance on a woman named Galarina for inspiration), while you probably don't know who I am talking about when I name a chapter for Remedios Varo, one of the most freaking genius surrealists of the twentieth century, who relied on herself for just about everything.

In 1989, the Guerrilla Girls—a pro-activist group that will be discussed at length in just a few short pages—addressed the question, "Do women have to be naked to get into the Metropolitan Museum?" Here are their findings:

> Asked to design a billboard for the Public Art Fund [PAF] in New York [City], we welcomed the chance to do something that would appeal to a general audience. One Sunday morning we conducted a "weenie count" at the Metropolitan Museum of Art in New York, comparing the number of nude males to nude females in the artworks on display. The results were very "revealing." (Guerrilla Girls, 1995, 61)

They designed a billboard depicting a reproduction of Ingres's reclining *Odalisque*, with a gorilla mask on her head and a dildo in the hand draped over her hip. Accompanying this image was the following statement: "Less than 5 percent of the artists in the Modern Art Sections are women, but 85 percent of the nudes are female."

Alas, the Public Art Fund and the Guerrilla Girl's *Odalisque* were not meant for each other.

> The PAF said our design wasn't clear enough and rejected it. We then rented advertising space on NYC busses and ran it ourselves, until the bus company canceled our lease, saying the image . . . was too suggestive and that the figure appeared to have more than a fan in her hand. (Guerrilla Girls, 1995, 61)

The difficulty in locating art made by women artists compared with the *impossibility* of avoiding art work created by men reflects *how women live* in this culture.

It is the absolute normal reality.

Cultural symbols that hold deep representational meaning for the community are shaped by the victors of history's present telling. The victors have a time-tested interest in controlling women's bodies, decimating civilizations, playing cops and robbers, keeping people of color and white women in our "proper" pigeonholed place and glorifying themselves through power plays with each other.

These interests are serviced through most television shows, movies, songs and music videos readily available. The interests of the victors project and reinforce absolutely *nada, zilch, nothing, zero,* that serves women.

Yet we view and absorb this art every livelong day.

And it hurts us.

Ouch.

Every day.

Here is a paragraph from the 1997 handbook for the Michigan Womyn's Music Festival:

> If you play recorded music that can be heard by others, please make it music with womyn only vocals. We come here to enjoy a womyn-only environment, part of which is hearing only womyn's voices. This is not a judgment on men or music, but a strong, positive desire to spend these few special days surrounded only by the sounds of womyn.

The Michigan Womyn's Music Festival is an unparalleled spiritual experience for—I'd be willing to wager—every woman who attends. It is a weeklong world created not so much without men, as with women. Women cook the food, play the music, guard the gates and drive the shuttle busses twenty-four hours a day. We see, speak, smell, taste and touch nothing but women. Every structure, artifact and song is of women's creation. It is not often one has the opportunity to exist in an entire community of women, wholly untouched by men, even for a day.

The only men who set foot on the festival grounds do so to empty out the Porta-Janes.

It can change a lady forever.

When I step outside my home, I am besieged by the creations of men. They designed the cars driving down the streets, indeed, they planned the placement of the streets. Since architecture is one of the many, many fields considered "male dominated," I trust that most of the buildings and residences I see come from the blueprints of men's minds. Ditto landscaping. The probably male-designed movie posters at the bus stops usually feature men, and if not, represent the labor of male producers, directors, sound engineers and camera operators. If I turn on the radio while I am driving down this male-made street, the voices of men selling their products and singing their songs about how much they love/hate/want to fuck women will promenade into into my male-designed automobile.

It is not difficult to appreciate the art of men.

In fact, it is dang-ola a chore to altogether evade it.

For two years in college, I read only books by women. I did not watch television or read magazines in the check-out line. I studied paintings, photographs, sculptures and films created solely by women.

George Bush Sr. got hisself inaugurated, Ted Bundy counted down the days to his execution and Somalia cried out in pain, but I was in Zora Neale Hurston's world. Leslie Marmon Silko kissed me good night. Sister Rosetta Tharpe sang lullabies into my sleep. Diane Arbus scared me giddy. Maya Linn was the Cinderella of my heart. Käthe Kollowitz made me cry and cry and cry.

It was only an experiment. I only meant it to be one of those let's-see-what-happens-if-I-do-this kind of things. But it turned into sort of a habit. I fully immersed myself in the expressions of women, exclusively, and felt so comfortable, I guess I just didn't leave.

I wouldn't venture to advocate a supreme, *lifelong* militancy about the gender specifics of art appreciation. I recently finished Laurence Leamer's eight hundred–plus page book, *The Kennedy Women: The Saga of an American Family*. Chet Baker croons through the speakers as I write. The taxidermy manual I read last month was written by a man, but I've forgotten his name, Jesse Charles or something. As far as I'm concerned, Samuel L. Jackson is a demigod and I'm never-endingly inspired by the garden of Mr. Young-Park, who lives next door.

It's not a bad idea, however, to focus *solely* on the artistic expressions of women for *at least* one year. That way you notice not only the horrifying prevalence of male artistic expression much more, but the mother lode of inspiration and brilliance our grandmothers, mothers and sisters have produced.

I loathe special sections for women just as much as the next lady. It will forever bug the shit out of me that there's a "W" before "NBA." This designation makes certain we know that all basketball involves men, unless it's this special, *exceptional circumstance* which can only be qualified as "women's basketball."

Schools have classes called "women's studies," and "African-American literature" because the standard for *existence* set by white men has yet to be rescinded in this age. "Normal" history is the history of a certain class of white people, from the perspective of men. All the other histories are precisely that: other.

I wish that when I said "rockstar," the kneejerk status quo association was Me'Shell "Brilliant Goddess Lovechild" NdegéOcello instead of Keith "Piece of Shit" Richards.

I wish when I queried "Great American Writer?" most people standing on the street would respond, "Oh, yes, well *obviously* Flannery O'Connor and Louise Erdrich," instead of, "Why, John Steinbeck and Ernest Hemingway, of course."

But that is not the case at all.

There is subsequently an unfortunate—yet urgent—need for something I'll refer to as a "Cuntlovin' Women's Art Movement." At least, until our culture no longer recognizes women within a male paradigm, and language and perception have broadened enough to imply the [art] world's inclusion of and dependence upon women.

Also, not to sound like a total wet blanket.

The *multitude* of acclaimed cuntlovin' artists bustin' fine round womanly asses getting honest reflections of us into the world *thrills me beyond measure.* Women populate the stages, giving acceptance speeches for Nobels, Grammys, Pulitzers and Guggenheims like never before. With each passing year, it grows easier and easier to immerse oneself in the expressions of women.

The singular detail here is to *immerse* yourself in the expressions of women; to *create* a Cuntlovin' Women's Art Movement with your friends, sisters, lovers and daughters; to be part of the community that defines art.

Cuntlovin' Women's Art Movement
Item #C.W.A.M.-1: chant

> You are what you eat.
>
> You meet who you greet.
>
> You head where you tread.
>
> You dead when not fed.

Cuntlovin' Women's Art Movement
Item #C.W.A.M.-2: womanifesto

the neverending "she taught me" womanifesto

. . . diamanda galás.
she taught me.
all the pain and joy of the whole wide world is inside my body.
my dna never forgets.
her voice in my body is the inquisition, all slavery ever, all rape,
all war, AIDS. her voice brings all that pain into my body—
which hurts—but the fact that she offers me the opportunity to
physically perceive the complexities of this pain, which exists in
the world in her voice, means it exists in the world in my body,
too. knowing this, the ball's in my court to take responsibility,
which gives me power.
all the pain and joy of the whole wide world is inside my body.
my dna never forgets.

leslie marmon silko.
she taught me.

if i want it to, history can mean his story. but mostly and much
moreover, history means
hi, story.
she said hi, story, and i understood what the vietnam war was
from her perspective, which mirrors my own much more
closely than the textbooks i read in school. she told me cowboys
and indians are people i see in my everyday life, the *nahual* flies
overhead, slavery is a business based on male sexuality and
home is where the heart is.
if i want it to, history can mean his story. but mostly and much
moreover, history means
hi, story.

pippi longstocking.
she taught me.
don't you worry about me, i always come out on top.
she reigns supreme over the police, mean boys, pirates, nosey
parkers, uppity snoots, the education system, monsters and
rascally impositions of her culture. the wonders of just simply
being alive in the world are limited solely by her imagination.
she was one of the first fashion inspirations of my life, and when i
grew up, her stories became the vortex of my feminist rhetoric.
don't you worry about me, i always come out on top.

remedios varo.
she taught me.
i am what i eat.
she painted pictures of magic happening, which are also what
her paintings, themselves, are. her life, her cosmology and her

product are three mirrors peering into one another at the same time, infinity. her precise science is based on the findings deep inside her consciousness and it is irrefutable. what comes from her is what she is because she is what she comes from.

i am what i eat. . . .

Cuntlovin' Women's Art Movement
Item #C.W.A.M.-3: http://www.guerrillagirls.com

The Guerrilla Girls have been an exemplary part of this culture for over a decade. Here is their mission statement:

> The Guerrilla Girls are a group of women artists and arts professionals who make posters about discrimination. Dubbing ourselves the conscience of the art world, we declare ourselves feminist counterparts to the mostly male tradition of anonymous do-gooders like Robin Hood, Batman, and the Lone Ranger. We wear gorilla masks to focus on the issues rather than our personalities. We use humor to convey information, provoke discussion, and show that feminists can be funny. In 10 years, we have produced over 70 posters, printed projects, and actions that expose sexism and racism in the art world and the culture at large. Our work has been passed around the world by kindred spirits who consider themselves Guerrilla Girls too. The mystery surrounding our identities has attracted attention and support. We could be anyone; we are everywhere. (www.guerrillagirls.com)

The Guerrilla Girls are one of the most internationally recognized activist groups on the planet. Though they'll never get due credit, the Guerrilla Girls' poster style is a huge inspirational prototype for the strong-image/in-your-face text combo that has become formulaic in everything from Nike ads to blockbuster movie trailers.

Their tactics are clever, humorous and highly effective. They attack specific issues at specific locations. Guerrilla Girl propaganda is clearly and concisely worded. The vivid, often co-opted images grab the attention of non-English-speaking people, those unable to read and the completely jaded, alike.

Were the Guerrilla Girls originally a bunch of seventeen-year-old kids who bullshitted a mission statement into being, got their act together and poetically terrorized the art world after they finished their homework every afternoon?

Are the Guerrilla Girls really a smattering of disgruntled career gals who realized how very, very pissed off they were that they had "sold out" instead of pursuing their passions as artists?

Are Chelsea and Hillary Clinton Guerrilla Girls?

How weird must it be for men who work with women in New York's finest museums and galleries *not to know* if one of their colleagues, bosses or subordinates is one of an increasingly powerful group of women who undermine everything they allegedly work towards together during business hours?

It is very delicious that so much surrounding this group is a matter of conjecture.

Here's a conservative guess:

The Guerrilla Girls originated as seven to twenty-eight

women who decided to do something together instead of sitting back and witnessing the horror.

Talk about an inspiration to the nation.

Here is the recipe for starting an activist group in your hometown:

a. pictures

b. words

c. a reproduction and distribution system

d. women friends with imagination, focus and motivation—especially ones who work at Kinko's.

Put it all together.

On your marks,

get set.

Go.

Cuntlovin' Women's Art Movement
Item #C.W.A.M.-4: disbursement of revenue

Get CDs and books at the library when appreciating the work of men. Rent their movies. Watch their sporting events on TV.

Buy CDs and books by women. Go to the theater to see films by women, and purchase videos for your gorgeously expanding library. Buy tickets to our basketball games.

Disburse revenue into the women's art world in your community and afar. Each cent spent on work by men is money taken away from the Cuntlovin' Women's Art Movement.

Who Mammon Is

The ceiling isn't glass, it's a very dense layer of men.
—Anne Jardim

 I love money.

I love money so much I can hardly contain my passion for it.

Money rules.

Besides shelter, featuring a warm cushy bed, heat, electricity, a pot to piss in and a floor to watch my period blood drip onto, money equals: time to work on my book, presents for people I love, a sumptuous, satin-lined, floor-length, pink, polyester fur coat with matching bikini, mango mochi ice cream, a telephone line and an e-mail account, a three hour luxuriation and massage at the communal women's baths, new books and CDs, industrial-sized rolls of double-sided tape, sheets of stickers with my face next to an alien's, fancy dinner dates and that divine three tiered cocktail table at the antique store.

Lordisa yes, money is grand.

Making,

managing and

generating

yet more money in a cuntlovin' way that makes me smile from earlobe to earlobe is an absolute different story.

There are two ways to make money in a capitalist, patriarchal setting:

1. Fuck other people over faster and more efficiently than they fuck you over.
2. Whore.

I'm too much of a sucker for the wrath of karma to excel at #1, so that leaves #2. In this context, Whoring consists of selling some aspect of one's being in order to survive. Sometimes this is selling one's dexterity at the espresso machine and other times it's selling one's ability to seduce people into buying things they don't want. Sometimes we think we can escape corporate Whoredom by becoming artists or owning our own businesses.

But no.

To make money, we gotta associate ourselves with a corporate pimp somewhere along the food chain.

This ain't circumventable.

Any kind of Cuntlovin' Women's Economic System that's implemented in this society will have to answer to the capitalist patriarchy because the buck stops there. It is downright illegal to ignore the IRS. Please inform me if there's a single behemoth insurance company owned and operated by women, but I'm quite certain the New York Stock Exchange floor has never been grid-locked by cuntlovin' ladies vying to invest in the education of our children.

So be it.

At the 1997 Michigan Womyn's Music Festival, I met a writer for a popular American magazine. We got to talking, and duly realized that we totally disagreed on pretty much every mien of existence. This in no way hampered our mutual fascination and respect for one another.

I will never in my life forget her candor when she said to me (of all people) in an unabashedly woman-centered community (of all places), "I am totally seduced by male power."

In context, it was one of the most brutally honest statements I'd ever heard—even though (and indubitably because) I could not relate on any spectrum of cognizance. She'd put great and highly intelligent thought into her choice for survival, which involved investing all of her power and trust in the capitalist patriarchy economic model.

Which makes perfect sense.

The proof is in the pudding.

The largest, most successful women-owned companies in the United States are cute little unicorns that play in the rainbow compared to the village-stomping dragons like Microsoft, GE and Disney.

I ain't never heard tell of an internationally recognized multimedia production company, chain of car dealerships, real estate conglomerate, advertising agency or garbage-collection firm owned and operated solely by women. There are no states

r
e
c
o
n
c
i
l
i
a
t
i
o
n

with women in all positions of political office, from the governor on down to the postmaster in each city. If mafias are needed to keep the economy humming along, there certainly aren't any matrifocal ones testifying to the truth of this.

This has been the economic reality since time out of my grammy's mind. Past and present cuntlovin' businesses are inherently at odds in this reality. Subsequently, they must fight like the devil in order to remain solvent.

Cunt would never have become a product accessible to consumers if it weren't for the rippling effect of one woman's struggle and tenacious dream. One woman's unwavering standard to employ and serve women creates a cuntlovin' consciousness that bolsters every person who works for—or comes in contact with—her company. Rest assured, pretty much any product purchased from a cuntlovin' business benefits all women in a similar manner.

Cuntlovin' businesswomen are consistently on the economic defense because—at present—we aren't the ones who foment the rules and codes of supply and demand. Women have no modern history of managing commerce on the civic, county, state or federal level.

I am a sharecropper on the patriarchy's land.

I can dress this up with all the modes of independence imaginable, but if I want my mail every day, I am at the mercy of the United States Postal Service. The electricity for my computer is compliments of the Pacific Gas and Electric Company, which still often boasts repair signs that remind me of the fact that this society is run by a series of "Men Working."

Furthermore, individual women are systematically shot down when we make a stand in the name of anything that defies the white male standard of existence. To my dying day, I'm gonna be cranky about the fact that Dr. Jocelyn Elders got canned for testing our society's puritanical tolerance level about sexuality.

Women who acquire the courage, will and/or money to secure positions of high-octane power and prestige *must conduct business* within the same "mainstream designations" found in the art world. Likewise, in order to become and remain a hugely successful organization, woman-owned companies must alienate women.

Marjorie Merriweather Post, for example.

Her father, C. W. Post, of Raisin Bran fame, was right there at the crest of the breakfast and advertising economic revolutions here in America. He insisted his only child be involved in the intrigues of business. Marjorie was raised much differently than other girls of her generation. She grew up with a sense of entitlement and independence, believing her gender was certainly no hindrance in getting what she wanted. Undoubtedly, this is more a reflection of C. W. Post's money, whiteness and love for his only child, than the philosophies of the women's movement at the time. The result was, nonetheless, a strong-willed woman who controlled a huge corporation after her father kicked. Almost until the day she died, Ms. Post ran the family business, and she did so under the same model as every other "successful" corporation in America. Men held positions of power and decision. Women were secretarial mom-wife-Whore-sis sycophants.

I reckon if the breakfast-cereal industry hadn't been revolutionized by C. W. Post and the Kellogg brothers until, oh say 1960, and Marjorie Merriweather Post was raised in the '70s and took over in the '90s, Post Cereal would've ran its course along pretty much the same gender lines. There would, as a concession to existing mainstream designations, perhaps be a smattering of men and women of color and white women secreted away in a few executive positions.

It's doubtful that Marjorie would have employed only women, provided child care, self-protection courses, profit sharing, investment groups and generous retirement plans for her employees. Neither would she have played Tori, Nina Simone, Me'Shell, Shonen Knife, Sinéad and Yma Sumac over the factory loudspeakers to boost morale, meanwhile revolutionizing the advertising industry's image of women and children with her sheer buying power.

Good businesswomen just don't take risks like that.

So let's, shall we, define risk:

*A maneuver which has neither a past
nor a guaranteeable future
generating profits
is a risk.*

It's a risk for women to run the show because the show was designed to be run by an elite group of white men.

Women will never be an elite group of white men, so the show was not designed to be run by us.

Deedle dee doo, Catch-22.

When I feel defeated or frustrated or just dang upset because there is simply no sidestepping this shitty reality, I sometimes call my sister. She says, "Count your blessings, ya' lucky hooker. Don't be bitter. Your face gets all ugly when you're bitter."

I represent maybe .0001 percent of cuntlovin' ladies throughout history who have been and continue to be bored to death with the plights of this reality.

Sometimes though, I *feel* like being bitter because I wake up in the morning and just have to face the fact that within this economic model, *it makes perfect sense* for Kevin Costner to spend more money on a single, fully lunkheaded movie that contributes absolutely nothing to society than the entire nation of El Salvador sees in one year.

My face gets all ugly and I call my sister and she reminds me I'm a lucky hooker when I think about the multitudes of women who are creating desperately needed and appreciated products that have no *physical place* within the capitalist, patriarchal economic model and—like women artists—struggle to prove our *existence* long before advancing upon the struggle to *survive.*

I work with a woman named Kathleen Gasperini who publishes *W.I.G.* (Women in General) magazine. *W.I.G.* is focused on giving women a place to write about our fabulous lives and adventures living them, the music and sports that move us, our poetry and stories, interviews with other women living their fabulous lives and our battles with cancer, violence, poverty, racial and sexual hatred, drugs and/or eating disorders.

Ms. Gasperini has a difficult time finding investors because her magazine does not reflect standard "women's interests" found in other culturally accepted "women's magazines."

Here is what potential investors say to Ms. Gasperini, "There's no section for your magazine in the stores. It can't be in the sports section. It's not just about fitness and health. Neither is it for new mothers, brides-to-be, lesbians or feminists. If you focused more on fashion and make-up, we'd be happy to invest because then we'd know how to market it and people would know where to find it."

The fact that *W.I.G.* is one of a handful of like-minded, brilliant magazines—*Bitch, Bust* and *Hues* come readily to mind—doesn't seem to inspire any thoughts about a market of consumers who represent an acute demand for what these magazines supply.

Once upon a time, Kathleen Gasperini spent two months begging her printers to be patient for the money she owed them, as a gentleman who runs a major magazine publishing company had expressed an interest in investing in *W.I.G.* Week after week they played phone tag, Kathleen's heart lodged in her throat.

When she finally met with him, he had the following nugget of inspiration to impart:

"You are the wrong gender for what we are focusing on at this time. The market is going crazy for young men right now."

Circulation for the first issue of *W.I.G.* was five thousand.

Circulation for *W.I.G.*'s fourth issue was fifty thousand.

For a market that does not exist, fifty thousand consumers is a pretty heady figure, considering *W.I.G.* sales are dependent upon word of mouth in lieu of national advertising and promotion. Stores do not have a section for magazines such as *W.I.G.* because it is by, for and about women, on our terms.

Our culture does not provide a place for that.

There is—*literally*—no place for products of this kind.

A small amount of research in American history illuminates how just about every "right" and "freedom" people of color and white women achieved was the result of economics. The Civil War was not about compassion and decency, it was about real estate. The alleged "rights" of "land settlements bestowed" upon Native tribes are also real estate. Granting white women and people of color the "right" to vote was about creating a class of peon workers who were less able to grumble over the poor pay and working conditions when they had such a glorious "right" as casting ballots that placed a variety of white men in office.

Hoop dee doo.

In our society's time-tested economic model, men make and women consume. Our fingernail polishes, snowboards, vacuum cleaners, computers, clothes—pretty much most of our stuff— was manufactured by male-dominated and -owned companies. Utilities and credit card companies claim yet another portion of our income for the male producers that make stuff for us ladies.

Accordingly, one of our most promising stakes of power is our indisputed role as consumers.

As consumers, we exist.

This is a resource that is presently part of our reality.

Exploit the fuck out of it.

Cuntlovin' Consumerism

Time and money are power.

Conscious decision-making about the expenditure of both nourishes a market that is somehow considered "fledgling," although it represents 51 percent of the population.

Many phallocentric religious organizations, from the Promise Keepers to the Church of Latter Day Saints heartily extol the benefits of keeping money in the community of the brethren.

Patriarchal society never has to bother preaching the benefits of keeping the money with the men because, at present, there's no place else for it to go.

In the marketplace of the patriarchy, the "competition" tends to be people living in Mexican, Latin American, South African and Southeast Asian communities (often referred to as "guerrilla terrorists"), fighting for the right to live on the planet with an identity other than that of expendable factory worker-slaves.

It sounds *terribly* ideological to say women's power as consumers is a major economic stronghold, but it seems the most promising strategy that does not involve retreat.

Cuntlovin' Consumerism is a matter of research and potential inconvenience.

It requires no thought to amble to the Mega Food-O-Rama and buy a name-brand loaf of bread. Finding a bakery in your community that is owned by a woman struggling to bring up three children by herself may take a bit of phone work. Because this baker does not produce and distribute on the massive scale of Wonder Bread, her product will be of higher quality and nutritional value, but it may also be more expensive.

Cuntlovin' Consumerism is a matter of common sense.

When it becomes the custom to visit only women gyne-cologists, naturopaths and midwives, the clientele of male doctors will fluctuate precariously, and cuntcare will eventu-ally become the sole women-dominated field in the medical industry outside nursing.

Cuntlovin' Consumerism is a matter of commitment.

The only women-owned bookstore you know of is twenty-five miles away from your house. Once a month, you and your friends make a special trip to this store instead of bopping into the local Mega-Book-O-Rama whenever you happen upon disposable income.

Try this experimental test.

You will need a sheet of gold stars to conduct it properly.

Stand in the middle of your kitchen. Scan every single appliance, work of art, food product, fixture and piece of furniture in the room. Place everything in one of three categories:

1. Definitely/probably produced by women or a woman-run corporation.
2. You aren't sure.
3. Definitely/probably produced by men or a male-run corporation.

Every time your vision rests upon something that falls into category #1, put a gold star on it. After you have perused the contents of every cupboard and drawer, count up the number of gold stars.

Unless you have already researched the matter and actively

c
u
n
t

sought out products made by women, your kitchen will not be very golden starry.

Conduct this experiment in every room of your house.

Now, live your life from this day forward with the objective of filling your home with as many gold stars as possible.

The day you got gold stars on most all of your stuff will be the last day of the patriarchal age as far you, the consumer, are concerned.

Cuntlovin' Investment Portfolio

An investment is a portion of capital (money or time) that is spent now for bigger, better results later.

There are a number of different kinds of investments.

One is the personal investment. This is where you buy a coffee maker that you set before you go to bed, so that in the morning, you will have time to do yoga, which in turn, centers you for the day ahead and subsequently helps you make optimal decisions that improve the quality of your life day by day.

Another investment is the pain-in-the-ass-job investment. This is where you sacrifice X amount of time each and every week Whoring yourself at some meaningless job in order to finance your life so you can, say, finish your book.

Yet another kind of investment, the kind we're concerned with here, is a group investment. This involves getting your women friends or family members together and figuring out how much capital you have, collectively, to invest.

First you determine how much time you have to invest in your investment group.

Then you figure out money and resources.

If each of you has five dollars, and there are ten of you, that is fifty dollars. *The amount of money you have is not important.* What *is* important is how you answer the following question:

How can we make this fifty dollars into one hundred dollars?

This is the beginning of a Cuntlovin' Investment Portfolio.

The best way to have a productive investment group is to exploit the resources you already have available to you, rather than expending energy looking for the resources you imagine are necessary. I'm gonna say this again in a few moments because it's a fundamental rule here.

Perhaps two women in your group are seamstresses, one has an industrial sewing machine in her closet, another inherited a garage full of fabric from her great-grandmother, you happen to be a genius at computer design and the remaining three are very talented songwriters and musicians.

Hmmmm.

Seems like the eight of you should be able to bring all those things together in a lucrative manner.

How?

I haven't the faintest clue.

That is where the brilliance of your investment group comes in.

An investment group meets on a regular basis and focuses energy on the process of making collective capital experience gains.

Your group may decide to start a business, play the women-owned companies that have gone public on the stock market, present an investment proposal to your local woman-run record company, have bake sales or throw huge, elaborately themed parties where you charge people to get in.

Once again, I underscore the following: The challenge for an investment group is exploiting the resources you have readily available. This yields *much better results* than agonizing over how to make something out of a good, but presently inaccessible idea.

When an investment group gets enough capital, it pays dividends to the group's members, which helps improve the quality of life; it re-invests or loans money to woman-run businesses or production companies; it starts a scholarship fund or buys an entire city block to provide housing to young women athletes, scholars and artists who are fighting like the devil to survive and fulfill dreams at the same time.

Time and money are power.

When women pro-actively seize both, we take power.

Every iota of power women claim and use to the advantage of our sisters brings the destructive patriarchal age that much closer to its timely, timely, timely end.

It has been a long time, but the Goddess is waking up from her nap.

She's yawning, stretching her muscles and scratching her big beautiful butt. Rest assured, the Goddess has a thing or two to say about man as the maker. When the Goddess gets the sleep out of her eyes, I daresay my face won't have many opportunities to get all ugly about cultural atrocities like Kevin Costner movies.

But my sister will probably always remind me I'm a lucky hooker.

P.S.
You're a Big Cunt now.
You find out who Mammon is.

reconciliation

Who the Old Woman with Black Eyeballs that Swallow You in Love Is

the end

The end of this book came to me in a message from an old woman in a dream. What follows is a verbatim account of this dream, written in my journal directly after waking up.

In Dream that woke me up.

I am a thirteen-or-so-year-old Latino boy. I am freaking out in some room that feels like a place where the community gathers, but it's not a church. I—the young boy—am angry beyond orange, beyond red, beyond white. People are futilely trying to physically restrain me. Some white men have served an unnamed injustice to my people. *Mi familia.* I want to kill. I want their blood to stain my hands. I want to pull their hearts from their chests. No one can control me.

An old woman walks into the room. All attention falls upon her. I feel her black eyes bore into my being, but still, I thrash and fight to get to the white men, outside the place where I am.

The old woman walks directly up to me. She takes my wrists in her hands, and my strength—which has defied every woman, child and man in the room—is useless against her.

Holding my wrists, she gently brings my arms down to my sides and begins to cry, oh, she cries from the depths of every soul that has ever graced this planet.

Through her tears, she calmly, soothingly whispers, "Don't you know, don't you know, only our stories can fight against these men. Only our words. You must say, 'Excuse me, sir, but I would like to tell you this story about my grandmother.' And the man will listen, our words will enter his heart, and kill his power from the inside."

She stares into me.

"Only our stories. Only our words."

She continues crying as she says all this, she is crying for ancestors, for grandchildren, for all the civilizations which have been decimated.

Her crying is in my body.

My sleeping, dreaming body.

Her crying storms through the core of my heart. Her crying, *the feeling*, not the sound, her crying wakes me up.

There are no tears on my face.

Her crying is inside me.

This is the message from the old woman with black eyeballs that swallow you in love and make you understand there is nothing to fear.

r
e
c
o
n
c
i
l
i
a
t
i
o
n

231

c
u
n
t

Blessed Be.
Grandmother.
Cunt.

afterword

It's been almost a decade since I first set out to write this book, and I am honored and thankful that a second edition is in order.

Fucken rad.

Writing a book called *Cunt* is a very odd experience.

Just today I was laughing about how I always get emails with subject headings like "My Big Cunt" and "Northern Whores." I make wagers with myself about whether or not they're spam porn.

Like the two above, they're often not.

While working on this book, my world was two things: writing and surviving. It took three years to write *Cunt*. I estimate I spent a year and a half actually working on the book. The other year and a half was devoted to survival—in this case, finding and getting fired from jobs every three or four months.

After *Cunt* came out, I was totally ecstatic, depressed and confused. What is one supposed to *do* after their first book is published?

Thankfully, right around this time, I interviewed Dorothy Allison for *Bust* magazine. I asked her what she did after *Bastard Out of Carolina* hit the streets. She told me that her press had socked away three thousand dollars for book promotion, and

planned to spend the whole wad on an ad in some fancy
newspaper. Dorothy told them, essentially, "*My ass* are you
gonna spend three grand on one ad," and used the money to go
on a national tour.

"Honey," Dorothy said, "you need to get out there and
promote that book."

So I, Miss Genetically Logistically Impaired, planned a
national tour. Besides challenges engendered by thinking, say,
Chicago is "on the east coast," I also had not one red cent.

But I am a Taurus, and when you are a Taurus, you just
forge ahead and do things anyway. Continuing to get fired from
jobs, with all my stuff in storage and living with friends, I put
together a tour.

The money eventually, miraculously, showed up.

Yes, a month before the first scheduled reading, my friend
Cedric Ross handed me a theretofore hypothetical—even
mythical—check. I cried a bucket when he gave me that piece
of paper. This act of kindness will awe me for the rest of my
days.

Cedric, thank you.

In one of the most striking ironies of my life, by the time I left
for tour in the fall of 1999, my self-esteem was lower than it had
been since pre-adolescence, and I found myself in rooms full of
people who thought I had done something wonderful.

This was bewildering, to say the least.

I had hoped that people would like my book, but I had no
idea what it *would mean*. I had no experience going to strange

cities and sitting in (locally owned, independent) bookstores surrounded by people who knew intimate details of my life and so shared with me intimate details of theirs. I had no experience signing books. Most of all, I had no experience taking responsibility for putting something in the world that wasn't there before.

When my sister had a baby last year, her humility, anguish and joy resonated deep in my heart.

A book is not a baby, but also, it is.

I have learned many things from the experience of writing a book called *Cunt*.

There is a part of myself that positively itches to insert new paragraphs, edit whole sections and otherwise "update" the original text of this book.

One of the things I have learned, however, is that *Cunt* is a spirit that came through me. Though it may sound strange for the author of a book to say this—I believe I have no right to tamper with it.

I love this book and I don't want to change it, but I have changed and things have changed.

So here are some changes.

Women With Dicks, Men With Cunts

When the general public asks me what *Cunt* is about, I used to say, "It's a women's studies book," and change the subject. By the "general public" I mean those who unquestioningly exist in a culture of consumerism, the teevee and denial. Most folks of this stripe aren't attracted to the ideas in my book, so I don't see much point in engaging about it.

Upton Sinclair said, "It is difficult to get a man to understand something when his salary depends on his not understanding it."

(Forgive him the male-centered language; Sinclair never saw the likes of Katherine Harris, Gale Norton and Condoleezza Rice in action.)

I study occupational vocabularies so I can convincingly fabricate an identity when I am in social situations (like weddings) where the fucken annoying question, "And what do *you* do?" is likely to come up.

Lately, I've been an underwater welder and a cake designer.

Don't get me wrong.

I'm not a reticent person. It's just that the corporate work ethic has completely infiltrated U.S. culture and created a pathologically unhealthy atmosphere for self-actualization and open-mindedness. I'll talk a blue streak with self-actualized/open-minded folks. I can spot a self-actualized person from a mile away, and have gotten into breathtakingly beautiful cunt-versations with open-minded cowboys and marines.

Once I was in Flagstaff and my buddy Dawn Kish asked some friends of hers if they had read a book called *Cunt.* One of them, a man, kinda chuckled and said, "No. What's it about?"

Without missing a beat or even looking askance at me, she said, "Freedom."

I was delighted. Dawn inadvertently provided me with something to say to members of the general public who manage to find out I wrote a book called *Cunt*.

So, freedom.

The all-purpose, common-denominator, one-word synopsis of *Cunt* that I like best. *Cunt* is a product of my freedom and my need to be in a free world with free people.

Cunt spoke of freedom to a young woman I met in Virginia who'd recently been raped and found out she was pregnant. She happened to be reading *Cunt* when she got the test results back, and subsequently induced a miscarriage. Affecting her destiny in such a powerful way helped her to survive and thrive after being sexually assaulted.

It spoke of freedom to the two women who opened Ruby's Pearl, a woman-positive sex store in Iowa City. Not long after reading *Cunt*, Lauren Crassley, Kymbyrly Koester and her baby Vivian took stock of their economic realities and their community. Ruby's Pearl is the result of bringing these factors together.

Cunt spoke of freedom to the wealthy patriarch who came to a reading in Texas and asked me to sign copies for his wife, his daughters and all of his grandchildren.

It speaks of freedom to bookstore employees all over the country who take great joy in asking if there are any *Cunt*s in stock over the in-house PA system.

I lived in a small town for the first nineteen years of my life, and I was not free there. It was no secret to me. Towns like

Santa Maria are tried and true petri dishes for cultivating incredibly oppressed adolescents.

When I was growing up, "feminism" and "vegetarianism" shared similar, extremely peripheral roles. I could probably have given you a definition for both terms, but it never occurred to me that "feminism" and "vegetarianism" were *actual realities* that happened in the lives of *actual people.* I had absolutely no experience with either term until I was almost twenty years old, when people started calling me a "feminist" and I found out how grocery store chickens die.

As a teenager, I had one, and I mean ONE resource informing me that there existed sound-assed reasons for feeling imprisoned in my community—an album called "Penis Envy" by the U.K. band, Crass.

It was, evidently, enough to kick-start a life of political resistance which shows no signs of petering out, but really, "Penis Envy" was all I had. The end. Nothing else.

Crass is a social movement/band of vegan anarchist punks who created their own record label, a community center/school and other such amenities in the early era of the punk movement. "Penis Envy" sent me scurrying to the dictionary, puzzling together phrases like "rituals of repression." I listened to that album every day, over and over.

Loudly.

In my room with the door closed, but thudding.

How does one go from being a pissed-off little punk rocker holed up in her bedroom to being a pissed-off writer who gets to experience fucken rad things like freedom?

It's a long process. I live in flux. Nothing stays the same here.

By the time I sat down to write *Cunt,* I was at a point where I'd read a lot of books, interviewed a lot of people, written poems, songs, articles and stories, and, *crucially,* had almost ten years experiencing life in communities where women were, for example, on stages talking/singing/rapping serious-assed shit and starting night patrols to see people home safely. I was sick of being pigeonholed as a "feminist" just because I asserted myself. I was also angry about the prevalence of and ambivalence towards sexual assault (among many other things). I wanted to write a book that could, feasibly, speak of freedom to all girls and women.

And—in my wildest dreams—to boys and men as well.

What I did not consider—and this is totally a result of my socialization—is that the world is made up of more than women and men, boys and girls. In writing *Cunt,* I completely overlooked the realities of gender-variant people.

This was brought to my attention a year after *Cunt* came out.

At the 1999 Michigan Womyn's Music Festival, issues of transgender inclusion exploded within the queer community. As the story goes, some trannyladies attended the festival that year, thus defying the festival's "Womyn Born Womyn" policy.

While one of the "trans-gressors" was taking a shower, other festival attendees saw her dick and people freaked out and started running around screaming "There are PENISES on The Land!!!"

(I am not making this up.)

A few months after this brouhaha, I started being questioned about what my "position" on trans-inclusion was. In particular, some readers had problems with the sentence, "All women have cunts," which appeared in the introduction to the first edition and led many trans-folks to feel expressly (and rightfully) excluded from *Cunt*.

The events in Michigan set off a firestorm, and I was pressured to defend my book in ways I'd never anticipated. I was confused—kicking myself for inadvertently alienating an entire sector of humanity, and at the same time, being patient because learning never ends.

Learning is endless.

A woman named Zabrina Aleguire from the wonderful land of North Carolina wrote me a long, incredibly intelligent email about gender and trans-inclusion.

Here is an excerpt:

Dear Inga,

Tearing through your book "Cunt" was incredible for me——an experience I've wanted to share with many other gals. . . . I'd like to thank you for helping me get back in touch with my body, my passion, my silliness and my fighting feminism. Your book helped inspire me and some other cunt-lovin women to resurrect women's health and art collectives, in the tradition of groups like Magical Pussy from Chapel Hill.

In addition to letting you know how much your words have inspired, ignited and entertained me and my friends, I want to share some thoughts about an omission from Cunt. What I'm talking about is transgender identity and gender nonconformity. In the intro to the book I was stopped short by the words "womankind is varied and vast. But we all have cunts."

Do we? I thought. Aren't there women without cunts? Or, what about the tranny boys in my life who have cunts but don't consider themselves women—despite years of assigned female gender? I wanted their inclusion in this declaration of independence, this feminist manifesto. And yet, "the anatomical jewel which unites us all" and "the only common denominator . . . that all women irrefutably share" didn't seem to imply that room for inclusion. . . .

I'll tell you about my experience being a bridesmaid in my friend's huge country-club, limousine-princess, "you don't want to know how much I paid for this gown" wedding. It was the first wedding I'd been to since coming out the year before and subsisting on a really small salary doing queer activist work. By the time we reached the reception, I was feeling so strange amongst the wealth and heterosexism that I was almost physically ill. But I burst into a smile when I saw our waitress Joy. Noticeably a male-to-female trans-woman, Joy had short hair, a bunch of earrings, long press-on nails and a long, pleated black skirt. She was our headwaiter for the wedding party table, and I felt relieved and a little less isolated to know I wasn't the only queer in the ballroom.

Then other guests noticed her. Little cousins and the groomsmen began whispering, pointing and asking, "Is it a boy? Is it a girl?" Then she became a snicker, a joke, a snide remark. Some were "weirded out." Some were "appalled." Some were "disgusted." Toward the end of the evening the intoxicated matron of honor, Cynthia, exploded, "I don't know what the hell he's doing! I'm gonna call him George. Why does he call himself Joy? It must give him joy to wear a skirt." She spat her words: "He's sick!...That man/woman whatever." I stood by stunned and pissed off by such a venomous diatribe against Joy, who was quite lovely—and a helluva good waiter at that. Looking back I wish I had asked Cynthia what made her so angry. Instead, I have just been wondering the question on my own since. . . .

My guess is that Cynthia was feeling it that weekend——the pressure of conformity. Compared to the bride, nothing about herself must have felt good enough——not her house, her car, her job, her husband, her family, her appearance. Damn, I was feeling it too—— inadequacy, comparison, even shame. And there was Joy, intentionally, blatantly not conforming in an environment where Cynthia required it of herself and doubted her own worth among the wealth, beauty and (perceived) acceptance of those around her. This experience illustrated to me how we stick to gender conformity as strongly as, if not stronger than, any other norms. We get hell when we——as women or men or trans or androgynous people——diverge from those norms. It's in these moments that I see how tightly feminism, queer and trans liberation are connected.

Our culture's stringent male/female gender codes are inextricably linked to our oppression as women, our materialistic capitalist culture, and the rigidity and denial of self-expression that is characteristic of white people (particularly those holding on to significant power). We are culturally accepted and even celebrated if we stay within established power differentiation. That's how Cynthia gets hers—being a seasoned hetero beauty. That makes her "better" than people like Joy. How dare Joy challenge the system that Cynthia knows deep down has gotten her at least somewhere, with a husband, a sorority membership for life and a home of her own away from that crowded middle-class house of her childhood in the Midwest.

In my mind it makes sense for feminists and progressive transgender folks to be united——and in many of our communities this is the case. But there is still such serious division, as we see from the Michigan Womyn's Festival. I think it's work like yours that can help bridge this division. Clearly there needs to be more challenge put to feminist communities who don't acknowledge trans-identity as authentic, as well as to transgender communities who don't engage with gender privilege and oppression. From what I have observed, your ability to inspire cuntlove in so many people makes me think that you can really help this effort. I look forward to hearing back from you. In solidarity,
Zabrina Aleguire

I feel really blessed that such an incredibly smart person would take time out of her life to write me such a beautifully articulated letter.

Thank you, Zabrina.

This multifaceted issue raised a lot of questions in my heart.

I called my friend Lynnee Breedlove, a woman who—as lead singer for the band Tribe 8—has had her dick sucked on stage by hundreds of people. This surely merits an entry in the Guinness Book of World Records by anyone's standards except for, evidently, the people at Guinness.

Anyway, I needed answers and Lynnee is a person who often has good ones.

And she did, but not like how I thought her answers might go.

She said:

"It's question time, pal. It's not a time for answers. It's a time for questions."

This was one of those moments where gold lamé banners unfurl from the sky in my mind and trumpets blare in the dawn's early light of my consciousness and I say, "Oh. But of course."

Question time.

What if someone who was born a "boy" feels like a "girl" almost always?

If s/he dates girls, is s/he heterosexual or homosexual?

What if someone who was born a "girl" feels like a "boy" five months out of the year like clockwork?

If s/he dates girls is s/he bisexual?

What if someone who grew up to be a "man" felt like being *more* than a woman every Friday night at the local cabaret?

What if this "man" was happily married to a woman and had three kids?

What if this "man" was happily married to a man and had three kids?

What if someone who grew up to be a woman felt like being a man when she went out for solo nights on the town?

What if, as this man, she developed an endearingly cantankerous personality? And what if she loved this personality and loved having two completely different sides of herself that she manifested through changes in dress, thinking, environment and comportment?

What if a kid felt completely NOT the specific gender that society assigned him/her throughout life, and so decided to get an operation or take hormones when s/he grew up so that his/her physical appearance would mirror the self-image s/he holds dearest to his/her heart?

What is wrong with any of this?

What, exactly, does it mean to be a "woman?"

What, exactly, does it mean to be a "man?"

Why shouldn't one's gender be as fluid as one's life should be, if it's a happy life, I mean.

If it's a life where freedom happens.

I wrote *Cunt* from my experience as a white woman who grew up on the west coast of the U.S.A. in a working-class single-parent home. I grew up in a culture that hates cunts, hates women, hates everybody who isn't white and/or white-identified and hates all of us over here in what Eddie Murphy and I lovingly refer to as "the faggot section." (*Eddie Murphy: Comedian,* 1983)

When I found out that the word "cunt" once held emphatically non-derogatory meanings in cultures all over the world, I saw this huge link in the way both women and this word have been denigrated over time. It took *thousands of years* to get women to believe we were such silly things as "the weaker sex." I was seeking freedom from this history for myself and for everyone who is afflicted with it. My experience of being a woman was, and is, greatly influenced by my cunt: a maligned part of my body that bleeds, that can be raped, that was the focal point of two harrowing vacuum abortions; a cunt that produces grand, smashing orgasms.

I never thought my cunt was what *made me a woman,* but I knew that many of my experiences as a woman were (and continue to be) centered around my cunt.

I considered defying society's prescription for how we treat our bodies to be a revolutionary act of nonconformity. It is *political resistance* to learn self-protection, to masturbate, to fuck whomever you want, to take control of your body's functions and fluids. All of these things are in direct opposition to how society deems we should act and feel. I still believe this with all my heart, but in the last few years, I've been inspired to think about gender variance in a broader context. This has really shaken up my whole notion of how I perceive the world—and my book.

As a child, I took umbrage against being repeatedly told I was "such a pretty little girl until you open your mouth," but I was also perfectly content doing things little girls weren't "supposed" to do, such as fighting, cussing and challenging my teachers. Through all of this, though, I never felt a conflict about my assigned gender.

I knew I wasn't like the "good" girls at my school who cried if you hit them with a muddy dodge ball. I knew I was a "bad," "loud" and "aggressive" girl.

But still, a girl.

Before people started asking me about trans-inclusion, I simply took it for granted that I was a biological woman. When I stopped to think about it on a daily basis, however, I seldom consciously think, "I am a woman." I am most often aware that I am a woman when I feel threatened, or when someone— through actions, body language or words—points out that I am a woman.

When I am riding my skateboard late at night and see a group of (potentially drunk, repressed and sexually frustrated) men outside a bar on the sidewalk, I feel like a woman. I am faced with a number of choices, all based on survival. Should I cross the street? Should I yell, "Coming through, fellas!" and plow forward? Should I turn back and go around the block before they notice me? Should I hop off into the street and coast around them?

At decision-making times like these, I am acutely aware of being a woman.

When I am in the airport and a security person hollers, "FEMALE," so I can be wanded, I feel like a woman.

When I am on my period and aggressively shun loud-mouthed men and their radio stations, I feel like a woman.

In the final analysis, I think of myself as *a woman* only in specific circumstances.

The rest of the time I am just me.

Me, asking questions.

Me, in flux.

Isn't this the same for most people?

I mean, when you stop to think about it.

Whenever I go to the Midwest I feel very comfortable because I always think I am surrounded by dykes. To me, women in the Midwest are much sturdier and more assertive than women in other regions of the U.S. I know it is irrational for me to feel this way, but I am presently conditioned to view dykes as sturdier and more assertive than everyone else. This is not to say that I don't know a lot of kickass straight ladies and prissy lesbians, but in general, queer women are not people one wants to tangle with. Same with women in the Midwest. Hence, my comfort level rises there. Does this mean that women in the Midwest challenge gender roles more than women in other places?

No.

It means my perception of gender is in flux and affected by context.

In my experience, there is a certain demographic of gay men who are obsessive about their appearance, endlessly yap into cell phones and walk around like they are very, very busy, all, all, all the time. Subsequently, in Los Angeles, I often make the mistake of assuming straight men are this specific kind of flaming gay man. I am conditioned to perceive a certain kinda guy as a certain kinda gay, and I see this guy all over LA. In any other part of the country, he probably *is* gay, but in LA he is likely an ardent heterosexual.

Does this mean that men in Los Angeles challenge gender roles more than men in other cities?

Fucken, fuck no.

It means my perception is in flux and affected by context.

Everybody's perception is in flux and affected by context.

Gender is fluid and gender norms vary fantastically.

So when we talk about gender, we are all talking about something endlessly fractalized and fascinating to say the least.

I was born a woman and I live as a woman. In certain contexts, I deal with prejudice because I do not conform to what a woman "should" look like. I don't shave very often. I keep my fingernails clipped shorty short. I ride a skateboard. I often wear what many consider to be "men's" clothes and footwear. All of this is subtly—and not so subtly—unacceptable to many people.

In general heterosexual society, I sometimes feel ill at ease, but no one gawks at me or says stuff like "What are you?"

In the queer community, I am more or less a plain jane, a runna-the-mill white dyke who shops at thrift stores.

This has led me to wonder what it would be like to be treated by the queer community the way blindly heterosexual society treats me. What if I didn't conform to gender norms upheld by the queer community?

Well, a coupla things have given me some insights on what my life might be like.

The death of Sylvia Rivera led me to some pretty ugly aspects of history.

According to legend, Ms. Rivera was known as the person who instigated the Stonewall riots in New York City. This is something of a myth, but I like tall tales.

They say that when the cops raided the famous Stonewall Inn in June of 1969, Ms. Rivera threw a brick/her shoes/a bottle at them, thus inciting what would become a nationwide fight for queer—but, as we shall see, not tranny—rights.

What really happened is she, along with the whole crowd, reached critical mass and everyone got sick of the same fucking brutalization at the hands of the NYPD at the exact same time.

After Stonewall, she went on to become this huge activist and revolutionary. Along with Marsha P. Johnson and Angela Keyes Douglas, she was pivotal in organizing the Gay Liberation Front (GLF) and the Gay Activists Alliance (GAA). In 1970, she and Ms. Johnson started an organization called STAR (Street Transvestite Action Revolutionaries).

It kinda pissed me off that I never heard of any of these truly heroic women until I got five or so emails telling me that Sylvia Rivera had died. (Peacefully, in the hospital, surrounded by loved ones.)

I searched her name on Google and ended up at transhistory.org.

Here I learned that Ms. Rivera—a tireless crusader for queer and tranny rights—*lived on a fucking wharf* in New York City for a year and a half because she was also a crack addict and Rudy Giuliani's administration rendered her (and many others) homeless. During this time, Marsha P. Johnson was murdered. Her body was found in the Hudson and the police, insisting she committed suicide, refused to open any kind of investigation. Marsha P. Johnson was Sylvia Rivera's mentor and best friend. As far as I can find, the gay and lesbian community offered absolutely no support in pressuring the NYPD to open an investigation in her death.

For the rest of her life, Sylvia Rivera would wear a button photo of Ms. Johnson on her outer garments.

I do not doubt that she was murdered because her loved ones said she was not suicidal, she left no note, she was on her way home from the 1992 Pride March in NYC, and murder seems to be a pretty common way to die when you are transgendered.

For instance, on June 20, 2000, it was widely reported that cabbies and street vendors *cheered* while witnessing the brutal stabbing murder of 25-year-old Amanda Milan in front of the Port Authority Bus Terminal. Though there was no way for the police to claim Ms. Milan killed herself, newspapers (such as the *New York Times*) nevertheless served her the profound post-mortem injustice by reporting that, "A man was fatally stabbed in Midtown Manhattan yesterday after a dispute with two other men, the authorities said......The victim...was found on the sidewalk...dressed in women's clothing and stabbed once in the neck."

If you look up some photos of the stunningly gorgeous Ms. Milan, you will see that it would require an entirely deluded stretch of imagination to mistake her for a "man."

Six months prior to her death, one of Ms. Milan's dearest friends, Simone, died after being thrown from a five story window in San Francisco. Two years before that, their friend, Kim, who rounded out this triumvirate of soulmates, was found mangled beyond recognition at the bottom of a cliff in Australia.

She was identified by the serial number of her breast implants.

Do a web search. Google will give you 9,080 hits for "transgender murder."

I have a very difficult time believing Marsha P. Johnson decided to end her life by drowning herself in the Hudson River, no matter what the NYPD says.

Here's the part where I got really, really pissed off:

I found out that, as a queer biological woman, I inherited a part in a legacy of totally shunning and despising people like Sylvia Rivera and Marsha P. Johnson. It seems that in the 1970s, feminists, lesbians and gay men were vociferously intolerant toward transgendered people. Before founding STAR, Sylvia Rivera and Marsha P. Johnson were edged out of the GLF, an organization that they had been *instrumental* in forming. In a

stunning betrayal, the GAA wrote an anti-discrimination bill to
the New York City Council, that excluded transgendered people.

Being totally, totally shafted by a community that you
poured *all your activist genius into* would be incredibly heart
breaking.

It seems to me that everyone in the queer community has a
bit of accountability to face up to here. I truly believe that if Ms.
Rivera and Ms. Johnson were accepted, respected and supported for the work they were doing (and continued to do,
despite setbacks like micro-marginalization within a
marginalized community, poverty and homelessness), it is
possible that both of them would be alive today, helping
younger generations learn how to fight and kick ass and stand
up for ourselves.

Due to our own ignorance, fear and prejudice, we have
probably lost many leaders of this caliber.

Another woman who fell prey to trans-exclusion was a recording
engineer at Olivia Records. In 1977, Sandy Stone was one of the
most brilliant recording geniuses in the business, and Olivia
Records was an all-women recording studio. They were poised
to turn a profit for the first time that year, but a bunch of
separatist types (which comprised a very vocal demographic in
the 1970's women's movement) found out that Sandy Stone was
transgendered, and threatened to boycott Olivia Records. The
record company reluctantly fired Ms. Stone.

This story is notably ironic:

During the 1999 Michigan Womyn's Music Festival, a rumor somehow got out that members of the Butchies supported trans-inclusion while also respecting the Michigan Womyn's Music Festival's policy that only "womyn born womyn" attend this yearly event.

This led to a nationwide trans-activist boycott of the Butchies, and all other bands on the Mr. Lady record label. (Although, I must say, I don't see how punishing Mr. Lady for the MWMF's policy is fair. Wouldn't this reasonably lead to a boycott of every band, performer and organization that attends the festival?)

I think it is very interesting that twenty-odd years after one women's record company was boycotted for *including* trans-women on their staff, another women's record company was boycotted for honoring a festival's policy that *excludes* trans-folks.

That seems like 360 degrees to me, so it's time to start another chapter of history—one that is totally trans-inclusive.

The reason I didn't know about Sandy Stone, Sylvia Rivera, Marsha P. Johnson or any of these women is that they've been airbrushed out of queer, feminist and U.S. history. To find out about them, one has to research *transgender* history. (And I highly suggest you do so, by starting off at transhistory.org. Many thanks to Kay Brown for putting up this wonderful site.)

This answered the biggest question I was asking when I started getting my "trans-inclusion position" email queries: why *did* I exclude an entire sector of the population when I was supposed to be writing a book about freedom for all?

The answer is, simply, I didn't know.

And why didn't I know? Why did an avid reader like myself never come across references to trans-history?

For the exact same reason that "feminism" and "vegetarianism" were peripheral to my life in Santa Maria, California: it's not—or at least, when I was writing *Cunt,* it wasn't—a topic that came up much.

It's, uh, excluded.

The identities, realities, experiences, accomplishments and history of transgendered folks are not acknowledged in the marginalized cultures of queers and feminists, and are pathologically feared in the "general" culture of the United States.

Time after time, in its effort to appear "normal" to blindly heterosexual society and thereby gain "equal rights," the queer community has kicked its own in the ass. Tranny folks have been the lightning rod for straight *and* queer wrath because they shake up ideas about—to paraphrase a talk-radio windbag—the way things oughta be. Like Cynthia in Zabrina's wedding experience, if you can't put someone in an easily identified box, then how do you know where *you* fit in?

Margaret Cho said something wonderful in the June 2002 issue of *Lesbian News* in an interview with Kathleen Wilkinson: "If you are a woman, if you are a person of color, if you are gay, lesbian, bisexual or transgender, if you are a person of size, if you are a person of intelligence, if you are a person of integrity, then *you* are considered a minority in this world." Margaret Cho is always saying wonderful things.

I would like to mention here that most of the people who have challenged me about tranny rights have been white. I am not aware of the ways in which race factored into Ms. Rivera and Ms. Johnson's exclusion in the queer community (both were women of color). I do not doubt, however, that it did indeed factor in.

For the past three years, I have been working on *Autobiography of a Blue-Eyed Devil,* a book which deals with race and whiteness. I have had many conversations with many, many people about how the white queer community exoticizes, marginalizes and stereotypes queers and trannies of color. I am not paying lip service to racial complexities by mentioning this. The infernally kaleidoscopic nature of race and the perception of race is confounding, to say the least. Rather, I would like white trans-activists to look at how they themselves may perpetuate ideas of exclusion and "otherness" by taking whiteness for granted.

I don't know how anybody—trannyfolks, queers of all colors, people of color, white women, feminists, fags, retirees, farmers, workers, really, I could go on—can stand around with our heads up our asses, expecting rights to be handed to us on a silver platter, when we are so terribly busy oppressing as we are oppressed.

But this is, like I say, a subject for a book.

Throughout the annals of queer and feminist history, transgendered folks have been misrepresented, feared and marginalized to the point of perceived non-existence.

Through dialogue, grassroots efforts and legislation, trans-exclusion seems to be on its way out the door.

On April 30, 2002, the New York City Council amended the city's Human Rights Law to include transgendered people. Thirty-one years after the GAA royally shafted Sylvia Rivera, Marsha P. Johnson and Angela Keyes Douglas, transgendered people have the same rights to housing, jobs, benefits and justice as everyone else in New York City. Similar laws have been enacted in Minnesota and Rhode Island, as well as thirty-seven other cities and two counties in the U.S.

Unfortunately, on the state level in New York, a law that will probably be passed this year called the Sexual Orientation Non-discrimination Act (SONDA) does not include transgendered people:

"The decision of state legislators and the Empire State Pride Agenda not to include transgender people is a real loss," said [Paisley] Currah, who was part of the legislative task force for the New York City bill and has extensively researched and written on transgender rights legislation. "When the leading gay rights group in the state will not support state-wide equality for transgender people, it shows the prevalence of discrimination against transgender people, and just how necessary passing this kind of legislation is for the transgender community."

(Transgendered Law and Policy Institute Press Release, April 24, 2002)

In the spirit of Sylvia Rivera mythically instigating the Stonewall Riots by throwing a brick/her shoes/a bottle at cops, things changed in 1999, by a single event in an outdoor shower area, by the laughter inspired at the thought of people freaking out and yelling, "There are PENISES on The Land!!!"

People may not recognize this as a historic event quite yet, but after the festival that year, tranny-folks and their many allies started calling people (like me) to task in the queer and feminist communities.

Trans-inclusion is spiraling out into the "mainstream" culture of the general public.

So be ready for that.

A Clarification: I Am a Pro-life Baby Killer

On September 12, 2001, I, like most folks, was installed in front of the teevee. Since I have never owned a teevee, and since I needed to hear news of what was going on in New York City and the rest of the country, I had become a kind of temporary roommate at a teevee-owning friend's home.

During this evening, another friend popped by and began watching teevee with me. It is difficult for people to watch teevee with me because my viewing criterion is inclusive of infomercials, religious shows and non-English-speaking programs. The lifestyle of not watching teevee makes watching it a very fascinating excursion into the collective consciousness of America for me. And on this date, it was all about the news. The friend who popped by wanted to watch a specific news program, deeming it "better" than others. I thought they were all completely biased and full of shit, and wanted to see what was on other channels.

During this time, the clicker stopped on a 714 Bible Show. Lots of such shows are taped in Orange County, California, at Trinity Broadcasting, to be precise. On the bottom of the screen, the call-in number to give them your money often begins with the 714 area code.

I asked my friend (who had the clicker) to let me watch this for a minute.

Reluctantly, she did.

The show blew my mind.

It was set in a room made to look like a library, with "books" cleverly painted on the walls. Four people sat around a table: an intellectual-looking, savvy black woman whom I never got to hear talk; a white man who seemed to be hosting the show, as everyone addressed their attention to him, a white woman who looked like a hippie gone New Age and ever so subtly corporate; and another white lady who looked like Delta Burke heralding from a Houston suburb. The Delta Burke type did most of the talking in the short time that I saw the show. She emoted on birth control, about how god-fearing Christian women can learn to monitor their cycles and figure out when they are ovulating and practice "abstinence," or use condoms so that they don't get pregnant. The host looked uncomfortable—

slightly tortured, even—because the Delta-type uttered the word "vagina" a number of times, but for a 714 Bible Show host, he was pretty goddamn stoic.

I could not believe what I was hearing.

Then the ex-hippie lady started talking about how god put a number of herbs on the planet to help women keep their menstrual cycles "regular." (This is a common euphemism for saying down a bunch of pennyroyal tea if you think you are pregnant.) Then the Delta Burke lady started chiming in about how God Gave Us These Gifts and it is WRONG for us not to make use of them.

Then my friend changed the channel and, since I did understand her pressing need to hear information about what in the name of Lordisa was going on in the world, I didn't raise a fuss.

I have, consequently, been kicking myself ever since because I have no way of backing this story up, but I am telling it anyway because it is *the gospel truth.*

See, this 714 Bible Show solved a huge mystery for me.

Since *Cunt* first came out, I've heard from a number of people who consider themselves "pro-life" and have mystifyingly commended me on my "anti-abortion" stance. It seems my abhorrence for the vacuum cleaner used in clinical abortions has been confused with a "pro-life" position.

I assume a lot of the people who have congratulated me for being "pro-life" have been young Christian women who somehow happened upon my book. I've often wondered how fanatics like Operation Rescue manage to get so many young women out there on the front lines, protesting at abortion clinics. Operation Rescue's propaganda imagery focuses on the "barbarous" nature of terminating a pregnancy and relies on harrowing images of third trimester fetuses. The idea that women who opt for clinical abortions are heartless "baby-killers" seems to be a cornerstone of this movement, and it certainly plays on the emotions of young girls.

Since seeing the 714 Bible Show, I've been wondering how many young people in America haven't had a chance to critically examine this issue on their own, and instead have simply seen too many grisly abortion films in the basement of their church.

The show informed me that there is a crucial distinction between the *way* one aborts a fetus and the actual end result. It seems that in the minds of those subjected to Operation Rescue-style propaganda, taking herbs to keep ones period "regular" is a lot different than going to an abortion clinic.

So when I lambaste the vacuum cleaner at abortion clinics and discuss how I induced a miscarriage with herbs and other such "Gifts From God," then to some "pro-lifers," at least, I may sound like an ideological ally.

To set the record straight, I consider myself a "pro-life baby killer."

Last year, I was invited to speak at a Million for Roe benefit in Boston. While I am increasingly concerned about Roe v. Wade being overturned, and wanted to support this organization, I had a scheduling conflict. So, in lieu of an appearance, I wrote them a letter.

It appears below.

Dearest Everyone at Million for Roe,

I hope you are having a fabulous time at an event "celebrating" the deaths of thirty million unborn souls who have been systematically annihilated since the 1973 Roe v. Wade ruling.

I know if I was there, I would be kicking up my heels that I made the decision to murder three of these souls. Yes, it fills my heart with joy when I think about the three kids (aged fifteen, thirteen and nine) I would have had right now had I not been one of the many cold-blooded baby killers that live in America today.

But alas, I am a cold-blooded baby killer.

And I am walking free in society.

And one day soon, abortion may be illegal, and people like me will be criminals.

Today I read in the *Los Angeles Times* that a young girl was picked up by the police for placing her newborn child in a dumpster. She will go to jail for this offense, and I don't know who got her pregnant—whether it was her stepfather, a priest or a neighborhood boy who promised her love.

She is a cold-blooded baby killer too.

In James W. Loewen's book, *Lies My Teacher Told Me*, there is a quote from a 1517 letter from Pedro de Cordoba to King Ferdinand describing life for the Arawak Indians under Spanish colonial rule:

As a result of the sufferings and hard labor they endured, the Indians choose and have chosen suicide. Occasionally a hundred have committed mass suicide. The women, exhausted by labor, have shunned conception and childbirth...many, when pregnant, have taken something to abort and have aborted. Others after delivery have killed their children with their own hands, so as not to leave them in such oppressive slavery.

By 1555, the entire Arawak nation had been annihilated. The pre-Columbian population of Haiti is estimated to be around eight million people. The "natives" of Haiti now are descendants of African slaves who were brought there by the Spanish and the French. These slaves rebelled mightily, and Haiti has been in turmoil pretty much ever since.

When I read stories about Haitian history and present day upheavals, I often think about the souls of those eight million Arawak Indians, and the many millions of Africans and Haitians who have died horrifying deaths—both in slavery and fighting for their freedom since Columbus's landing. These souls are speaking to the world. They say, "Colonialism is murder, colonialism is genocide, colonialism is now called things like 'free trade in the new world order' but it is still colonialism."

When rabbits find themselves pregnant in times of severe environmental stress, they absorb their young back into their bodies.

After NAFTA was in force 1994, U.S.-owned factories called "maquiladoras" opened up all over the border of Mexico. One place that is very convenient to huge U.S. corporations is Ciudad Juarez, located just a few miles away from El Paso, Texas. The maquiladoras offer jobs and money to people who operate in a more pronounced economic apartheid than the one present in the United States. So people, primarily women—the poorest people in the world—flock to these shitass jobs in huge factories where no one gives a fuck about them.

Since 1993, at least 270 women have been found raped and murdered in Cuidad Juarez. Another 450 have disappeared. They have primarily been factory workers, attacked on the dark streets as they walk to and from work. (progressive.org)

Here is an excerpt from a February 2002 article on the Progressive Media Project's website:

> On Feb. 11, Chihuahua Governor Patricio Martinez Garcia
> said that he would seek assistance from the United
> Nations as well as from international police agents to
> solve these murders.
> Mexican women's-rights activists and the families of
> the murdered women have called attention to the murders
> of Mexican women for years. Their pleas have too often
> remained unheard by government officials and law-
> enforcement agencies. (progressive.org)

In June 2002, the U.S. Christian Right, Catholics and Mormons announced the creation of an alliance with Iraq, Iran and a number of other countries to create a powerful bloc within the U.N. Their focus? Squelching all talk of rights for queers, women and children throughout the world.

One imagines that Governor Garcia's requests fell upon deaf ears.

I wonder what it would be like to live in a world where people became outraged over the grisly murders of hundreds of women in Mexico. I wonder what it would be like if Jerry Falwell and Operation Rescue went down to Ciudad Juarez to protect the lives of people who have already been born, against the cold-blooded women killers and the factories that take no responsibility for their workers well-being.

I wonder.

If I had three kids, I would not have been able to write *Cunt*. All the love I have for those three kids went into that book. *Cunt* fomented in my heart for years before I ever sat down to get it all out. I produced *Cunt* to serve myself and to serve other people who are already born.

I am very pro-life.

I wholeheartedly support the lives of the living. And life is a goddamn complex thing, and it involves making difficult choices, and sometimes those choices lead to sacrifice. And sometime those sacrifices lead to a woman waking up one morning, her uterus in agony, and crying for the harrowing choice she has made.

Aborting a child is a painful thing to do, but in order to serve the living, it is sometimes necessary.

If Roe v. Wade is overturned, then where does that leave all the pro-life baby killers like myself?

Generations of women have grown up with legal, safe abortions available, and this has made us lazy. We have grown accustomed to living in a world where it is no one's goddamn business what insanely personal sacrifices and choices we make in our lives. We have had the wool pulled over our eyes so tight, we have no idea what is going on in Haiti and Ciudad Juarez. We read about little girls dumping newborn babies in garbage cans, we sigh sadly, and we turn the goddamn page.

If Roe v. Wade is overturned, then I am gonna celebrate because I know it will make people get off their asses and take a look around this post-1973 world we live in.

It will mean war.

We've all been getting our asses kicked since before Columbus sailed the ocean blue, and little "rights" like voting, working, freedom and abortions have blinded entire generations to this fact. Abortion is not a "right." It is not within the jurisdiction of men to decide whether or not women will be "allowed" this "luxury." We seem to have missed this point entirely.

At least if abortion is outlawed, more people will understand that the exact same war has been going on for over five hundred years, and there will be a lot more soldiers asking where they can line up.

With warm regards,

Inga M.

I read a version of this letter in January, when I spoke at Western Washington University in Bellingham. Afterward, a woman came up to me and introduced me to her three beautiful girls. From youngest to oldest, they were the exact ages of the children I would have had. There were tears in the woman's eyes as she told me that she and all three of her girls have read my book, and it has had a significant impact on their family. She told me I was right—I would have never been able to write *Cunt* with three kids. I was stunned into silence. I wanted to cry and hug her and thank her for putting those children on the planet, but there was a line of people waiting for me to sign their *Cunt*s, and I emotionally sandbagged the tidal wave of grief and joy that washed over me.

I still cry when this memory comes up.

I am crying now.

Life is so complex.

Taking Back the Morning, Noon and Night

Since writing *Cunt,* my position on sexual assault and violence toward women has also evolved considerably. In *Cunt,* I limited my focus to the rape of biological women, but I have since realized that rape affects all segments of the population. Rape isn't just about men raping women. It is about the powerful raping the powerless.

Every day one can read reports of children being stolen, raped and killed. The media tends to showcase stranger abductions, although the proclivities of Catholic priests have recently come to light. Neither of these situations addresses the likelihood of children being sexually assaulted by adults they know, love and trust. How many children in this world live with the horror of rape in their daily lives? How many grown-ups have buried deep the terror of "visits" in the night? Of getting up for school the next morning and facing a playground of kids, many of whom may have also had similar visits the night before?

We live in a culture that rapes its children.

Think of this in terms of, oh say, a college anthropology textbook on ancient Mayan culture. Here is a line from a hypothetical textbook called *United States Culture Five Hundred Years After Columbus:*

> One trait of twentieth and twenty-first century U.S. culture was the widespread rape of children. According to research done during the time, anywhere from 826,000 to three million children were abused in 1999. Abuse was categorized as "neglect," "physical" and "sexual." As many as one million children were reported as victims of sexual abuse during that year. At the time, this number was equivalent to or more than the *entire population* of many major cities, such as Seattle, Detroit, Houston or San Francisco. Exactly how many went unreported could never be substantiated.
>
> Something called "child pornography" also featured in the socioeconomic relationship between consumers and the business sector.

I can't think of any other culture that manages to rape so many of their children. I think it is weird to live in a culture that does this.

Of the four biological men I have been closest to in my life, *all* of them have been sexually molested and/or violently raped either as adults or as children. In other words, 100 percent of my closest biological male friends and ex-lovers have experienced varying degrees of sexual assault. This overwhelming percentage does not include the two male relatives in my family who were molested as children.

Every time I speak at a Take Back the Night rally, two or three men come up to me afterward and tell me, often for the first time in their lives, that they were raped, or thwarted a sexual assault, or have never spoken of their childhood ordeals of molestation with anyone in their lives.

Every time I speak, a few men muster the courage to break their silence, shame and fear clouding their eyes. I always wonder how many men were not yet ready to say anything.

Thanks to the anti-rape movement, many women feel freer to speak out about rape. This is still difficult for many women of color, Muslim-American women and women raised in poverty, but some improvement has been made. It is not generally acknowledged that men can be in positions of powerlessness, so it is even more difficult for them to speak out.

Rape is often viewed as a "punishment" for defying norms, as a way to ensure silence and conformity, so if biological women think we have it bad by being cast as "whores" who must have "brought on the attack," imagine the *veritable field day* lawyers, doctors, judges, reporters and cops have with those who endanger society's stagnant ideas of gender identity.

I have heard from many people, and read in books and articles that gender-variant women are forced to give police officers blowjobs as a matter of course.

Sylvia Rivera mentions this phenomenon in an interview with Leslie Feinberg:

When drag queens were arrested, what degradation
there was. I remember the first time I got arrested, I
wasn't even in full drag. I was walking down the
street and the cops just snatched me. We always felt
that the police were the real enemy. We expected
nothing better than to be treated like we were
animals—and we were. We were stuck in a bullpen
like a bunch of freaks. We were disrespected. A lot
of us were beaten up and raped.

Transgendered and/or effeminate men are victimized on a
whole different level of power and control, as the well-publi-
cized murders of Brandon Teena and Matthew Shepard horrify-
ingly illustrate.

Gender-variant people suffer untold humiliations in
emergency rooms, courthouses, police stations and morgues.
For transgendered folks who are sexually assaulted and live to
tell about it, there is no end to the brutality at the hands of
community officials.

One cannot assert that biological women suffer from sexual
assault *more* than anyone else. Biological women are the only
ones for which even non-conclusive statistics *exist*. There are no
widely published rape statistics on transgendered women.
There are no children's crisis hotline numbers explained and
handed out at schools. There are no readily accessible resources
for biological or trannymen. In this regard, biological women
have it a lot better than other genders and children—which isn't,
I assure you, saying much.

So, the focus on biological women being sexually assaulted no longer serves me. In this country, children, adolescents and adults are all raped, molested and sexually victimized.

According to my calculations, if I throw in everybody who is affected by the sexual assault of a loved one, this adds up to pretty much the entire population.

Much, much, *much* furthermore, it has become impossible for me to make distinctions between the rape of a human being and the rape of the earth.

And by "the earth" I do mean the plants, animals, waters, mountains and soil— but "the earth" also includes human civilizations, languages, religions and traditions that have been in existence for millennia.

Not long ago, I read *A Language Older Than Words* by Derrick Jensen. This book profoundly validated my entire existence, giving voice to many thoughts I have had about the role of rape in our culture—thoughts I have mulled over for years and years, but have not had the courage to articulate outside my heart.

Please, please.

Read this book.

Derrick Jensen grew up in a "privileged" white setting. His father was a powerful attorney and his mother, a homemaker. There are five kids in the Jensen family. The attorney father regularly beat the oldest three, while he sexually assaulted Derrick and his youngest sister on a regular basis.

Their mother was also routinely beaten and raped.

They showed the face of a happy, well-to-do white American family to all who witnessed their lives.

I can see their toothy family portraits without even closing my eyes.

I have seen images of happy families so many times in my life.

Mr. Jensen got a degree from the Colorado School of Mines, but soon veered off the path his background so effectively paves for him and his lot. He eventually became a writer and environmental activist. With his (to me) impressive background in math and science, he was able to look at the world around him and make precise conclusions, based on fractalized sociological patterns.

What he came to understand and communicate so courageously in his book is that abuse in a family operates under the exact same rules as abuse in our culture.

In March 2002, I read about the deaths of 250 million monarch butterflies in Mexico. The "news" reports laid the blame on the weather. There was, evidently, a sudden freeze.

But if one scratches the surface of this story, one finds that all of the trees that protected the butterflies from sudden weather changes were recently cut down.

The butterflies died because the forest was raped.

The trees, murdered.

This rape and murder was perpetuated by people who have been checkmated into poverty and despair by NAFTA.

Some of the very few people who benefit from NAFTA are also the ones who bought the trees from the checkmated Mexican community.

So we have here a situation where the abuser coerces the abused into abusing others and we end up with 250 million dead monarch butterflies, a community of people who have been thrust further into poverty and despair by getting shafted out of the tourist money that the butterflies used to bring, and a "media" that "blames" all of this on someone it whimsically refers to as "Mother Nature."

The abuser (in this, and most cases, "the abuser" is an amalgam of the few people who benefit from NAFTA, the International Monetary Fund, the World Bank, the Carlyle and Bilderberg Groups and so on) is far removed from the situation, and people in America are too "busy" to read through the lines and trace the blame backward down the serpentine reality of cause and effect.

People in the area tried to describe the stench of 250 million rotting butterfly corpses.

If 250 million people in America died, that would leave us with roughly thirteen percent of the present U.S. population.

But people are not butterflies, right.

People are, well, *more important than butterflies.*

We have *opposable thumbs,* hello.

You can't possibly compare the sanctity of a human's life with that of a butterfly. In our culture, you can and, indeed, must **quantify sanctity**, and butterflies have less than people.

✳

When I was younger, I found a place by the ocean where the monarch butterflies stopped in on their way to Mexico. Their stomping ground was a eucalyptus grove. It is hard to describe the beauty of millions—do you understand me: *millions*—of butterflies all in the same place at once. They hang from the trees in magnificently gigantic bunches, and the sky can barely peek through the fluttering of their wings. I went to the eucalyptus grove all the time, and never saw another person there. *Nothing* boosts a teenager's self-esteem like knowing they have a secret butterfly grove to look forward to every fall. Millions of monarch butterflies gave me the strength to trudge my ass through the high school years, but if I were to list them in the acknowledgments of my next book, most people would think I was a fucken flaky-assed tree-hugging crystal gazer.

I am, nonetheless, filled with a deep mourning and loss at the death of 250 million butterflies.

It is no less painful than when my brother died.

It's okay to be sad about my brother, but it's not okay to be sad about the butterflies.

I believe this loss resonated in the hearts of everyone on the planet, whether they were aware of it or not. And when people experience loss after loss after loss, but never acknowledge that anything is gone, well it makes for a fucked-up population that rapes and/or condones the rape of its children.

In Derrick Jensen's family, there was much sibling resentment.

He considered himself "lucky" that he didn't get the shit kicked out of him for the slightest transgression. This is how his father maintained control over the whole brood. The three eldest would never think to align their cause with the two younger ones, and they, in turn, were too filled with shame to talk to anyone at all.

In the context of the butterflies, trees and the people in Mexico, people in the U.S. are supposed to be considered the "lucky" ones. With our highly-touted full bellies of food and semblances of education and health care available for our children, we would never think to align ourselves with an environment and a population that has suffered from the abuse of the few who benefit from NAFTA.

I often hear biological women (for, again, we are the only ones who feel free enough to converse on the topic) say they have been "lucky" so far.

Meaning they haven't been sexually assaulted.

So far.

While the threat of rape is always present for any woman who doesn't have her head lodged up her ass and/or who can't afford bodyguards, women will still refer to themselves as "lucky."

This produces similar results as when we attempt to quantify sanctity.

It's fucking chickenshit bullshit denial that leads to neurosis.

If you live in a culture that rapes its children, you can, under no circumstances, consider yourself "lucky."

Are people in the U.S. "luckier" than people in Guatemala, Nicaragua, El Salvador, Rwanda, South Africa, Palestine, Iraq, Indonesia, Sierra Leone, Bosnia, Venezuela, Mexico?

Do you feel "lucky" to know that, according to Michael Moore in *Stupid White Men*, your garden-variety twelve-year-old in Guatemala can give you more information about the World Bank than your garden-variety U.S. "investigative reporter" can?

On a recent jaunt through the News of the Weird website, I found numerous instances of mental instability in our culture:

The U.S. Postal Service revealed in March that ten men had already been convicted as part of an Internet group that exchanged videos of themselves administering beatings to children (often their own). One man wanted to join the club but lacked an authentic video to contribute and so made one of himself administering corporal punishment to a small manne-quin. Among the group: a middle school teacher, a nurse, a former Boy Scout leader, and a former Sunday school teacher. (*Chicago Tribune*, 3/13/02)

A twenty-seven-year-old woman told reporters in January that when she called the Camarillo, California, police on Saturday, December 22, to report a sexual assault, she was told that the staff is limited on weekends and that she should call back Monday morning (and when she did that, detectives counseled her to report for a medical exam). (Scripps Howard News Service, 1/3/02)

Among the absurdities touching Enron was the report in February by a former employee, broadcast by NBC News, that the company ran a mock trading floor in its Houston headquarters, furnished with desks, large flat-panel computer screens and teleconference rooms, for the sole purpose of making visitors believe the company furiously traded commodities full-time. In reality, revealed the employee, the equipment was only hooked up internally, and the employee-"traders," who appeared to be frantically placing orders, were merely talking to each other. (*NBC Nightly News*, 2/27/02)

A State University of New York at Buffalo professor, in a recent ecology journal, expressed confidence that eventually butterflies could be genetically altered to permit advertising logos and other designs on their wings. (*Chicago Sun-Times*, 3/13/02)

It took me eight minutes to find these items, and there were plenty more to choose from. It was not difficult.

Let's go back and pretend biological women are the only ones who suffer from sexual violence in this country. If that were indeed the case, then isn't 33 percent of one half of the potential voting population still a pretty heady figure to be dealing with?

Doesn't it seem like that's kind of a crisis, and should possibly be discussed and acted upon?

What if one out of every three multinational corporation CEO's were raped every year? Don't you think that would raise kind of a ruckus?

People in power—those who broadcast "issues" and enact laws—*know* that women in America are systematically raped, killed, beaten and cowed into submission.

Doesn't it seem *odd* that—affecting such a huge percentage of the population—violence towards women isn't a loaded topic like abortion "rights," cloning and terrorism? How about the subject of white violence and corporate devastation on reservations? Police brutality in black neighborhoods? How about the fact that young black men comprise over 40 percent of the prison population in this country?

None of these issues are on the desks of the people who make policy and decisions because everything that keeps people down and hurt and struggling serves those in power.

It *serves* those in power to rule a population of people who are traumatized. That way, we are much too busy dealing with alcoholism, drug addictions, peer competition and post traumatic stress disorder to really pay much notice to how deeply we are being shafted. Those of us not dealing with any of these problems are very, very busy gazing at our lucky, lucky stars.

I am pretty fucken sure, however, that no one is free from violence and abuse.

If you haven't been directly targeted, someone in your family most certainly has. And if it has affected your family, it has affected you too, possibly in deeply personal ways, in phobias or neurosis, in anxiety or self-esteem issues.

No one is exempt.

Certainly not monarch butterflies.

Even if you are one of the "lucky" ones, who has somehow, magically survived life in this culture without the "taint" of sexual violence in your life, you nevertheless suffer from the complexities of being socialized in a culture of heinous abuse.

Maybe you think I am full of shit, but let me remind you that denial is one of the most common responses to heinous abuse.

People are constantly telling me, either directly or via the "media," to stop bitching about the white man and all of the "perceived" injustices he is responsible for.

I would like to clarify my position on this point.

I am not against the white man.

Robert Graves was a white man and if he hadn't written *The White Goddess,* I would simply not be as smart as I am today. White men constantly honor me by reading my book. Michael Moore is a goddamn pasty-faced corn-fed glowing white-assed man, and I hardly pass a day of my life lately without referencing him because he's such a gorgeous shit-talker.

My white brother is one of my favorite social commentators on the planet.

Greg Palast: white man, love him.

Henry Waxman and Dennis Kucinich: white men and fucken politicians; love them.

My three nephews: white as driven snow; love them, pray for them, will do anything to improve the quality of their lives, even, and especially if, that means reigning in the sense of entitlement and strict gender roles that will be thrust upon them by an unforgiving, mindlessly brutal and competitive culture.

You see, I have *no beef* with white men.

It *just so happens* that pretty much everyone I *do* have a beef with, is either a white man or on the white man's payroll.

I recently read Michael Moore's *Stupid White Men*.

I would have probably read and thoroughly enjoyed this book in any context, but I enjoyed it with a *particular glee* knowing that it has been on the bestseller list for over four months now. The bestseller list is a calibrated reflection of the American collective consciousness. I infer the interest in this book to mean that a lot of folks in this country are unhappy living in the world the white man has created.

Books like *Stupid White Men* and *A Language Older Than Words* are part of a healing process.

It makes sense to me that those whom many would identify as "part of the problem"—that is, white men—are in fact, making attempts to become "part of the solution."

I also imagine that the pressure white men are feeling at this point in their history is somewhat agonizing.

More fucken power to the white man, I say.

But seriously, folks, it's time to overthrow the government.

It's time for the Cynthia McKinney/Barbara Lee Administration.

It is time for everybody *besides* white men and those on their payroll to run the show. Michael Moore gives us a bit of insight about this in *Stupid White Men.*

I've been thinking about this a lot. There are tons of elected city positions and there is no reason whatsoever that y-o-u shouldn't be voted into office.

Like the water?

Then run for port commissioner.

Fair-minded Libra?

Run for city attorney.

Morbid Goth?

City coroner is the job for you.

Transgender folks should be writing the city's sexual harassment policies and running for sheriff.

Run for city council, postmaster or the board of education.

Moreover, support the fuck out of the very few people in political power who don't seem to be on the payroll of white men. Presently there are a few such people in Congress: Barbara Lee, Henry Waxman, Jan Schakowsky, Cynthia McKinney, Dennis Kucinich and John Conyers.

At present, it is of utmost importance to *support the fuck-all* out of politicians who have our backs, whether or not we live in their state. When you read about some Congressperson talking shit, email them. It's easy—just type their last name on any search engine.

Ultimately, we need all grandmothers, all the time.

c
u
n
t

A grandmother who has raised her children and/or other people's children is the perfect person to be in national office. Grandmothers have their life experiences to help them make sage judgments, they generally have more compassion than everyone else, and if the white men in power assassinate one grandma, they will not only have hell to pay for offing an old woman, but there are plenty more where she came from. Grandmothers also have the time to focus. No one has to worry about someone having to breastfeed during the State of the Union Address. And since the sexuality of elderly people is completely ignored in this culture, grandmothers won't have their energies taxed with sex scandals.

We are in dire need of a grandmother-based government.

We cannot transform the government unless indigenous people, people of color, queers, freaks, self-actualized revolutionaries and transgendered folks make some serious stabs at procuring power.

Recognize sexual assault of individuals for what it is: a minute aspect of a vast continuum of abuse that has taken place on the planet for over five hundred years.

Stop looking inward at your own individual reality.

Place yourself in the continuum, and act.

Do not, under any circumstances, put this book down and turn on the teevee.

The teevee debilitates our culture.

I know a Yaqui gentleman who abstains from drinking alcohol as an act of political resistance.

In a similar vein, I abstain from watching the teevee.

More perhaps than reading *The White Goddess,* my teevee boycott has made me smarter. My mind is sharp and my critical thinking skills are constantly challenged because I do not have a teevee deadening my brain, making me feel like things that are completely unacceptable are somehow okey-dokey.

It is not okay to pigeonhole, stereotype and tokenize people of color, but the teevee does it all the fucking time.

It is not okay to normalize whiteness or heterosexuality.

It is not okay to glorify the insignificant lives of people the teevee insists are important celebrities.

It is not okay that the teevee pays Jennifer Aniston more money for filming one episode of *Friends* than a sixth grade teacher will see in her entire career.

It is not okay to objectify all women, exoticize women of color and present transgendered people as caricatures, if at all.

In order to appear on the teevee, you have to make the teevee executives happy. In order to make the teevee executives happy, you have to make the white men who run the gigantic corporations that run the teevee companies happy. In order to make all these men happy, you have to be serving them in some capacity, however indirectly. If you do not serve these men, then you will not appear on the teevee.

This reality is mathematically precise.

In case you ever wondered, this is why I don't have my own late night talk show.

This is why the folks at International A.N.S.W.E.R. don't have their own news channel. This is why it's Larry King instead of Noam Chomsky, Jerry Springer instead of Jocelyn Elders, Eminem instead of Seeds of Wisdom and Martha Stewart instead of the Dalai Lama.

Maybe you are one of those people like my mom who says, "Oh god Inga leave me alone. I only watch the Discovery Channel." Well I've watched the Discovery Channel with her and what I learned is that the Discovery Channel serves the white men too. It shows us that there is no situation on this planet that is free from the prying, entitled eye of "civilized" human beings. Isn't it a very strange voyeurism that leads people to film polar bears fucking in the last corners of the world where they manage to eke out an existence? And maybe that tribe of indigenous people in the Brazilian rainforest really wouldn't enjoy knowing exactly how many millions of unknown and largely ignorant people are scrutinizing images of their lives.

My mom asks me why I always have to put a damper on things.

I say, "I don't know."

If you watch the teevee, you get information that serves the white men that are selling the earth so they can have a power that is an illusion in the first place but they don't know this and could give a fuck anyway.

And yes, they are white men.

And yes, you can find out their names and what they are up to and why.

But not by watching the teevee.

Turn the piece of shit off, or better yet, smash it to bits.

It's time to connect the dots folks, and it may not be the easiest thing to do, it may not be something that "lucky" people do, but I, for one, am sick and fucking tired of living in a culture of violence and destruction.

The violence is everywhere, we perpetuate it and we can stop it.

The time has come.

Fucken rad.

Long Postscript

For months now, I've danced around the whole prospect of writing this afterword thing.

The world appears drastically different than it did when I wrote *Cunt*. At that time, there were foreshadowings of a planet-wide corporate takeover—one going by innocuous-sounding designations such as "globalization" and "free enterprise." While I wrote *Cunt*, NAFTA, GATT and deregulation laws steamrolled a golden expressway of opportunity for huge, multinational corporations. Meanwhile, mindlessly brutal atrocities took place throughout the world. Bosnians, Haitians, East Timorese, Somalis, Hutus, Tutsis and the people of Chiapas are just some members of the world's population who could tell tales of what was going on while I wrote *Cunt*.

Every indian tribe and nation living in what is now called the U.S.A. has been under some kind of siege or another for the past five hundred years. Corporate and police forces all over the U.S.A. brutalize black men, women and children without so much as a slap on the hand. Jamaican, Southeast Asian, Latino, Haitian, Pacific Islander, African, Middle Eastern, Chicana, Central Asian, Cholo, Vato, Mestiza, Cuban, Puerto Rican, Asian, Hispanic, South American and Central American people are routinely marginalized, victimized and wantonly stereotyped as a matter of course in this country.

These trends continued as I wrote *Cunt,* and they continue today.

What is different now is it is difficult for me to focus on my work because I am completely obsessed with what is going on in the world, in this country. The sense of desperation that I was once able quell in the nether regions of my heart has exploded into my every day life.

In a recent article in the *Observer,* author, political commentator and self-described "hooligan" Arundhati Roy spoke about pointlessness. Ms. Roy lives in New Delhi, and the article, "Under the Nuclear Shadow" was a response to the threat of nuclear war between India and Pakistan. Here are her thoughts about foreign reporters asking her if she is working on a new book:

That question mocks me. Another book? Right now
when it looks as though all the music, the art, the
architecture, the literature, the whole of human
civilisation means nothing to the monsters who run
the world. What kind of book should I write? For
now, just for now, for just a while, pointlessness is
my biggest enemy. That's what nuclear bombs do,
whether they're used or not. They violate everything that is humane, they alter the meaning of life.
(Observer Worldview, June 2, 2002)

And I, American me, *I* should not feel this way. I shouldn't
consider pointlessness *my* biggest enemy. I'm a "lucky" one. No
one is talking about obliterating almost every single person *I*
have ever loved on this planet, myself included. No one is
talking about me looking into *my* mother's eyes as we sit at her
kitchen table and wait, because the buttons have just been
pressed.

My desire to write has presently been consumed by my
desire to understand—and perhaps anticipate—what is going on.

At present, I know a lot.

I know more than I have ever known in my life about U.S.
history, foreign policy and domestic policy.

I know names, dates, places, events.

But I have not felt much like writing, even though I know
very well what kind of book I should write. I have been working
on it for three years.

Pointlessness is my biggest enemy.

According to the freaky little white men running the show right now, my job as an American is not to concern myself with big, faraway things like the rest of the world. My job is not even to concern myself with my country. Most certainly, my job is not to spend endless hours scouring the Internet for actual news, and piecing together the fragmented hints reported in the mainstream "media."

My job is to consume the products that the world produces for me at breakneck speed, in sweatshops where folks are fired for failing a mandatory pregnancy test, or killed for trying to organize a union. My job is to watch teevee and allow it to shape my view. My job is to keep on the look-out for suspicious Muslims in my neighborhood.

If I adhered better to my job description, the desperation and pointlessness that haunts me would surely go away.

Conversely, part of the pointlessness I experience is *directly related* to how very well my fellow Americans are following the freaky little white man's idea of a job description.

We are ass-deep in shit, but the "media" keeps telling us that new, improved, compassionate shit no longer stinks. A gaping disparity between the daily myth and the daily reality is producing a form of collective schizophrenia.

I recently came across an article on PopPolitics.com, written by a lawyer named Steven C. Day. He describes how a trial in which he was involved gave him insight on how the bias of the mainstream "media" messes with public opinion and creates this kind of collective schizophrenia.

It seems the plaintiff's lawyer was buddy-chums with the reporter covering the trial. Every day, the local newspaper printed articles about how the trial was going in favor of the plaintiff. People would stop Mr. Day on the street and tell him he needed to seriously get his shit together. His only response was, "Don't believe everything you read in the newspaper." When the trial was over, and the judgment went for Mr. Day's client, people in the community were stunned. Based on the news accounts written by the other lawyer's pal, folks were pretty sure Mr. Day's side would lose.

From this experience, Mr. Day clearly saw how the U.S. "media" operates on a much grander scale:

> Am I stretching too far in trying to compare the actions of this Midwest legal reporter to those of the journalistic royalty of the presidential press corps? I don't think so. The truth is, the relationship between the White House and White House correspondents is every bit as symbiotic as the associations legal reporters build with certain lawyers. The Bush administration, like others before it, provides reporters with information and inside access that is critical to their jobs. By all accounts, Bush himself also provides them with a much-appreciated salve to their well-developed egos, by handing out nicknames and engaging in friendly chit-chat. In exchange, the reporters disseminate the administration's point of view to the public. (Steven C. Day, June 6, 2002, PopPolitics.com)

Walter Cronkite:

> I'm deeply concerned about the merger mania that
> has swept our industry, diluting standards, dumbing
> down the news, and making the bottom line
> sometimes seem like the only line. It isn't and it
> shouldn't be.

You know times are worth concerning ourselves over when a white guy who got rich reporting what was once considered "the news" sounds like a goddamn pinko revolutionary.

At this point in history, regardless of our race, gender or class, we are informed by homogenized "media" outlets that read us verbatim press releases from the Heritage Foundation, the present corporate government administration and whatever sponsor has a new product that ties in to a current event (such as Bayer Pharmaceuticals, makers of the much-touted Anthrax antidote, Cipro).

Here are a few of the media outlets that "inform" us:

1. Westinghouse/CBS
2. GE/NBC
3. Disney/ABC
4. FOX
5. AOL Time Warner
6. Gannett
7. Hearst Corporation
8. USA Today
9. Clear Channel Communications
10. Vivendi Universal

(Because of the cutthroat nature of the present economic model, any one of these monsters may at any time consume any other of these monsters. So excuse my error if, by the time you read this, the ten above named "media" corporations have glommed into four or three or two, or one.)

Here are a few more examples of how the "media" creates this debilitating form of collective schizophrenia:

1.   May 10, 2002. CNN has a small story on its website about "C-18," a one hundred and twenty-five-mile-long iceberg calving from the Ross Ice Shelf. In June, it's reported that Mt. Everest is melting.

May 10, 2002. Reuters runs an article where the man who is and, yet, is not, president emotes on the patent non-existence of global warming.

I am not a scientist, but I still feel really safe asserting that ice melts when it warms up. (From ssec.wise.edu/media/icebergC-19.html; for evidence of the Bush quote go to buzzflash.com archives for May 10th.)

2.   During a dramatic "dead or alive" manhunt for the most wanted international criminal known to modern history (which, for some reason, involved a "carpet of bombs" for a population also victimized by this selfsame man), the U.S. government flips the bird at the world's creation of an International Criminal Court.

3.   In May, the German magazine, *Der Speigel,* reports that Bush asked Brazilian President Fernando Henrique Cardoso, and I quote: "Do you have blacks too?"

On May 9, 2002, the *Miami Herald* reports on the deteriorating relationship between the present corporate government administration and Brazil. "What is beginning to look like an escalating diplomatic skirmish between Brazil and the Bush administration went up another notch this week, when a Brazilian diplomat claimed in an academic paper that the U.S. government's, 'irrationality and arrogance' could expose the world to a Nazi-style imperial power." Because I'd seen the translated *Der Spiegel* article, I know very well what the reporter is talking about when referring to the "escalating diplomatic skirmish." Many Americans, however, do not have this frame of reference, since Bush's quote was published only in "alternative" news sources.

Millions and millions of people rely on "alternative" news sources. How do all these people feel when Larry King interviews Anna Nicole Smith, and J.Lo's divorce makes headlines, while the country is going to corporate hell in a handbasket and the rest of the world is rabidly protesting our present government?

4. In June, BartCop.com published an article by Gene Lyons about the U.S. media's "selective" reporting of Bush's embarrassing behavior during his trip to Europe.

> Something the Washington press did report, if only because it involved one of their own, was Junior's bitchy response to what he apparently saw as NBC correspondent David Gregory's attempt to show him up by speaking French. At a joint Paris press conference with President Jacques Chirac, Gregory asked Bush about the perception that U.S. policies

were unpopular in Europe. He then directed the
same question to Chirac in his own language, a
courtesy generally followed by European reporters.

Bush bristled. "Very good," he snapped. "The guy
memorizes four words, and he plays like he's
intercontinental."

Insulted, Gregory volunteered that he could
continue in French.

"I'm impressed," the president sneered. "Que
bueno. Now, I'm literate in two languages."

The *New York Times* account emphasized how
tired Bush was, an excuse you wouldn't make for a
fifteen year-old. Which is exactly what Junior, kept
up past his bedtime by decadent European dining
habits, sounded like: a resentful preppie at a fancy
school on Daddy's money showing his contempt for
a brainy scholarship kid—pretty much how people
who went to school with Bush describe him.

For the record, it has been reported that Mr. Gregory considers
this interaction to represent the end of his career as a journalist.

Do you remember all the reports that Bush was "tired" during
his trip to Europe?

The *Washington Post* reported that President Chirac *surprised* Bush with a press conference after lunch one day. Bush
was completely unprepared to meet the press, and I suspect
President Chirac was well aware of Bush's need for totally
scripted "press conferences." That's right: the president of

France pulled a fast one on Bush, and the U.S. media's response was to report that a caught-off-guard Bush was "tired." How utterly humiliating for every U.S. citizen. The *Washington Post*, however, made no connection between the surprise nature of this press conference and Bush's embarrassing behavior.

5.   Since when does the Supreme Court decide who the president is? I wasn't the best student, but I enjoyed government and history classes. I paid attention. I read the textbooks. There was nothing about the Supreme Court deciding anything about who would be president.

EVERYONE KNOWS THIS.

But it has been palmed off since day one like it's this *perfectly normal thing* and you're just being a sore loser or a bitter partisan or an eco-terrorist if you insinuate anything close to a question on this never before heard of rule that the Supreme Court decides who the president is.

I mean, how weird and surreal is this?

I learned about "dazzle camouflage" from Lynda Barry in her work of staggering genius, *Cruddy*. Dazzle camouflage is from the Navy and it's where you do something really glaring and obvious to get your opponent's attention away from what you are *truly* doing.

I've developed a dazzle camouflage tactic for phone solicitors:

"Hi, this is Larry Laforge from the Fireman's Benevolent Vinyl Siding Association, how ya doing this evening?"

"Oh, hi. I don't speak English."

"Uh, you don't speak English?"

"No, no. Not a word. We don't speak English in this house."

"You sound like, uh, you speak pretty good English."

"Yeah, I know. People tell me that all the time. Thanks for the compliment!"

"Uh, so. Well, thanks."

"Sure, anytime."

Click.

Say people are starting to wonder about what you knew that might have stopped terrorist attacks on huge buildings filled with people. You don't want people to wonder about this at all. You think it is none of their business. Even though you received warnings from at least six international intelligence agencies and even though your attorney general stopped flying on commercial planes a few months before two airplanes slammed into the buildings (globalresearch.ca/articles/CHI205C.html), you really, really must insist that it is no one's business. So you find someone to blame and you hand out all these press releases/articles with fill-in-the-blank bylines, that lay irrevocable blame on the someone you picked, say the head of your bureau of investigations.

Maybe you even had this person all picked out in advance, because you figured one day people might start asking you questions, even if it takes, say, eight months.

Maybe this person became head of the your bureau of investigations only one week before the terrorist attacks, and actually allowed himself *to be placed in the position of blame for the express purpose of being blamed in your stead.*

I mean, you would always love them for taking the blame, and do everything in your power to make sure wonderful things happened for them, it's not like the person being blamed will necessarily even suffer for the terrorist attacks on huge build ings filled with people.

Maybe the person who catches the blame will, as a result, have more power than before.

Maybe it could be a win-win situation.

This is a dazzling example of dazzle camouflage.

It works.

All the blame and questions are simply too dazzling to see you in there anywhere, but you are there.

You are there.

> Mr. Mueller's childlike promise to work harder to "connect the dots" is designed to protect his political superiors from blame by changing the subject—to the notion that bureaucratic bungling, not political corruption, is the problem. (John R. MacArthur, "He Waved Away Warnings," *The Globe and Mail,* June 4, 2002)

> You can't believe Bush is truly a man of nuanced intelligence because that implies that he probably did know something about the possibility of a terrorist attack and how it could fortify his political career, but you can't call him flagrantly stupid because that's unpatriotic and un-American and embarrassing, and hence you're just left with this

feeling of unease and vague despondency about the
nation's overall direction and whatever happened to
your civil liberties. Ignorance is bliss. Ignorance is
patriotism. We don't want to believe the Bush
administration could've done something to prevent
the horrors of 9/11, can't imagine Bush would use
the tragedy to bolster his re-election hopes while
simultaneously pummeling Afghanistan into docility
in the name of oil pipelines and his friends in the
military-industrial complex. Increasing piles of
evidence be damned. It's just too painful. (Mark
Morford, June 7, 2002, SFGate.com)

What happens to people living in a society where everyone in
power is lying, stealing, cheating and killing, and in our hearts
we all know this, but the consequences of facing all these lies
are so monstrous, we keep on hoping that maybe the corporate
government administration and media are on the level with us
this time.

Americans remind me of survivors of domestic violence.

There is always the hope that this is the very, very, very
last time one's ribs get re-broken again.

There is another way in which this situation reminds me of
domestic violence. One of the most popular tactics of an abuser
is to isolate their victim from the community. The abuser
belittles family, friends and neighbors until they just stop
coming around.

If you read the newspapers and put together a comprehensive look at how the rest of the world feels about the U.S. right now, you will see that we are being isolated from the world in a very similar manner.

I think people in other countries are wise to this abuse tactic because all the protests I read about make a **huge and formal** distinction between the American people and the present corporate/presidential administration.

It seems like we should be reaching out to this community, and not allowing ourselves to be boxed in.

All in all, I wish we were more like the people of Venezuela.

I don't know what will be happening in Venezuela in the next few months—it could get ugly—but in April 2002, the Venezuelan population took to the streets and demanded the return of their president after an attempted U.S.-backed coup.

I imagine Venezuelans have experienced the U.S.A.'s version of how their country should be run enough to know that it doesn't serve them.

In 1998, they voted Hugo Chavez into office. His "platform" was the Bolivian Revolution, a reference to one of South America's heroes of independence, Simon Bolivar. President Chavez has spent the last four years giving Venezuela back to the people, after forty years of a two-party rule that represented the country's elite (sound familiar?).

Some of these elites—involved with Venezuela's oil industry—muscled Chavez out of office. (Wherever there's a problem, there's oil. Venezuela is our third largest supplier.) America was—as far as I've been able to discern—*the only country in the world* that did not report this as a coup. U.S. papers reported that Chavez had suddenly "resigned" because members of "civil society" were fed up with his silly nationalization of Venezuela's resources.

Bullshit.

In an interview on Buzzflash.com, journalist Greg Palast speaks on the bullshit nature of the U.S. press coverage of the attempted coup in Venezuela:

> There was a report straight out of the United States State Department that Hugo Chavez, on April 12th, had resigned as President of Venezuela. This is a complete fabrication, lie, garbage, nonsense. And the *New York Times*, the *Los Angeles Times*—every major paper in the United States ran it. And by the way, PBS ran it as a stone-cold fact. And the entire factoid—the entire garbage nonsense of this was nothing better than a false press release from the U.S. State Department. Pure propaganda.

The military revolted; the people took to the streets and nonviolently freaked.

Within two days, President Chavez was back at Mira Flores, the presidential palace. (There's a lot more to this story and it you want to check it out go to gregpalast.com.)

Venezuelans were willing to have a goddamn neon yellow canary when *their* government was taken away from *them,* even though the coup-backing "media" *broadcast sitcoms* while President Chavez was spirited off by greedy men the U.S. would much rather deal with. Mr. Chavez's main flaw seems to be his unwillingness to allow U.S. oil giants to plunder Venezuela's resources.

Our resources are being plundered too, but we don't have a President Chavez, and we don't have a population of people who are willing to turn off their teevee and stop this utter nonsense.

The day after Arundhati Roy broke my heart with her words, I went to a (locally owned, independent) bookstore where Robin D. G. Kelley was reading from his new book, *Freedom Dreams: The Black Radical Imagination*

This proved to be one of those instances where the universe decides it's time to save my ass from utter despair.

Freedom Dreams is about how the fight for freedom occurs in the mind. I have long suspected this, but *Freedom Dreams* (I am reading it as I write this postscript) is showing me exactly how.

An excerpt:

> Too often, our standards for evaluating social movements pivot around whether or not they "succeeded" in realizing their visions rather than on the merits or power of the visions themselves. By such a measure, virtually every radical movement failed because the basic power relations they sought to change remain pretty much intact. And yet it is precisely these alternative visions and dreams that

inspire new generations to struggle for change.

(Preface, p. vii)

We've been getting shafted for a long time now. We have fought, and the freaky little white men have prevailed. The stories of our fights are glossed over in the freaky little white men's history, which is partly how they have prevailed. Now they are poised to kill the earth, and this is not about signing petitions and attending protests. This is about eradicating fascinations with celebrities who contribute nothing to our imaginations. This is about telling our stories, poetically employing our imaginations in the actions of our every day lives. And this is about loving each other.

When I saw Robin D. G. Kelley reading, I wondered how frightening it must be to come out in public and talk to people about love and imagination. He is an academic, a noted historian, an analyst of social movements, a professor at New York University. He is not "supposed" to talk about the power of love and imagination. To do so places him in danger of being invalidated by his peers. Maybe I am projecting, for I have been publicly belittled for speaking of such things, but this book is obviously very close to his heart, and he is incredibly courageous for speaking of love in such hate-filled times.

What does it say about our culture when it is considered "dangerous" to talk about the power of love and imagination?

What really set a fire under my ass is when Professor Kelley discussed how social movements are not necessarily huge groups of people making things change:

"Sometimes, it just takes one person, like Ivory Perry of St Louis—a Civil Rights activist who sometimes chained himself to monuments or cars and blocked traffic for miles to draw attention to certain struggles for social justice."

Please read *Freedom Dreams*.

A young woman named Selemawit Tewelde hit this point home. Ms. Tewelde is a teenager in Philadelphia who does not want her school to be privatized, and thanks to her and a handful of other youth's actions, her school probably won't be.

A lot of students probably think, "I don't care, since nobody's asking me how I feel about what's going on with this," she says. That's how everything gets messed up. Young people start to feel powerless, but they're not. They're very powerful—and they need to understand that. (*Mother Jones,* May, 2002)

My only addition to this is that "young people" aren't the only ones who are very powerful.

Yesterday I felt like shit, so I rode my bike around town and repeatedly grafittied "The revolution is not being televised" in paint pen. It was a "pointless" action, but it nonetheless healed me to do this. It was an act of love for that "hooligan" Arundhati Roy. It was an act of self-love. I don't expect it to change the world, but on the other hand, I know it will.

Inga Muscio
Los Angeles, California
June 2002

Cuntlovin' Guide To the Universe
Revised and Updated World Domination Version

As Derrick Jensen so lovingly explained in his introduction, we're fucked.

We're more fucked now than when I first wrote *Cunt,* and back then I was primarily focused on women (though I inadvertently excluded tranny folks). I know that women are the poorest people on the face of the earth. I am more committed to the freedom of women than I ever have been. There are, however, many people who are not women, and I am committed to their freedom as well. The first Cuntlovin' Guide to the Universe was geared toward women creating community.

Everyone is in this together, now.

If a rich white frat boy from the Connecticut suburbs is willing to face himself and the past he represents in order to totally resist the forces that are shaping our world, then I am not of a mind to exclude him.

Since we're all fucked, I don't see any point entertaining any limitations.

This resource guide is not only more inclusive, but also bigger than the last one. I figure people need more resources this time around. I've included as many listings as I can possibly cram in, and in exchange, opted to forgo the lengthy descriptions I am so fond of.

If something is listed in here, rest assured, it proactively contributes to a world envisioned around the premise that life, lived realities and the planet are sacred and must be protected at all costs.

While the Cuntlovin' Guide to the Universe has expanded significantly, it is still not even close to a comprehensive listing of all the products, businesses, services, organizations and events working to end white male domination. The present universe of resistance and revolution is massive, to say the least.

We got us murderers, morons, neo-fascists and liars in our midst. It is not difficult to figure out what they're up to (making money) and how they are going about it (plundering the earth's resources) and what their goal happens to be at present (domination of the planet).

We are living in incredibly interesting times.

Saving the planet and everything on it is certainly a daunting task; but see, push has come to shove.

Every moment you choose inaction, a freaky little white man carves a few more days off our collective life span.

Let's roll.

The News

Guerrilla News Network

GNN rules. In-depth interviews, analysis, special investigative reports, the works. Vociferously anti-corporation and anti–freaky little white men. guerrillanews.com.

Independent MediaCenter

News and views from around the world and your own backyard. Sites in most major cities in the world report on protests, actions and atrocities the mainstream media steers right clear of. indymedia.org.

yellowtimes.org

Yellowtimes.org offers readers an alternative to "the exploitation of public figures, the distortion of real world problems, and the exaggeration of unimportant events."

Buzzflash

The quintessential news source, with links to articles and news sites all over the world. Buzzflash also features articles from the English-speaking European and Indian press. They have a pro-Democrat slant, which I'm not inclined to trust, but they feature the largest, most comprehensive listing of articles available. buzzflash.com.

worldpress.org

The site for *World Press Review* magazine, a compilation of articles from newspapers around the world. The print version makes intensive forays into specific issues, while the website is updated daily. Special rates for educators and students.

Center for Public Integrity

Featuring investigative articles from around the world. publicintegrity.org/dtaweb/home.asp.

mediawhoresonline.com

Whistle-blowers on lame-assed journalists who suck corporate cock instead of reporting the goddamn news.

mediatank.org, mediachannel.org, mediaed.org
Organizations with opportunities to get involved in activities
and events challenging and changing destructive media images.
Seize the news.

butchdykeboy.com
This is not a news site per se, but the news they do post is so
comprehensive and up-to-date, I am including it here in the
news section. ButchDykeBoy is a massive, sprawling trans-
activist site filled to the gills with inspiration, stories, information, events, and daily local postings. Part of the ButchDykeBoy
Empire. I love, love, love butchdykeboy!!!!!

Common Dreams
"Breaking news and views of the progressive community."
Compilations of articles from some of the thinkingest thinkers
of our time. Links to most major shit-talking publications in the
world. Updated daily. commondreams.org.

democraticunderground.com
DU has breaking news, analysis, columnists ("Ask Auntie
Pinko"), links to other reliable news sources and up-to-the-
minute discussion threads. Also, they sell cool T-shirts.

americaheldhostile.com
Everything you ever wanted to know about what the Bush
administration is up to.

Magazines & Zines

AWOL

The Revolutionary Artists Workshop. The print version of this magazine comes with a full-length CD of music and poetry, and it's only five bucks. Perhaps inspired by the now-defunct *Blu* magazine (RIP) in its awe-inspiring vision. The website has articles, art, merchandise and, most importantly, links. Consider all of the links part of this guide—they include *Redwire* magazine, *Redeye* magazine and the Black Panther Collective. 1515 Cherry Street, Philadelphia, PA 19102, (800) NO-JROTC, awol@objector.org, awol.objector.org.

Hip Mama

Never was and never will be just for mamas. In a country where "three million parents have attended training sessions to make their families more like mini-corporations" (according to *Stay Free!* magazine), *Hip Mama* remains the most important magazine in America. P.O. Box 12525, Portland, OR 97212, hipmama.com.

Stay Free!

This incredibly witty, politically astute magazine comes out around every ten months. I love *Stay Free!* They'll send free bulk issues to schools, so demand that your school order it. Also, subscribe. P.O. Box 306, Prince Street Station, New York, NY 10012, stayfreemagazine.org.

Danzine
A zine, store and networking organization for folks working in the sex industry. danzine.org.

Moxie
A wonderful magazine, with links to many other wonderful sites. moxiemag.com.

Colorlines
Race, culture, action. Published quarterly. In-depth analysis of current events, activism and general ass-kicking. A brilliant periodical from cover to cover. PMB 319, Oakland, CA 94611-5221, (510) 653-3415, arc.org/C_Lines/ArcColorLines.html.

Bamboo Girl
"Pro-Filipina/Asian/Asian mutt, pro-female, pro-fuck oppression." I am *such* an ass for forgetting about *Bamboo Girl* in the first edition of the Cuntlovin' Guide to the Universe. How could I have forgotten about this total mainstay? Please forgive me, *Bamboo Girl.* bamboogirl.com.

War Times
A bimonthly newspaper in English and Español, of which I am a proud distributor. Vital, vital, vital. EBC/War Times, 1230 Market Street, PMB 409, San Francisco, CA 94102, (510) 869-5156, war-times.org.

Alice

One of my current favorite magazines, *Alice* intelligently and artfully covers an astounding array of topics in each issue. Their clever tagline: "For Women on the Other Side of the Looking Glass." alicemagazine.com.

Clamor

"New perspectives on politics, culture, media and life." Issue #14 is concerned with the power of youth. *Clamor* is a Become the Media project; BtM also organizes the annual Underground Publishers Conference, "A weekend devoted to educating ourselves about reclaiming media resources," in Bowling Green, Ohio. Subscribe to this vital and ambitious magazine. clamormagazine.org

Soapboxgirls!

A great webzine outta Canada. soapboxgirls.com.

Muffy!: New Girly Life

Cultural criticism, realistic sexual discussions, advice and personal essays for teens. Puts together cool events. The site's not extensive—subscribe to the print version. *Muffy!* magazine, 4941 Winchester Drive, Sarasota, FL 34234, muffymagazine.com.

mysistahs.org

A site by and for young women of color. Includes a gallery with poetry, essays and short stories, as well as information on body image, STDs, teen pregnancy, HIV testing and emergency contraception. This is not technically a magazine—it's more of an organization—but they have lots of feature articles. Check it out.

A Gathering of the Tribes
Through its programs and publications, this organization creates a performance venue and a space for artists and audiences to meet across artistic disciplines, levels of complexity and definitions of difference. A Gathering of the Tribes publishes *Tribes* magazine and hosts events and readings in New York City almost every weekend. (212) 674-5576, info@tribes.org, tribes.org.

Venus (magazine)
A massive, intergenerational resource for black lesbians, gay men and their families. Unlike most "gay" mags, *Venus* is all-gender inclusive. venusmagazine.com

Venus (zine)
Not to be confused with *Venus* magazine. This *Venus* is girls and rock 'n' roll. venuszine.com.

Multiple Shades of You
A multifaceted e-zine for women of color, from ages five to twenty-five. Brilliant. msoyonline.com.

To-Do List
The magazine of meaningful minutiae. P.O. Box 40128, San Francisco, CA 94140, todolistmagazine.com.

Doula
See *urbanthinktank.org* in the Kickass Organizations section.

Bitch
2765 16th Street, San Francisco, CA 94103, bitchmagazine.com,
(415) 864-6671, bitchmagazine.com.

Bust
P.O. Box 1016, Cooper Station, New York, NY 10276, bust.com.

Girljock
P.O. Box 882723, San Francisco, CA 94188-2723, (415) 282-6833,
girljock.com.

Anything That Moves
Internationally distributed bisexual magazine containing stories,
poetry, news and other information of interest. Theme-based
and quarterly. 2261 Market Street #496, San Francisco, CA
94114, (415) 626-5069, anythingthatmoves.com.

Les Voz
Les Voz, la revista lésbica de México. A lesbian feminist site and
print magazine, in glorious Español. Huge site with many
listings, links and resources. lesvoz.org.mx.

Fat!So?
It's a book, it's a zine, it's a social movement. Marilyn Wann is a
hilarious genius. P.O. Box 423464, San Francisco, CA 94142,
fatso.com.

Yell-Oh Girls

"Emerging voices for Asian-American girls." Also a book, a zine and a social movement. yellohgirls.com.

Z

Everybody knows about *Z* magazine. Read all of Arundhati Roy's articles tonight. zmag.org.

Monolid

"For those who aren't blinking." The current issue, "Fear and Loathing in the New Millennium," examines the culture of fear and hate post-9/11. monolid.com.

Hardboiled

A student-run Asian/Pacific Islander issues news magazine at UC Berkeley. Sponsors cool local events. 201 Heller Lounge, Martin Luther King, Jr. Student Union, UC Berkeley, CA 94720, hardboiled.org.

Tongues

This queer Latina webzine features erotica, essays, poetry and political resistance, and sponsors events in the Los Angeles area. tonguesmagazine.org.

Dollars & Sense

The magazine of economic justice, run by a collective of graduate students, journalists, professors and activists. Comes out six times a year and also publishes books. This mag engagingly explains the world of global economics. 740 Cambridge Street, Cambridge, MA 02141, dollarsandsense.org

Nervy Girl!
P.O. Box 16601, Portland, OR 97292, (503) 25-NERVY, nervygirlzine.com.

Rockrgrl
A feminist music magazine that's been around and adored for a long time. Organizers of the Rockrgrl conference in Seattle, WA. rockrgrl.com.

Aviva
Webzine run by an international group of feminists in London. Free monthly listing service for women and groups worldwide. Click on their map of the world to see what's shakin'. 41 Royal Crescent, London W11 4SN, United Kingdom, aviva.org.

grrrlzines.net
A really great all-around resource.

Dream/Girl
Encourages creative genius in girls. dgarts.com.

panderzinedistro.com
Pander founder Ericka Lyn Bailey says, "I distribute wonderful zines by wonderful kids from all over the world," and she does, indeed. She also prints a biannual catalog and hosts a pretty dang extensive website.

idealpolitik
This bilingual zine is a joint effort between "Chile and the U$A," involving folks from independent, revolution-minded record labels and other organizations. idealpolitik.org.

Independent Bookstores and the Publishing World

My first choice in bookstores are the ones owned by women, but I am also an avid supporter of bookstore collectives, which go above and beyond the call of duty in serving their communities. Bookstore collectives often organize teach-ins, protests and other community events. I have not been able to find an online listing of nationwide bookstore collectives. The incredibly popular Slingshot Daily Planner has the most comprehensive listing of bookstore collectives I am aware of; you can get one at slingshot.tao.ca. Other collectives can be found by hitting the links at the Lucy Parsons Center (tao.ca/~lucyparsons/).

Feminist Bookstores Index
This listing of women-owned bookstores primarily focuses in the United States and Canada, but has listings from all over the world. I don't know how often they update this site because New York City's Bluestocking Books is not listed, and they opened in 1999. igc.org/women/bookstores.

bookhousecafe.com
An online bookstore and community for black, gay, lesbian, bisexual, transgender and same-gender-loving folks. Contains a gigantic listing of books, a book club and many other amenities.

booksense.com

You can enter your zip code to find all the independent book-stores in your area. Keep in mind that just because a bookstore is locally owned does not make it a proactive community forum. It was, after all, a female independent bookstore owner in Flagstaff who abruptly cancelled a scheduled reading by telling me that *Cunt* "did not promote family values."

Underground Publishers Conference
See *Clamor* magazine. This is another Become the Media project.

Pacific Asian American Women Writers–West
A nonprofit arts organization fostering artistic development in women writers of color and promoting, perpetuating and preserving Asian American and Pacific Islander literature, history and arts. paawww.org.

Context Books
Any company that has the courage to publish Derrick Jensen's *A Language Older Than Words* and *The Culture of Make Believe* is tops in my book. contextbooks.com.

mosaicbooks.com
A quarterly print and frequently updated online publication showcasing writers of color. Contains a gigantic listing of kickass links to organizations, people-of-color-owned bookstores and book clubs all over the U.S. and, for some reason, Italy.

Seal Press/Avalon Publishing Group
But of course! Check out Seal's great list o' books at
www.sealpress.com. Avalon Publishing Group, of which Seal is
now a part, also has some fabulous and subversive stuff. They
can be found at avalonpub.com. Seal is still independent and
not owned by some big, bad media conglomerate but by Avalon
Publishing Group which consists of five imprints, Carroll & Graf
Publishers, Thunder's Mouth Press, Marlowe & Company, Seal
Press and Blue Moon Books. All five are independent presses
that have been combined under Avalon.

Soft Skull Press
"Fearless, progressive punk-rock/hip-hop literature." Publishers
of *The Battle of Seattle, Fortunate Son* and many other important
works. softskull.com.

Spinsters Ink
One of the few independent women's publishers in the United
States. P.O. Box 22005, Denver, CO, 80222, (800) 301-6860,
spinsters-ink.com.

chicanawriter.com
A networking site for Chicana writers.

Independent Publishing Resource Center
The name says it all: the IPRC offers everything you need to
self-publish, but you gotta go to Portland. 917 SW Oak Street
#218, Portland, OR 97205, (503) 827-0249, info@iprc.org,
iprc.org.

Eve's Eye Press

Eve's Eye offers an online mag (*Unpopular Opinions*), a catalog of the books they publish, and kickass links. P.O. Box 5003, Glendale, CA 91221, customer_service@eveseye.com, eveseye.com.

Aunt Lute Books

A multicultural women's press publishing such important works as Gloria Anzaldúa's *Borderlands/La Frontera: The New Mestiza,* Audre Lorde's *Cancer Journals* and the anthology *I Remember: Writings by Bosnian Women Refugees.* Aunt Lute stands out as one of the oldest, most dynamic independent presses in the country. P.O. Box 410687, San Francisco, CA 94141, (800) 949-LUTE, auntlute.com.

Bookmobile Project/Projet Mobilivre

The Bookmobile Project was founded by the Bookmobile Collective, a group of emerging North American artists and community activists. The group travels around the U.S. and Canada in an Airstream trailer stocked with independently published books and zines, visiting community centers, prisons and remote regions all over eastern North America and the U.S. Midwest. They also facilitate free bookbinding and zine-making workshops, discussions, video screenings and related educational forums. Support Bookmobile/Mobilivre! The more support they get, the more places they can go. C/O Space 1026, 1026 Arch Street, Philadelphia, PA 19107, info@mobilivre.org, mobilivre.org.

The Way Multi-Media Oughta Be

radio4all.org

"Connects you to the movement to reclaim the airwaves." With micro news radio archives, micro radio station information and links to micro stations all over the country. Will help you start your own low-power FM radio station. Part of the wonderfully revolutionary digitaldisaster.org network.

Free Speech TV

This is the only U.S. teevee station I'm aware of that actually gives you news and assumes its viewers possess intelligence. Full-time satellite on the Dish Network: channel 9415. Part-time cable: check your local listing to see if you have it. Affiliate channels all over the country. P.O. Box 6060, Boulder, CO 80306, freespeech.org.

bringthenoise.com

Underground world Internet radio with news, shows, top ten countdowns and grassroots resistance concerts and events.

Listen Up!

Since January 1999, Listen Up! has helped more than a thousand young people from diverse backgrounds research, write, produce, edit and distribute their own media, organizing conferences, festivals, internships and funding for projects. 6 E 32nd Street, 8th floor, New York, NY 10016, (212) 725-7000, listenup.org.

mediawatch.com

"Challenging racism, sexism and violence in the media through education and action," Media Watch distributes videos, media literacy kits and newsletters to help create more informed media viewers. A great resource for everyone, especially educators, concerned parents and students.

Telemanita AC

A Mexican website helping women in video production organize and educate. En Español. Apartado Postal 199, Tepoztlán, Morelos, CP 62520, (52) 739-516-56, laneta.apc.org/telemanita.

infoshop.org

An anarcho-media site with a reading room, coverage of anti-capitalist movements, and many other resources. Just insanely comprehensive. They even have quotes of the week from geniuses like Eduardo Galeano.

5050summit.com

A website with info on historical women filmmakers, stats on women film directors, director interviews and great links.

standby.org

Provides cheap post-production services to video filmmakers. Also publishes *Felix,* a great journal for video makers.

Paper Tiger Television

Smashing the myths of the information industry. Support Paper Tiger! 339 Lafayette Street, New York, NY 10012, (212) 420-9045, papertiger.org.

Deep Dish Television

A national satellite network (Free Speech TV is on it) linking producers, programmers, independent video makers, activists and people who support a progressive teevee network. Same mailing address as Paper Tiger Television. (212) 473-8933, Igc.org/deepdish.

Jean Kilbourne

An analyst of advertising images of women, a public speaker and the creator of the documentary *Killing Us Softly* (and others). Lordly & Dame, 51 Church Street, Boston, MA 02116, (617) 482-3593, jeankilbourne.com.

graffiti.org

Showcases graffiti artists from all over the world, with information, history, resources and events.

gendertalk.com

Home of a Boston talk-radio program on gender issues, featuring over 250 inspiring, entertaining, informative programs covering every aspect of gender. Includes an extensive resources section.

Mad Screenwriter

Writing, film, music, history, technology, resources, links, casting calls, a reference desk and multimedia galleries. madscreenwriter.com/womens.htm.

Women in the Director's Chair

941 W Lawrence #500, Chicago, IL 60640, (773) 907-0610, widc.org.

About-Face

A San Francisco–based nonprofit that promotes positive self esteem in girls and women of all ages, sizes, races and backgrounds through their spirited approach to media education, outreach, poetic guerrilla activism tactics and much more. about-face.org.

Video Data Bank

A resource library of videotapes by and about contemporary video artists. Founded in 1976, at the beginning of the U.S. media arts movement. 112 S Michigan Avenue, Chicago, IL 60603, (312) 345-3550, vdb.org.

Asian Media Access

AMA's mission is to "connect the disconnected," challenging the traditional isolation of Asian-American communities by helping Asian-Americans realize the media can be an effective tool for communication and education. amamedia.org.

Sisters in Cinema

Sisters in Cinema is a resource guide for African-American women filmmakers. The site has (among other cool things) clips from Yvonne Welbon's documentary *Sisters in Cinema,* an overview of African-American women filmmakers from the 1920s to today. sistersincinema.com.

Women Make Movies
Get their catalog to create a film festival in your town. 462 Broadway, Suite 500WS, New York, NY 10013, (212) 925-0606, wmm.com.

CFMDC
The Canadian Filmmakers Distribution Centre. 37 Hanna Avenue, Suite 220, Toronto, Ontario, M6K 1W8, Canada, (416) 588-0725, cfmdc.org.

Zeitgeist Films
A catalog of great independent films from all over the place. 247 Centre Street, Second Floor, New York, NY 10013, (212) 274-1989, zeitgeistfilms.com.

First Run Features
First Run Features was recently honored by MOMA for its more than twenty ass-busting years of indie-homo film distribution. 153 Waverly Place, New York, NY 10014, (800) 229-8575, firstrunfeatures.com.

Third World Newsreel
Founded in 1967 as Newsreel, TWN is one of the oldest alterna-
tive media organizations in the United States. TWN has trained
over 250 film and video artists through its annual Advanced
Film and Video Production Workshop. 545 Eighth Avenue, Tenth
Floor, New York, NY 10018, (212) 947-9277, twn.org.

mediarights.org
A community website that helps media makers, educators,
nonprofits and activists use documentaries to encourage action
and inspire dialogue on contemporary social issues. The site
offers documentaries on issues facing most everyone who lives
in the real world.

The Video Activist Network
Everything for the established and aspiring video activist.
videoactivism.org.

Frameline
Frameline provides access to films dealing with issues related to
sexuality and gender. Each year they present the San Francisco
International Lesbian and Gay (but not transgendered???) Film
Festival. frameline.org.

Music Type Stuff
Michigan Womyn's Music Festival
The big, gorgeous kahuna. michfest.com

Camp Trans

A trans-inclusive response to the Michigan Womyn's Music Festival's trans-exclusion policy. Camp Trans happens during the second weekend in August, just off the property of the MWMF. camptrans.cjb.net.

Hip Hop Congress

An annual national conference connecting music, communities and social movements. Music is only one aspect of the hip hop movement, and the essays, science section, interviews and calls for action illustrate this quite clearly. hiphopcongress.com.

womensfestival.com

A global listing of women's festivals all over the world.

ladyfest.org

Links to those lively Ladyfests all over the country.

Mujerfest

Held in South Texas. chicanastuff.com/mujerfest.

gogirlsmusic.com

"Cuz chicks rock." An online community of indie women musicians.

gogirlsmusicfest.com

A U.S. tour with bands varying from city to city.

insound.com

The best online store for indie CDs.

Rock 'n' Roll Camp for Girls

They have a sliding scale from $50.00 to $1,000.00. *No girl is turned away for lack of funds.* P.O. Box 86633, Portland, OR 97286-0633, (503) 771-4789, girlsrockcamp.org.

Freedom Fighter

The first compilation album put out by this label, *Shame the Devil: Hip Hop Tells the Truth about the Prison-Industrial Complex,* has eleven songs and interviews with anti-corporate prison organizers. Revolutionary music for these times of duress. freedomfighter.ws.

Garment District

An online store with a fairly comprehensive listing of a bunch of (mostly eastern seaboard) independent record labels, including Villa Villakula Records. garment-district.com/store/music.

Higher Octave Music

Puts out an astounding amount of world, Latin and cross-cultural music. higheroctave.com.

Heartcore Records

heartcorerecords.net.

Chainsaw Records
chainsaw.com.

Kill Rock Stars
killrockstars.com.

Righteous Babe Records
righteousbabe.com.

Mr. Lady Records & Video
mrlady.com.

papayarecords.com
This is where to get *Cuban Hip-Hop Allstars, Vol. I.* The history
of Cuban rap is fascinating and teaches Americans a lot about
our consumer habits. Look for Instinto, Cuba's number-one all-
women hip-hop group.

rapstation.com
It would be nice if this site featured more women artists, but the
site is still pretty cool. They're connected to a bunch of indie
hip-hop labels, and have radio shows, news and many other
such life-affirming things.

Madness Factor Music Collective
A not-for-profit resource network for women seeking careers in
the music biz. One of the many cool organizations found on
Home Alive's website. (206) 675-9948, homealive.org/arts.htm.

Ye Olde Sex Shoppes

It's wonderful to announce that women- and trans-positive sex stores are popping up everywhere. Even some bookstores (like Book Garden, in Denver, Colorado, and Common Language in Ann Arbor, Michigan) have little sex areas discreetly tucked away.

Good Vibrations

The grandmother of all sex shops. Now there's two. San Francisco: 1210 Valencia Street, San Francisco, CA 94110, (415) 974-8980. Berkeley: 2504 San Pablo Avenue, Berkeley, CA 94702, (510) 841-8987. (800) 289-8423, goodvibes.com.

Toys in Babeland

With winsome public relation tactics like the Masturbate-A-Thon, the women at Babeland have great senses of humor. They put everyone at ease. Seattle: 707 E Pike Street, Seattle, WA 98122, (206) 328-2914. New York: 94 Rivington Street, (212) 375-1701. (800) 658-9119, babeland.com.

It's My Pleasure

This store moved right after the first edition of *Cunt* came out, so their address was wrong for a long time. One of the most beautiful sex shops in the country. 3106 NE 64th Avenue, Portland, OR 97213, (503) 280-8080.

A Woman's Touch

600 Williamson Street, Madison, WI 53703-4509, (888) 621-8880, (608) 250-1928, a-womans-touch.com.

Grand Opening!

Kim Airs, the owner of this august establishment, is a goddamn miracle worker. She has singlehandedly increased the sexual openness and awareness in her legendarily puritanical neighborhood. When I went there for a reading, she saw Mike Dukakis and got him to give me his autograph. 318 Harvard Street, Suite 32, Brookline, MA 02446, (617) 731-2626, grandopening.com.

Eve's Garden

119 W 57th Street, Suite 1201, New York, NY, 10019, (800) 848-3837, evesgarden.com.

Ruby's Pearl

13 S Linn Street #3, Iowa City, IA 52240, (319) 248-0032.

Healing

Boston Women's Health Book Collective

Publisher of *Our Bodies, Ourselves* and its Spanish translation, *Nuestros Cuerpos, Nuestras Vidas.* BWHBC also facilitated translation of the book into seventeen other languages. P.O. Box 192, Somerville, MA 02144, (617) 414-1230, ourbodiesourselves.org.

Association of Asian Pacific Community Health Organizations
AAPCHO works to provide low-cost heath care to everyone in
Asian-Pacific communities. aapcho.org.

sexuality.org
This is a huge, sprawling site dedicated to human sexuality.
They've got links to almost every cool sex store in the country,
an antique vibrator museum, sex toy guides and a nationwide
calendar of events. They publish books and a magazine, and
they have amazing educational programs. The all-around best
sex site I know of. Part of the sex education web circle.

The Coalition for Positive Sexuality
The coalition asserts that all teenagers have the right to complete and honest sex education. CPS is a grassroots, not-for-
profit activist organization that provides sex education,
resources and support for youth of all races, genders, sexualities
and ethnicities. P.O. Box 77212, Washington, DC 20013-7212,
(773) 604-1654, positive.org.

scarleteen.com
"Sex Education for the Real World." Another really wonderful,
inclusive site that supports and educates teens who want to
know more about sex, birth control, AIDS and more.

survivorproject.org
A nonprofit dedicated to addressing the needs of intersex and
trans survivors of domestic and sexual violence through "caring
action, education and expanding access to resources." See also

transfeminism.org in the Kickass Revolutionary Organizations section.

The Native American Women's Health Education Resource Center
Your all-around extensive resource and education site for Native and First Nation women. You can support NAWHERC by purchasing T-shirts, postcards, Dakota language books and tapes, and works by community artists. P.O. Box 572, Lake Andes, SD 57356-0572, nativeshop.org/nawherc.html.

geocities.com/capitolhill/9118/mike.html
This site documents NAWHERC's report on coerced sterilization of Native American women carried out by the Indian "Health" Services, Job Corps and other agencies. The site also includes a bookstore, search engine and comprehensive bibliography.

ultimatebirthcontrol.com
Extensive links to information about birth control.

National Black Women's Health Project
NBWHP provides wellness education, services, health information and advocacy. Lots of wonderful links, and cool positive affirmations like "I have the power within me to contribute to my personal healing." 600 Pennsylvania Avenue SE, Suite 310, Washington, DC 20003, (202) 543-9311, nationalblackwomenshealthproject.org.

Feminist Women's Health Center
FWHC has regional offices in a number of locations, mostly on the west coast, and is a massive resource for information about women's health. Did you know, for instance, that every man, woman and teenager can get free birth control in Washington state? Not through the humiliating DSHS, either. Site is in English and Español. fwhc.org.

National Asian Women's Health Organization
Founded in 1993 to achieve health equity for Asian woman and their families. The site features a huge listing of health resources. nawho.org.

The Blood Sisters Project
As ever, the most wonderful menstrual activism group for everyone. Blood Sisters is based in Montreal. They offer zines, links, pads and other wonderful "urban armor" menstrual gear. bloodsisters.org.

Lunapads
More Canadians hard at work improving the quality of life for bleeders and the planet. Lunapads come from a clothing designer who got sick of the way we poison our bodies with the toxins commonly found in disposable pads and tampons. Lunapads are by far my favorite pad. lunapads.com.

GladRags

Comfortable, well-designed cloth pads and other goodies. They
also have a great little book called *Passage: A Girl's Guide,*
written for the newly bleeding. I highly recommend this book
for any parent or school that wants to give their girls a chance to
see periods in a positive way from the get-go. gladrags.com.

thekeeper.com

The site explains all the virtues of this ingenious little device.

adiosbarbie.com

A body image site á la that mortal genius, Ophira Edut.

GINE Web

Site en Español for online health and well-being information.
Serves as a hub for hundreds of links and resources. unizar.es/
gine/hola.htm.

Center for Research on Women with Disabilities (CROWD)

This is more of a research resource than a practical, hands-on
site. But it has extensive information on sexuality, reproductive
health, chronic conditions, mental health, alternative medicine,
surviving sex abuse, getting access to health care, and community living. 3440 Richmond Avenue, Suite B, Houston, TX 77046,
(800) 44-CROWD, (713) 960-0505, bcm.tmc.edu/crowd.

annelawrence.com

Really good and informative medical site for trans-women, by
Anne Lawrence, MD, Ph.D.

Barbara Robertson's Women and Disability Resources
For all women with disabilities. Information about economics,
sexuality and general resources. According to the site, "Looking
at disability through the lens of a feminist, and at feminism
from a disability perspective, enriches both feminism and
disability studies with fresh insights." members.tripod.com/
~Barbara_Robertson/Women.html.

National Abortion Referral Federation
On Home Alive's site. In fact, the links and resources on Home
Alive's site should be accessed by all. (800) 772-9100,
homealive.org/resources.htm.

fight4choice.com
This NARAL site keeps watch on the Bush administration,
Congress and the courts. Send letters to state representatives,
sign petitions, donate, and get involved locally. Includes
previous advocacy results and one hundred ways to fight for
choice.

Cunt Mall-O-Rama

The National Mayor's Convention convened in Madison,
Wisconsin, this year to discuss how corporations and civic
localities can better "cooperate." They've even invented a new
word for "cooperation" on this scale: "glocalization."

It is *fucking imperative* that people figure out ways to shop
locally. I've heard all the arguments that Target is cheaper and
Wal-Mart has such intensely time-saving one-stop shopping, and

all I can tell you is that we have to learn completely different consumer habits and belief systems.

My mother recently told me that around four years ago, a lady showed up at her front door and asked if there were any flowers that she could pick. Her name was Maria and she made bouquets from people's yards and sold them. My mother—who thinks people who hoard their flowers miss *the entire point* of gardening—told her she was welcome to pick whatever. Since then, every June and December, Maria has harvested some of the flowers in my mom's garden. A few days later, a gift of food or candles—or even small flower bouquets—appears on my mom's front porch.

By recontextualizing a plentiful resource, Maria is able to create an income. By not being materialistically attached to the flowers she grows, my mother receives love-filled gifts from an almost total stranger.

This is an example of thinking differently about economics. Here is another:

A few months ago, I realized I didn't know what happened to my coffee table. I had one once, but I lost it, or gave it away, so I needed another. There are many creative ways of procuring a coffee table, from running into Starbucks and grabbing one (their employees are forbidden to give chase), to spending an entire weekend garage sale-ing, to building one out of found objects. I opted for a tactic I use when holiday shopping: I pick one store whose owners I like and want to support, and I buy everything there. A thrift store in my neighborhood that specializes in furniture is owned by a husband, wife and baby. The wife and baby run the front and the husband refinishes furniture in the back. I like them. I stalked this thrift store for two months before I found a coffee table. The one I found was gorgeous and much less expensive than one from a corporate furniture outlet. Furthermore, 100 percent of the profits went to a struggling family.

And I can hear many an American shopper say, "You waited *two months* for a coffee table?" To which I would answer: "What kind of delusional force is ruling your heart that inspires you to think that two months is a long time to wait for some fucking decorative material good that does not involve life or death?"

When applied to holiday shopping, the "focus on one store" tactic is quite the stress reducer as well. I have one toy/book store for my nephews, and I pick a new business/product for adults every year.

There are thousands of consumer beliefs that we uphold which make no sense whatsoever, and serve no one but huge, uncaring corporations.

Shopping locally does not mean spending more money. Go to breadhours.org to see what one city is doing to create an alternative economy. Local businesses are much more inclined to barter time and goods, but this involves communication and dialogue. Being a responsible consumer is letting go of the idea that money talks.

Money doesn't talk, people do.

thehumanbean.com

The Human Bean's motto is "Putting human values before profit values." They are fine purveyors of Café Chiapas Zapatista coffee, fairly traded, transitional organic, shade-grown coffee "for the autonomous indigenous communities of Chiapas, Mexico." This also happens to be the best coffee I have ever had. The coffee is nine dollars a pound, which is pretty steep. However, if you are holiday shopping, spending nine dollars on each of your coffee-drinking friends and family is not so much, is it? Also, the coffee is sold for $6.20 a pound for ten pounds. If you got together with a few of your friends and bought a bulk quantity of coffee, you'd be paying less than most whole bean coffees in the grocery store. The site also has a great history of the Zapatista movement and links to many other organizations.

simpletreats.com

Featuring the best brownies I have ever tasted on Lordisa's good earth. They also sell (and ship!) cookies and other treats. All vegan, all the time. Simple Treats will be publishing a cookbook soon, too. (866) 33-VEGAN.

Autonomedia

This is where to find the Sheroes calendar. It costs an astounding *five dollars.* That means fifty bucks and you got birthday gifts for all your friends for the entire year. The calendar has a different woman for each day of every month and a short bio about how she fought for her people—whoever "her people" may be—all over the world and throughout history. I have learned so much from this calendar. I keep it by the phone and read it instead of getting annoyed while I am on hold and would otherwise be subject to a "samba" version of "Born to Be Wild." Autonomedia also has an impressive stable of books that they publish and distribute. autonomedia.org.

thelunapress.com
The most wonderful lunar calendar in the English-speaking world.

craftswomen.com
This is the hub for many of the women who sell stuff at the Michigan Womyn's Music Festival. Here, you can purchase many handmade or locally created products. Look for Maat Dompim, Magic Mountain Mama's Spices, Amoja ThreeRivers' insightful book *Cultural Etiquette* and Amy Wang's exceptionally beautiful clocks made from recycled/discarded items. You can find clothes, quilts, jewelry, candles, pottery, soaps, sandals and all kinds of other stuff. Many of the women are open to bartering time, goods or services.

buyolympia.com
Multicolored vegan pleather purses, wallets and belts designed by you and made by Queen Bee. Calendars and art by the amazing Nikki McClure and many other artists, musicians and activists in Olympia. This site is a template for connecting artists and responsible consumers in every town.

Sublime Stitching

Hand embroidered goods by Jenny Hart in Austin, TX. You can
have your portrait stitched! Sublime Stitching, P.O. Box 8345,
Austin, TX 78713, sublimestitch.com.

Sparkle Craft

Hand made home decor, journals, purses, belts, guitar straps,
accessories, potty room stuff and consignment shop. Tina
Lockwood, P.O. Box 163961, Austin, TX 78716-3961,
sparklecraft.com.

Naughty Secretary Club

An online zine and jewelry store, also Austin-based. (Sublime
Stitching, Sparkle Craft and Naughty Secretary Club comprise a
little craft mafia collective called Hand Made House—another
economic model worth emulating.) naughtysecretaryclub.com.

Double Dare Ya

Working with artists to further their message and work, including literature, music, crafts—distributing through communities
by independent retailers and online. 325 W 45th Street #602,
New York, NY 10036, doubledareya.net.

chicanastuff.com

A tiendita and networking resource for Chicanas and women of
color, offering zines, chapbooks, spoken word CDs, artwork and
artesanías.

piscescatalog.com

This is the "home of do-it-yourself creativity," with handmade items made mostly by teens and young women, but some grandmas, too. The catalog is run by Kerith Henderson, who is one enterprising and hilarious person. Evidently a Pisces, she sells clothes, undies, housewares ("Silly Bunny" and "Funky Owl" nightlights for $3.50, and "Witchy Little Special Jars") and more. The site has a rad selection of items, and a link over to pisces-soap.bigstep.com, where you can find dirt-scented garden soap with real gardens sticking out of them (must see), crispy-dill-pickle-shaped (and -scented) soap, and beautiful cunt soaps (only she calls them "kitty" soaps).

Media Action Alliance
Stickers to stick on stuff that pisses us off. Call or send for catalog. P.O. Box 391, Circle Pines, MN 55014-0391, (612) 434-4343.

Mamarama
Hello!!!!!! Handmade baby gear and hip gear for mamas-to-be and proud already-mamas. More than an online store, the site links to other great mama sites and stores. 3528 Emerald Street, Suite 5, Torrance, CA 90503, (310) 793-0696, mamaramastyle.com.

She Shoots, She Scores!
Featuring the "Bud the Silver Naked Trucker" sticker, one woman's clever response to the naked girl on the back of semi-truck mud flaps. Rachel Bachman, 2611 NW Upshur Street #207, Portland, OR 97210, (503) 243-7988.

One Angry Girl Designs

"Taking over the world, one shirt at a time." One Angry Girl also sells bumper stickers ("I Blame the Media," and "Fuck Your Fascist Beauty Standards") as well as Rachel Bachman's "Bud the Silver Naked Trucker" stuff. P.O. Box 745, Old Saybrook, CT 06475, oneangrygirl.net.

Co-op America

"Practical steps for using your consumer and investor power for social change." Co-op America publishes the National Green Pages; their programs include Green Business, Boycott Action News, Become Woodwise, Invest Responsibly, and End Sweatshops. Buy stuff at the Green Pages Store. 1612 K Street NW, Suite 600, Washington, DC 20006, (800) 58-GREEN, (202) 872-5307, coopamerica.org.

responsibleshopper.org

Learn more about the companies behind the products. Compare companies and investigate industries. Search by brand, product or company name. You can also contact companies through this site. Brought to us by Co-op America and Working Assets.

Social Investment Forum

For those of you with money to invest: do it right. Socially responsible investing. socialinvest.org.

diysearch.com

Do-it-yourself info on everything under the sun. Buy, barter, sell, post your product.

Kickass Revolutionary Organizations

The following listing of resources is a goddamn motley crew, to say the least. I considered "organizing" it by creating categories, something I know my editor would desire. But when I thought about it, the website that teaches us with cunts how to pee standing up is no less revolutionary and kickass than organizing with workers in Mexico and bringing their product directly to U.S. and Canadian consumers.

Coming up with "categories" is a divisionary act, and I don't have a lot of interest in divisions. Part of the problem with our culture is the need to "categorize" everything. I intend this extensive listing of websites and organizations to be *read,* as a story, as a mural of resistance.

After all, everyone's essentially saying the same thing.

"All we are saying is . . . 'fuck you, life is precious and this is our home, you mindlessly greedy piece of shit.'"

(My apologies to John Lennon. Maybe back then peace was enough. Presently, I want a world dominated by the wisdom of grandmothers.)

Not In Our Name

Join fellow Americans like Alice Walker, Yuri Kochiyama, Mos Def, Laurie Anderson and Edward Said in endorsing the Call. Have your whole family take the Pledge of Resistance, in English and Español. Not In Our Name organizes actions all over the country, and is working to get the mainstream media to recognize the will of the American people. notinourname.net.

International ANSWER

This organization has everything you need to understand what is going on with this so-called war and what you can do about it. Their extensive news reports are just one small part of this site. International ANSWER (Act Now to Stop War and End Racism) organizes the biggest anti-war and anti-racism actions in the United States. Support this vital organization. internationalanswer.org.

Maquila Solidarity Network

MSN works to promote solidarity with activists, workers and other groups in North America and Asia. Get news reports and updates from their site on sweatshops, actions, protests and union organizing. Search links from around the world. Hold excellent events like the "Sweatshop Fashion Show." This is yet another reason to appreciate Canadians. 606 Shaw Street, Toronto, Ontario, M6G 3L6, Canada, (416) 532-8584, maquilasolidarity.org.

Home Alive

Home Alive's site has so many links! This wonderful group is inclusive of all ages, races, religions and genders. Invite them to your town to teach folks how to protect themselves. 1122 E Pike Street #1127, Seattle, WA 98122, (206) 720-0606, homealive.org.

urbanthinktank.org

"For the body of thinkers in the hip-hop community." They pick up the slack-jawedness the Heritage Foundation inspires in the living majority. We need more think tanks!!! They also publish

Doula magazine, the journal of rap music and hip-hop culture. Women are totally represented in this mag.

aimovement.org

The American Indian Movement's official site, which features a live webcast, news, actions and resources such as declassified FBI/CIA documents. The AIM store has a lot of political resistance posters, T-shirts and more. Lots of links and a special area dedicated to the freedom of Leonard Peltier. The U.S. says we have "no political prisoners." My ass.

chicanas.com

A Chicana feminist site with a great listing of magazines, events and resources. Articles and profiles on Chicana sheroes, past and present.

transgender.org

Links to groups all over the country.

feministcampus.org

The site of Choices Campus Community, a project of the Feminist Majority Leadership Alliances, helps women start a pro-choice feminist group on campus. It also lists information on affiliated programs, such as Pro-choice Public Education Project and Rock for Choice. Find a feminist career, learn about the well-organized, well-funded right wing opposition to women's rights, start a mentoring program and more.

Madre

An international human rights organization supporting women and their families in combat zones around the world with medicine, counseling and justice programs. Find out what our country has been doing all over the world, and get involved with this very important organization. madre.org.

illegalvoices.org

A hub of anarchist sites, including Justice for Katie Sierra (Sierra is the fifteen-year-old girl who, sometime in October 2001, showed up for class at Sissonville High School in Charleston, West Virginia wearing a T-shirt with the hand-lettered message, "When I saw the dead and dying Afghani [sic] children on TV, I felt a newly recovered sense of national security"). Her entire community—including that bastion of free speech, the media—excoriated her. Can we please stick up for our children?

gender.org

Promotes gender education and advocacy, and educates about issues facing gender-variant people and society as a whole.

indiegURL.com

Serves as a hub for a number of indie gurl sites (technodyke.com rules) and lots of links for webmaster resources, technical website help, free fonts and much more. Figure out how to seize the Internet here.

Dads and Daughters

DADs provides tools to strengthen dads' relationships with daughters, with information on fathering, parenting, body image, media, sports, economic literacy and sexuality. P.O. Box 3458, Duluth, MN 55803, (888) 824-DADS, dadsanddaughters.org.

Sakhi

A community-based organization in the New York metro area committed to ending exploitation and violence against South Asian women. P.O. Box 20208, Greeley Square Station, New York, NY 10001, (212) 714-9153, sakhi.com. Hotline: (212) 868-6741.

National Gay and Lesbian Task Force

Without them, the world would be a lot more homophobic and clueless than it is, and in 1997, they formally included transfolks into their mission statement—but sooner or later, they're gonna hafta make their name trans-inclusive as well. ngltf.org.

GenderPAC

A national conference on gender. These folks have their shit together. Their Gender Tour travels all around the United States; they lobby, publish an annual report, and educate, charm and disarm for congressional advocacy. 1743 Connecticut Avenue NW, Fourth floor, Washington, DC 20009-1108, (202) 462-6610, gpac.org.

bilderberg.org
Find out how one of the most powerful organizations of freaky little white men works. Up-to-the-minute history on this incredibly influential, clandestine group of wealthy people.

Kearny Street Workshop
The workshop archives and showcases art that enriches and empowers Asian-American communities. kearnystreet.org.

Black Mesa Indigenous Support
Black Mesa is located in Arizona, and the government wants the resources that are located on sacred Indian land. The Peabody Western Coal Company, in particular, wants the uranium inside of Big Mountain, which many (including me) believe to be one of the earth's heart chakras. Find out how to help in this struggle for the earth. The site fills you in on this history and offers many ways to get involved in this imperative resistance. blackmesais.org.

Transgender Law and Policy Institute
These folks mean business: lobbying, litigation watch, hate crime law information and news. Paisley Currah runs their site, and she means even more business. Just ask Mayor Bloomberg. transgenderlaw.org.

transgenderlegal.com
Legal resources for gender-variant folks, on a site run by Phyllis Randolph Frye. In 1980, Ms. Frye singlehandedly changed the anti-cross-dressing law in **Houston**.

youthresource.com

For gay, lesbian, bisexual, transgender and queer youth all over the country. A veritable *mall* of resources and opportunities to create community.

ambientejoven.org

Youth Resource's site in glorious Español.

Third Wave Foundation

Young women activists and their organizations can apply here for funding, or pool resources and energy in support of other people's projects. Cool public education campaigns like "I Spy Sexism," news, resources, the works. 511 West 25th Street, Suite 301, New York, NY 10001, thirdwavefoundation.org.

Not Bored!

A witty-assed "anarchist, situationist-inspired, low-budget, irregularly published, photocopied journal." It's not in the magazine section because there are all kinds of fascinating activist activities going on here. This is where to find The Surveillance Camera Players—guerrilla programmers of video surveillance equipment. SCP C/O *Not Bored!*, P.O. Box 1115, Stuyvesant Station, New York, NY 10009, notbored.org.

girlstart.org

A nonprofit based in Austin, TX, encouraging and empowering girls in math, science, technology and engineering. They have a summer camp, with no price listed. I am assuming it is free.

tgender.net
The transgender network. Many sites are hosted by this
organization, including It's Time, America, and all of their
chapters. Rad.

corpwatch.org
Offers citizen policing of corporations and info on how to get
involved in their downfall, which you should probably do if you
want anything resembling a future to look forward to.

flag.blackened.net/revolt/zapatista.html
An index to a huge variety of resources and information on the
EZLN, the Zapatistas and the struggle for indigenous rights in
Chiapas.

tgfmall.com
Contains resources for finding local trans support groups.

sistahspace.com
A resource site with links to movies, travel companies, online
communities, classified ads, bulletin boards and much more. A
beautiful, simply designed site for young black women.

queerbychoice.com/masculinewomen.html
An extensive list of gender-variant vocabulary from all over the
planet, including word origins, which are always an excitement.

Reciprocity

Reciprocity helps community organizations learn how to work together, repair entrenched problems (such as racism and homophobia), and heal frustration and burnout. A very cool organization primarily focused on, but not limited to, the southeastern states. P.O. Box 25244, Raleigh, NC 27611, (919) 832-7406, creatingreciprocity.org.

glamdykerescueunit.org

The fabulous misses genderfuckers and their winsome manifesto. They offer an entire philosophy and activities for all things glamorous.

Zuna Institute

The Zuna Institute is a national advocacy organization of black lesbians, with a site that links to all the biggest queer conferences in the United States. 6114 LaSalle Avenue #527, Oakland, CA 94611, (510) 482-1671, zunainstitute.org.

National Black Herstory Task Force

They publish a quarterly newsletter, the *Herstorian,* and organize the annual Black Herstory Conference. Take the Herstory Quiz! I got six out of ten (B-). P.O. Box 55021, Atlanta, GA 30308, (404) 508-8040, blackherstory.org.

Mothers from Hell 2

A huge network of women who fight for the rights of their disabled children. "Our name was something that was bestowed

upon us for daring to stand up for our kids."
mothersfromhell2.org.

transfeminism.org
Home of The Transfeminist Anthology Project, intended to
facilitate communication between intersex people,
transfeminists and their allies. With news, links and feature
articles. This site is brought to you by Emi Koyama and Diana
Courvant, who are involved with the Survivor Project.

Fantasia Fair
The longest standing transgender educational event in the
world, Fantasia Fair started in 1975 in Provincetown, Massachusetts. More serious-minded folks call it Transgender Week.
Happens every fall. Daily educational and social programs,
events, shows, speakers and parties. Sponsored in part by the
Provincetown Tourism Fund, which shows how cool P-Town is,
huh. fantasiafair.org.

United Lesbians of African Heritage
ULOAH organizes an annual Sistahfest Retreat. Their site is
extensive, with many links and resources. They plan outings
into the beautiful areas surrounding Los Angeles. 1626 N Wilcox
Avenue #190, Los Angeles, CA 90028, (323) 960-5051,
members.aol.com/uloah/home.html.

Institute for Global Communications
A progressive networking organization that's been around since
1987. igc.org.

hanksville.net/NAresources

A comprehensive index of Native American resources, with links to sites on history, languages, health, art, jobs and activism.

Institute for Multiracial Justice

Founded in 1997, the Institute for Multiracial Justice works toward eroding white supremacy. If you think "Aryan Resistance" when you hear the term "white supremacy," it's time to hit the history books. They print a newsletter and organize a wonderful film festival. These folks are focused on building alliances. multiracialjustice.org.

The Disability Rights Activist

Their site is dated, but the information is still great. The links alone make up for the datedness. There's also a huge listing of research in government laws and policies about disabled folks. disrights.org.

ibsgwatch.org

Indian Burial and Sacred Grounds Watch features daily updates (Because daily updates are needed; because corporations are sundering sacred burial grounds at an unprecedented rate) on actions, protests and threats to sacred burial grounds. A culture that disrespects death can never, ever, ever respect life.

amboyz.org

The American Boyz are organizers of the national True Spirit Conference; their site has listings of events and a lot more.

herwebbiz.com

A networking and support community for businesswomen and women who'd like to start a business. A huge resource.

Malcolm X Grassroots Movement

A brilliant organization out of Central Brooklyn. MXGM has chapters all over the United States. They sponsor programs to feed, clothe and educate people in their communities. They offer protection by organizing programs like Cop Watch. Part of MXGM's mission is to "defend the human rights of our people and promote self-determination in our community." I can think of many, many groups and organizations that would benefit from patterning themselves after this movement. malcolmxgrassroots.org.

restrooms.org/standing.html

A woman's guide on how to pee standing up.

bigbadchinesemama.com

"The #1 mock mail-order bride/Asian porn spoof site in the world." Read the "Memoirs of an Anti-Geisha" section, then find Arthur Golden's email and tell him what a piece of shit he is. This is a cathartic and hilarious site that gives vengeance a fabulous name.

Gabriela Network

The Gabriela Network is the Philippine-U.S. Women's Solidarity Organization. They work on issues arising from U.S. policy decisions which negatively impact women and children in the Philippines. With chapters in the Bay Area, Chicago, Los Angeles and Washington state. Gabriela Network USA, P.O. Box 403, Times Square Station, New York, NY 10036, (212) 592-3507, gabnet.org.

Citizens Against Homophobia

Citizens Against Homophobia uses mass media campaigns to diminish homophobia. They provide materials mostly free of charge. 324 Shawmut Avenue, Boston, MA 02118, (617) 576-9866, actwin.com/cahp.

womensmemorial.org/NAHM.html

The Native American Women Veterans site. Over eight hundred Native American women served in the military during World War II. Very little is known about the history of Native women serving in the armed forces because "history" shoves Rosie the Riveter and G.I. Joe down our throats. This site helps set the record straight. The Women's Memorial is located at the Ceremonial Entrance to Arlington National Cemetery. (800) 222-2294.

Coalition Against Trafficking in Women

CATW is a non-governmental organization promoting women's human rights. The coalition works internationally to combat sexual exploitation in all its forms, especially prostitution and trafficking in women and children. CATW is composed of regional networks and affiliated groups and individuals. Their website has a factbook on what's going on in countries all over the world. catwinternational.org.

Women Against Military Madness
WAMM's site is huge and well connected. Not to be confused with wamm.org, which is Wo/Men for Medical Marijuana. Women Against Military Madness is celebrating its twentieth anniversary; I wish there wasn't a NEED for this organization to have been in existence for twenty years, though WAMM is indeed something to celebrate. 310 E 38th Street #225, Minne-apolis, MN 55409, (612) 827-5364, worldwidewamm.org.

janes.com
This site is a bit, uh, different from what you might consumeristically associate with the word "Jane." I hesitated before including this site, but while organizations like WAMM are an imperative aspect of our survival, so too is knowing what the freaky little white men are up to. Jane's is named after a U.K. battleship annotater, Fred T. Jane, and it has everything you never wanted to know about war and weaponry. Know thine enemy, babe.

actlab/utexas.edu/~geneve/zapwomen
Mujeres Zapatistas/Zapatista Women. Honoring women who have given their lives to the Zapatista Movement. Forum, history, links.

Funding Exchange

"The Funding Exchange is a partnership of activists and donors dedicated to building a base of support for progressive social change through fundraising for local, national and international grantmaking programs. FEX supports progressive community-based organizations that address the root causes of social problems, reaching beyond direct services to directly address the underlying conditions that foster inequity, lack of opportunity, discrimination and economic exploitation." In short, they give money to kickass organizations. 666 Broadway, Suite 500, New York, NY 10012, (212) 529-5300, fex.org.

Women's Venture Fund

The Women's Venture Fund is a nonprofit micro-lender that focuses on women entrepreneurs in urban communities. They also offer a calendar of events and business classes. 240 West 35th Street, Suite 201, New York, NY 10001, (212) 563-0499, wvf-ny.org.

People United for a Better Oakland

PUEBLO has fought for justice for Oakland's low-income communities and communities of color since 1989. peopleunited.org.

afrocubaweb.com

Connect with the people of Cuba. Learn about the fascinating Cuban hip-hop movement here; find out which musicians are on tour and coming to the United States. Learn about Assata Shakur, the warrior goddess of the hip-hop movement and exiled American political prisoner.

c
u
n
t

freepeltier.org, afrikan.net/sundiata, mumia.org, prisonactivist.org
Find out what the U.S. is doing in prisons besides letting
corporations buy them up and turn them into slave-labor
enterprises. Fight to free Leonard Peltier, Sundiata Acoli, Mumia
Abu-Jamal and thousands of other framed/illegally detained
political prisoners on U.S. soil. Sundiata Acoli is one of the
lesser known, but by no means more justifiably incarcerated,
political prisoners in America. If you want to know what
freedom really truly is, read *Prison Writings* by Leonard Peltier.

Have a nice, cuntlovin' day.

Selected Bibliography and Reading List

Acker, Kathy. *In Memoriam to Identity*. New York: Pantheon, 1992.

Acker, Kathy. *Blood and Guts in High School*. New York: Grover Weidenfeld, 1989.

Allen, Paula Gunn. *Spiderwoman's Granddaughters*. Boston: Beacon, 1989.

Allison, Dorothy. *Bastard Out of Carolina*. New York: Dutton, 1992.

Allison, Dorothy. *Two or Three Things I Know for Sure*. New York: Dutton, 1995.

Angelou, Maya. *I Know Why the Caged Bird Sings*. New York: Random House, 1970.

Angelou, Maya. *Just Give Me a Cool Drink of Water 'Fore I Die: The Poetry of Maya Angelou*. New York: Random House, 1971.

Atwood, Margaret. *The Handmaid's Tale*. Boston: G. K. Hall, 1987.

Block, Francesca Lia. *Weetzie Bat*. New York: Harper & Row, 1989.

Block, Francesca Lia. *Girl Goddess #9*. New York: HarperCollins, 1996.

Brown, Judith C. *Immodest Acts: The Life of a Lesbian Nun in Renaissance Italy*. New York: Oxford University Press, 1986.

Brownmiller, Susan. *Against Our Will: Men, Women and Rape*. New York: Simon & Schuster, 1975.

Bufwack, Mary A. *Finding Her Voice: The Saga of Women in Country Music*. New York: Crown, 1993.

Burgos-Debray, Elisabeth, ed. *I, Rigoberta Menchú: An Indian Woman in Guatemala*. London, U.K: Verso, 1984.

Cameron, Anne. *Daughters of Copper Woman*. Vancouver B.C: Press Gang, 1981.

c
u
n
t

Caprio, Frank S., M.D. *Female Homosexuality: A Psychodynamic Study of Lesbianism.* New York: Citadel, 1954.

Carter, Angela. *The Bloody Chamber and Other Stories.* New York: Harper & Row, 1979

Carter, Angela. *The Old Wives' Fairy Tale Book.* New York: Pantheon, 1995.

Castillo, Ana. *The Mixquiahuala Letters.* Binghampton, N.Y: Bilingual Press, 1986.

Ceronetti, Guido. *The Silence of the Body: Materials For the Study of Medicine.* New York: Farrar, Straus & Giroux, 1993.

Chicago, Judy. *Beyond the Flower: The Autobiography of a Feminist Artist.* New York: Viking, 1996.

Cohen, David, ed. *The Circle of Life: Rituals from the Human Family Album.* New York: Harper, 1991.

Crawford, Joan. *My Way of Life.* New York: Pocket Books, 1972.

Dunn, Katherine. *Geek Love.* New York: Warner, 1983.

Dunn, Katherine. *Attic.* New York: Warner, 1990.

Eisler, Riane T. *The Chalice and The Blade: Our History, Our Future.* Cambridge, MA: Harper & Row, 1987.

Eisler, Riane T. *Sacred Pleasure: Sex, Myth and the Politics of the Body.* San Francisco: Harper San Francisco, 1995.

El Saadawi, Nawal. *Woman at Point Zero.* London, UK: Zed Books, 1984.

Ellison, Katherine W. *Imelda: Steel Butterfly of the Philippines.* New York: McGraw-Hill, 1988.

Erdrich, Louise. *Love Medicine.* New York: Holt, Reinhart & Winston, 1984.

Erdrich, Louise. *Tracks.* Boston: G. K. Hall, 1989.

Findlen, Barbara, ed. *Listen Up: Voices from the Next Feminist Generation.* Seattle: Seal, 1995.

French, Marilyn. *Beyond Power: On Women, Men, and Morals.* New York: Summit, 1985.

French, Marilyn. *The War Against Women.* New York: Summit, 1992.

Galeano, Eduardo. *Memory of Fire* (a trilogy): *Genesis, Faces and Masks, Century of the Wind.* New York: Pantheon, 1985.

Gilbert, Olive. *Narrative of Sojourner Truth.* Mineola, NY: Dover, 1997.

Green, Karen and Taormino, Tristan, eds. *A Girl's Guide to Taking Over the World.* New York: St. Martin's, 1997.

Golub, Sharon. *Periods: From Menarche to Menopause.* Newbury Park, CA: Sage Publications, 1992.

Graves, Robert. *The White Goddess.* New York: Farrar, Straus & Giroux, 1966.

Graves, Robert. *Mammon and the Black Goddess.* Garden City, NY: Doubleday, 1965.

Griffin, Susan. *A Chorus of Stones: The Private Life of War.* New York: Doubleday, 1992.

Guerrilla Girls. *Confessions of the Guerrilla Girls.* New York: Harper Perennial, 1995.

Harding, M. Esther. *Woman's Mysteries, Ancient and Modern.* New York: Harper & Row, 1976.

Haver, Ronald. *David O. Selznick's Hollywood.* New York: Knopf, 1980.

Hine, Darlene Clark, King, Wilma and Reed, Linda, eds. *We Specialize in the Wholly Impossible: A Reader in Black Women's History.* Brooklyn, NY: Carlson, 1995.

Hite, Shere. *Women as Revolutionary Agents of Change: The Hite Reports and Beyond.* Madison, WI: The University of Wisconsin Press, 1994.

Holiday, Billie (with William Dufty). *Lady Sings the Blues.* Garden City, NY: Doubleday, 1956.

hooks, bell. *Ain't I a Woman: Black Women and Feminism.* Boston, MA: South End Press, 1984.

hooks, bell. *A Woman's Mourning Song.* New York: Harlem River Press, 1993.

hooks, bell. *Wounds of Passion: A Writing Life.* New York: Holt, 1997.

Hulme, Keri. *The Bone People.* Baton Rouge: Louisiana State University Press, 1985.

Hurston, Zora Neale. *Their Eyes Were Watching God.* Urbana: University of Illinois Press, 1978.

Hurston, Zora Neale. *I Love Myself When I'm Laughing...And Then Again When I'm Looking Mean and Impressive.* Old Westbury, NY: The Feminist Press, 1979.

Jackson, LaToya. *Growing Up in the Jackson Family.* New York: Dutton, 1991.

Kaplan, Janet. *Unexpected Journeys: The Art and Life of Remedios Varo.* New York: Abbeville Press, 1988.

Khashoggi, Soheir. *Mirage.* New York: Forge, 1996.

Leamer, Laurence. *The Kennedy Women: The Saga of an American Family.* New York: Villiard, 1994.

Lerner, Gerda. *Black Women in White America: A Documentary History.* New York: Vintage, 1972.

Lindgren, Astrid. *Pippi Longstocking.* New York: Viking, 1950.

Lindgren, Astrid. *Pippi Goes On Board.* New York: Puffin, 1977.

Lindgren, Astrid. *Pippi Sails the South Seas.* New York: Viking, 1959.

Lord, M.G. *Forever Barbie; The Unauthorized Biography of a Real Doll.* New York: Avon, 1994.

Lorde, Audre. "Uses of the Erotic: The Erotic as Power" in Sister Outsider: Essays and Speeches. Trumansburg, NY: The Crossing Press, 1984.

Lorde, Audre. *I Am Your Sister: Black Women Organizing Across Sexualities.* New York: Kitchen Table, Women of Color Press, 1985.

Lunardini, Christine, Ph.D. *What Every American Should Know About Women's History.* Holbrook, MA: Bob Adams, Inc., 1994.

Lynn, Loretta (with George Vecsey). *Coal Miner's Daughter.* Chicago: Regnery, 1976.

Mankiller, Wilma (with Michael Wallis). *A Chief and Her People.* New York: St. Martin's, 1993.

Marx, Karl. *The Woman Question: Selections from the Writing of Fredrick Engels, V.I. Lenin, Joseph Stalin and Karl Marx.* New York: International Publishers, 1951.

Maus, Cynthia Pearl. *The World's Great Madonnas.* New York: Harper, 1947.

Mitchell, Margaret. *Gone With The Wind.* New York: MacMillan, 1939.

Morgan, Marlo. *Mutant Message Downunder.* Lees Summit, MO: MM Co., 1991.

Morrison, Toni. *Sula.* New York: Knopf, 1974.

Morrison, Toni. *Tar Baby.* New York: Knopf, 1981.

Morrison, Toni. *Beloved.* New York: Knopf, 1987.

Morrison, Toni. *The Bluest Eye.* New York: Knopf, 1993.

Nagel, Jill, ed. *Whores and Other Feminists.* New York: Routledge, 1997.

O'Connor, Flannery. *Wise Blood.* New York: Farrar, Straus & Cudahy, 1952.

O'Connor, Flannery. *Everything That Rises Must Converge.* New York: Farrar, Straus & Giroux, 1965.

Orenstein, Peggy. *SchoolGirls: Young Women, Self-Esteem, and the Confidence Gap.* New York: Doubleday, 1994.

Palmer, Rachel Lynn and Greensburg, Sarah K., M.D. *Facts and Frauds in Woman's Hygiene.* New York: The Vanguard Press, 1936.

Piercy, Marge. *Woman on the Edge of Time.* New York: Knopf, 1976.

Presley, Priscilla (with Sandra Harmon). *Elvis and Me.* New York: Putnam, 1985.

Queen, Carol. *Real Live Nude Girl.* San Francisco: Cleis, 1997.

Raymond, Janice G. *Women as Wombs: Reproductive Technologies and the Battle over Women's Freedom.* San Francisco: HarperSanFrancisco, 1993.

Redding, Judith M. and Brownworth, Victoria A. *Film Fatales: Independent Women Directors.* Seattle: Seal, 1997.

Roseanne. *Roseanne: My Life as a Woman.* New York: HarperCollins, 1989.

Rothblatt, Martine. *The Apartheid of Sex: A Manifesto on the Freedom of Gender.* New York: Crown, 1995.

Sasson, Jean. *Princess Sultana.* New York: Morrow, 1992.

Sasson, Jean. *Princess Sultana's Daughters.* New York: Doubleday, 1994.

Scholz, Suzette, Stephanie and Sheri (with John Tullius). *Deep in the Heart of Texas: Reflections of Former Dallas Cowboy Cheerleaders.* New York: St. Martin's Press, 1991.

Sen, Mala. *The Bandit Queen.* New York: HarperCollins, 1995.

Sharp, Saundra. *Black Women for Beginners.* New York: Writers & Readers, 1993.

Silko, Leslie Marmon. *Almanac of the Dead and Ceremony.* New York: Simon & Schuster, 1991.

Silko, Leslie Marmon. *Ceremony.* New York: Penguin, 1986.

Smith, John M., M.D. *Women and Doctors: A Physicians Explosive Account of Women's Medical Treatment- and Mistreatment- in America Today and What You Can Do About It.* New York: Dell, 1993.

Solanas, Valerie. *S.C.U.M Manifesto.* London, U.K: Phoenix Press, 1991.

Tan, Amy. *The Joy Luck Club.* New York: Putnam, 1989.

Tan, Amy. *The Kitchen God's Wife.* New York: Putnam, 1991.

Taormino, Tristan. *The Ultimate Guide To Anal Sex for Women.* San Francisco: Cleis, 1997.

Tea, Michelle. *The Passionate Mistakes and Intimate Corruptions of One Girl in America.* New York: Semiotexte, 1998.

Walker, Alice. *The Color Purple.* New York: Harcourt, Brace, Jovanovich, 1982.

Walker, Alice and Parmar, Pratibha. *Warrior Marks: Female Genital Mutilation and the Sexual Blinding of Women.* New York: Harcourt, Brace, Jovanovich, 1993.

Walker, Barbara G. *The Women's Encyclopedia of Myths and Secrets.* San Francisco: Harper & Row, 1983.

Walker, Barbara G. *Crone: Woman of Age Wisdom and Power.* San Francisco: Harper & Row, 1985.

Winterson, Jeanette. *Art and Lies.* New York: Knopf, 1995.

Winterson, Jeanette. *Sexing the Cherry.* New York: Atlantic Monthly Press, 1990.

Winterson, Jeanette. *The Passion.* New York: Atlantic Monthly Press, 1988.

Woods, Beatrice. *I Shock Myself.* San Francisco: Chronicle Books, 1988.

Woods, Donald. *Biko.* New York: Vintage, 1979.

Woodson, Jacqueline. *Autobiography of a Family Photo: A Novel.* New York: Dutton, 1995.

Woodson, Jacqueline. *I Hadn't Meant to Tell You This.* New York: Delacorte, 1994.

X, Malcolm and Haley, Alex. *The Autobiography of Malcolm X.* New York: Grove, 1965.

Yoshimoto, Banana. *Kitchen.* New York: Grove, 1993.

Zahavi, Helen. *The Weekend.* New York: Donald I. Fine, 1991.

Zinn, Howard. *A People's History of the United States, 1492-Present.* New York: HarperPerennial, 1995.

Credits

EXCERPTS, AS SUBMITTED, from THE WOMAN'S ENCYCLO-
PEDIA OF MYTHS AND SECRETS by Barbara G. Walker.
Copyright © 1983 by Barbara G. Walker. Reprinted by permission
of HarperCollins, Inc.

Selection from *Mutant Message Down Under.* Copyright © 1991.
From Mutant Message Down Under by Marlo Morgan. Reproduced by permission of M M Co.

Lyrics from "Buttons" by Kinnie Star. Copyright © 1996 by Kinnie
Starr. Reprinted by permission of Kinnie Starr.

Selection from *Immodest Acts: The Life of a Lesbian Nun in
Renaissance Italy.* Copyright © 1986. From *Immodest Acts: The
Life of a Lesbian Nun in Renaissance Italy* by Judith Brown.
Reprinted by permission of Oxford University Press, Inc.

Selection from "She's Gotta Have It: An Interview with Nina
Hartley" by Marcelle Karp (aka Betty Boop), co-editor, *BUST*
magazine #10.

Selection from *"The Progressive* Interview: Desmond Tutu,
February 1998." Reprinted by permission of *The Progressive.*
Selection printed as it appeared in the *Utne Reader,* May/June
1998.

c   Selection from the interview with Leslie Feinberg from the

u   Copyright Workers World Service. For more information contact

n   WorkersWorld, 55 W. 17th Street, New York, NY 10011,

t   info@workers.org.

Gracious Thanks

Writers tend to put acknowledgment pages in their books because—unless authored by the very vain or very hermetic—books do not come to fruition without the support and love of many, many individuals.

In college, I learned the value of unqualified support from a single human being. Dr. Leo Daugherty read my stories, poems, essays and interviews with a sensitivity and insight I hadn't experienced since elementary school, when Mrs. Lingle and Mrs. House—my second and third grade teachers, respectively—prodded my imagination with a gusto I was wholly unappreciative of at the time. I extend my deepest regards to these three educators.

From the outset of this book, Holly Marie Morris was the single human being who believed in me so much my heart *positively swells*. Trust and respect are huge gifts. I do not take lightly Holly's inspiration for bringing these gifts into my life. *Cunt* would never, ever, ever have been written if I hadn't seen · her that day in New York, gliding 'cross the room in her cream linen suit like grace was a word made 'specially with her in mind. Holly, I love you dearly.

My mother was the first person to read an early draft of *Cunt*. Because her experiences are so integral to my writing, I hoped to procure her blessing before venturing on to a rewrite. Not only is my mother from a different culture, but many of my beliefs are difficult for someone of her generation to understand. Regardless, she never paused in support of my words. She did not ask me to edit out a single iota of her life experiences. Her courage overwhelms me. I am honored to be her daughter.

I gave the final draft of *Cunt* to my brother, Joe B., and my sister, Elizabeth, for Christmas 1997. A man of few words, my brother left a concise message on my voice mail two weeks later, "It's killer," he said. "Goddamn, this is just killer." My sister, a person I have aptly nicknamed "Hard Customer," called me at least twice a week for a month, gushing with excitement and love.

Obviously, Joe B. and Liz are my siblings and lot of people might think, *"Of course* they had nice things to say," but it is an absolute veracity that my brother and sister would never say things to spare my feelings. If there's shit to be talked, rest assured, they are the first to talk it.

I don't thank them solely for reading my book with such care and devotion, I thank them for letting me know I am as precious to them as they are to me. It is extremely painful that we learned the preciousness of life through the death of our brother, but all the same, I am glad we learned this.

Jennie Goode and Faith Conlon. Goode and Faith, need I say more? Their Goode Faith in *Cunt* deserves accolades of candy and champagne forever. I know it is considered a "risk" to publish this book, and they, along with the entire staff of Seal Press—Lee Damsky, Ingrid Emerick, Laura Gronewold, Kate Loeb, Lisa Okey and Lynn Siniscalchi—rose to the occasion like prima ballerinas aloft. And don't even get me started on Jennie Goode's paranormal levels of comprehension. Lordisa.

Likewise, many thanks to Leigh Feldman. Her belief in this

project was—given the aforementioned "risk" factor—astounding. I will never forget the day she told me she felt like standing on the rooftop screaming "cunt" at the top of her lungs. Thank you. You rule.

Loraine Harkin, naturopathic physician, kindly read the manuscript and shared her knowledge. Her input and support for *Cunt* were greatly appreciated.

When it was time to get jacket and press photos taken, I went with a gut feeling and called Rebecca McBride. The resulting photographs freaked me out. It was as if she prowled around in my dreamworld and somehow duplicated the precise images I could conjure only nebulous words to describe. Rebecca is a genius.

Sybil, Paul, Memphis, Erin and Christopher were so kind to me during a very difficult time. Ditto Peri Heydari Pakroo, Oh My!, Turtle, Parisha and Jason Speewhoreski.

Lisa Vogel and the Michigan Womyn's Music Festival inspired me and goaded me on in ways I'm sure they are completely unaware of.

Whenever I feel like maybe there's no magic in the world, maybe I've been wrong this whole time, I just think of Panacea and Mr. Quintron, and I know there are always spells to cast and pussycats to cavort with.

Om. Her voice, her love, her letters from Japan. How I love Om. Elizabeth Faye spoils her women with laughter and massages. Gasperini sends her women skateboards in the mail, which makes them have total spontaneous orgasms of joy.

c
u
n
t

Dawn Kiss, the beautiful, passionate snowboarding punk rock valkyrie ablaze.

Bridget Irish, 100 percent Irish, born on St. Patrick's Day. Bridget tells me I can do anything I want. When voices in my head say stuff like, "Inga, you *can't* call him 'Keith "Piece of Shit" Richards,'" Bridget's face floats into my frontal lobe, and I *know*, I can call him "Keith 'Piece of Feral Dogshit Smeared on the Washington Monument' Richards," if I want.

I am intensely grateful for the support and love of dearest Kotexi, Bart, Mrs. L. and Dr. Flusty.

If home is where the heart is, my heart is where Bambi, Shug, Sini and Alisun are. All four of my housemates listened to me wrestle with various chapters, put up with my freakish hours and respected the importance of bunny ears. My week *sucks* if Bambi and I don't have our Sunday morning coffee 'n smokes session. Shug's bright, blazing smile is a pillar of our community. I could listen to Sini's hilarious stories for hours on end. Alisun's logical mind has improved the quality of my life hundreds of times. She never misses a *follicle* of inconsistency.

I love you all so very much.

And the genius filmmaker, Harperetta Carter. My heart *grieves* for those who underestimate her scathing perspective on life and society, which she cleverly hides in her sweet, sweet smile and grandmother-spiced tenderness.

At three o' clock in the morning, when I *hafta* share something, to cry or hear a beautiful story, I call Riz, my sunshine in the dead of night. He never gets mad at me even if I wake him up. He is groggy for a few minutes and then swings right into a tirade about love, Oprah, his Grandmother. If I was stuck on my book, I always knew somehow or other Riz would unstick me.

The psycho-enchanting and beautiful Ali Ø. brought into my life—among many exemplary things—the following sentence: "You don't get what you deserve, you get what you negotiate." For that little gem alone, I am forever indebted to her.

Kinnie Starr, Toni Childs, Diamanda Galás, Me'Shell NdegéOcello, Sinéad O'Connor, Tracy Chapman, the Immortal Caruso and Chet Baker: I wore out their CDs working on my book. I wore out the repeat button on my CD player. I disgusted neighbors who wondered what kind of freckin' fruitcake would listen to the same goddamn CD for six hours straight, night after night. I thank them for making music in the world. Diamanda, especially, helped me with the chapter on rape. It was the most painful one for me to write and without Diamanda's presence in my kitchen, I don't know how I could have managed.

I extend my deepest gratitude to Dr. Daniel Schiff, but ask his forgiveness for not including him in the acknowledgments last time around.

There are a number of other folks that I forgot to thank, chief among them, my Aunt Genie. How I neglected to acknowledge her is a mystery to me. I also didn't thank my Grammy, who died in February 2001. Let it be known that both of these women have served as role models to me my entire life and I would not know the first thing about asserting myself had I not been blessed with the honor of experiencing them in action since day one.

Jessica Roncker did a bunch of amazing work to update the "Cuntovin' Guide to the Universe" and I greatly appreciate her taking the time.

c
u
n
t

Many thanks to Zabrina for setting me straight.

I am filled with thanks to all of the people who've read *Cunt.* I've received many emails and letters from folks and I am very grateful that people have taken time out of their lives to let me know my book has had a impact.

Locally-owned independent bookstores, newspapers, websites, zines and magazines have been very kind to *Cunt,* and I thank them with all my heart.

Support your local bookstore.

Likewise, I'd like to thank the "mainstream" media for largely ignoring this book. I am deeply honored to have not garnered much space in this forum, and I truly hope the new edition reflects a continuation of this trend.

Lastly, I would like to thank all librarians, everywhere. My worship of librarians dates back to the age of four. Since I have become a published author, my reverence for librarians knows no bounds. Librarians are unheralded revolutionaries, and without them, all semblances of "civilization" that this country still manages to muster from time to time would be shot to shit.

Long live librarians!!!

Bios

Inga Muscio is a public speaker and author, presently working on a new book, *Autobiograpy of a Blue-Eyed Devil.* She lives on the west coast. Website: ingalagringa.com.

Betty Dodson went public with her love of sex in 1968 when she had the first one-woman exhibition of erotic art in New York City. Whether she is drawing, painting, writing, teaching or producing videos, sexuality has been the subject of her life's work. Her first book *Liberating Masturbation* was self-published in 1974 and became a feminist classic. *Sex for One: The Joy of Selfloving* published in 1987 and revised in 1996 became a bestselling Crown paperback. Her latest book *Orgasms for Two: The Joy of Partnersex* will be available in the fall of 2002. She has a private practice in New York City and maintains an active website: www.bettydodson.com.

Derrick Jensen is the author of *A Language Older Than Words,* and most recently *The Culture of Make Believe.* His work has appeared in magazines as varied as *The New York Times Magazine, Audubon, The Sun, Green Anarchy* and *The Earth First! Journal.* The central question of his life and his work is: If the destruction of the natural world and the immiseration of the majority of humans isn't making us happy, why are we doing it?

Selected Titles from Seal Press

Listen Up: Voices from the Next Feminist Generation edited by Barbara Findlen. $16.95, 1-58005-054-9. A revised and expanded edition.

Shameless: Women's Intimate Erotica edited by Hanne Blank. $14.95, 1-58005-060-3. Diverse and delicious memoir-style erotica by today's hottest fiction writers.

Sex and Single Girls: Straight and Queer Women on Sexuality edited by Lee Damsky. $16.95, 1-58005-038-7.

Chelsea Whistle by Michelle Tea. $14.95, 1-58005-073-5. In this gritty, confessional memoir, Tea takes the reader back to the city of her childhood: Chelsea, Massachusetts.

She's A Rebel by Gillian Garr. $19.95, 1-58005-078-6. The new and expanded edition of this breakthrough history of women-in-rock.

Breeder: Real-Life Stories from the New Generation of Mothers edited by Ariel Gore and Bee Lavender, foreword by Dan Savage. $16.00, 1-58005-051-4. A hilarious and heartrending compilation from the editors of *Hip Mama*.

Body Outlaws: Young Women Write About Body Image and Identity edited by Ophira Edut, foreword by Rebecca Walker. $14.95, 1-58005-043-3.

Seal Press publishes many books of fiction and nonfiction by women writers. Please visit our Web site at **www.sealpress.com**.